Praise for *Kenn..*

Kenneyism is more than the political biography of one man; it is a history of the populist far-right formations that have been gaining ground in Canada since the 1980s — in which Jason Kenney has been a central figure. The story of this movement's chaotic and destructive rule in Alberta —told by one of the country's most astute political journalists — should serve as a warning to other Canadians about the real agenda of this movement and the dangers of its further radicalization.

— LAURIE ADKIN, professor of political science, University of Alberta

Jeremy Appel's *Kenneyism* is an insighful, comprehensive investigation and explanation of the rise and sudden fall of Jason Kenney — one of Canada's most consequential conservative activists of the 21st century. Appel manages to intertwine Kenney's religious and ideological beliefs in order to explain his driving political ambition. The book chronicles Kenney's rise from a young man on the periphery of Liberal politics to his accession as the ultra-conservative premier of Alberta and his eventual resignation and exile from political life. *Kenneyism* is more than a narrative history. It is an explanation of how someone with such far-right views could wield such power in Canada. Placing the former Alberta premier in the neoconservative camp, Appel describes Kenney's goal of dismantling the modern state and reshaping society and government with a harsh free market ideology. For anyone wanting to understand the Canadian right, *Kenneyism* is required reading.

— KEITH BROWNSEY, professor of economics, justice, and policy studies,
Mount Royal University

Jason Kenney spent three decades in elected office and dramatically reshaped Alberta politics with the creation of the United Conservative Party, yet he remains an enigma to many political watchers. Jeremy Appel's *Kenneyism* takes one of the first in-depth looks at Kenney's rise and fall in Canadian politics and dissects the branches of conservatism and adherence to hierarchical social order that drove him to become a political animal unlike anything Alberta politics had seen before.

— DAVE COURNOYER, writer, *Daveberta*

Appel provides a detailed description of Jason Kenney's beliefs and approach to politics, digging up a few golden nuggets along the way. Kenney is revealed as a too clever-by-half who rode to political success on a mix of faux populism, ideological rigidity, cruelty, authoritarianism, and deviousness. Appel traces with unsparing candor how a politician who saw himself as the smartest man in the room proved instead incompetent to hold high office. Ultimately, however, the fall of Jason Kenney is not a tragedy. The tragedy lies in the wreckage he has left in his wake.

— TREVOR HARRISON, author, *Of Passionate Intensity: Right-Wing Populism and the Reform Party of Canada*, and professor of sociology, University of Lethbridge

Jeremy Appel's deep dive into the political life of Jason Kenney illuminates the life and intentions of an important though confusing political operative. All political watchers owe Appel a great debt for this in-depth look at such an elusive figure.

— NORA LORETO, author, *Spin Doctors: How Media and Politicians Misdiagnosed the COVID-19 Pandemic*

Jeremy Appel has written a thoughtful, well-researched, and accessible book that sheds sorely needed light on the pervasive political influence of Jason Kenney. *Kenneyism* is essential reading for anyone interested in how Canada arrived at its right-wing-populist descent into necropolitics.

— STEVE SLADKOWSKI, musician, PUP

Appel rigorously tracks the rise and fall of one of Canada's most prominent politicians. It's all here: what motivated Jason Kenney, how he became such a successful political strategist, and why he was eventually toppled by his own party. A compelling read by a journalist with keen insight.

— GILLIAN STEWARD, columnist, *Toronto Star*, and former managing editor, *Calgary Herald*

Kenneyism is as close to a biography as we're going to get unless Kenney writes his own story. But even then, he'll have to work hard to top this. Provocative, insightful, and meticulously researched, Jeremy Appel takes us on an absorbing journey through the political paradox that was Jason Kenney's self-sabotaged career.

— GRAHAM THOMSON, freelance columnist and long-time Alberta politics observer

Appel's tale of Jason Kenney's rise and fall reads like a two-part ghost story: on one hand, how the former premier's outsized influence still haunts the conservative movement; on the other, how the politician's lesser angels got the best of him, his parties, and his movement. *Kenneyism* delves deep into the public life and ideology of one of Canada's most prominent yet enigmatic politicians. Offering a nuanced and critical examination of his New Right philosophy, Appel chronicles how Jason Kenney's unwavering dedication to neoliberalism, neoconservatism, and authoritarian populism shaped his political journey from Ottawa to Edmonton to obscurity (for now). While other authors allow Kenney's controversial positions on human rights, the environment, immigration, and public services to cloud their judgment, Appel's research reveals the ideological underpinnings of the man's political doctrine. The result leaves Kenney's opponents and followers with a better understanding of, if not empathy for, his rise and fall. *Kenneyism* is a must-read for those wanting to make sense of Canada's contemporary conservative movement, the divided right in Alberta, and the premier's policy legacy.

— JARED WESLEY, author, *Code Politics: Campaigns and Cultures on the Canadian Prairies,* and professor of political science, University of Alberta

Everyone interested in the politics of the Canadian conservative movement or Alberta politics will find *Kenneyism* an interesting and informative read. It tells the story of the rise and fall of this enigmatic politician, tracing his journey from young anti-tax crusader to the hero who united the right, and then the chump who fell victim to the very populists whose support he courted. In this lively and readable account, Appel makes sense of Jason Kenney's ideology and the legacy he leaves in Ottawa and in Alberta.

— LISA YOUNG, professor of political science, University of Calgary

KENNEYISM

KENNEYISM

JASON KENNEY'S PURSUIT OF POWER

JEREMY APPEL

DUNDURN
PRESS

Publisher and acquiring editor: Kwame Scott Fraser | Editor: Michael Carroll
Cover designer: Karen Alexiou
Cover image: Jason Kenney image: Wikimedia Commons/Robert Thivierge; frame: jason cox/shutterstock.com, background: bernard hermant/unsplash.com

Library and Archives Canada Cataloguing in Publication

Title: Kenneyism : Jason Kenney's pursuit of power / Jeremy Appel.
Other titles: Jason Kenney's pursuit of power
Names: Appel, Jeremy, author.
Description: Includes bibliographical references and index.
Identifiers: Canadiana (print) 2023053855X | Canadiana (ebook) 20230538568 | ISBN 9781459752658 (softcover) | ISBN 9781459752665 (PDF) | ISBN 9781459752672 (EPUB)
Subjects: LCSH: Kenney, Jason, 1968- | LCSH: United Conservative Party. | LCSH: Premiers (Canada)—Alberta—Biography. | LCSH: Politicians—Canada—Biography. | LCSH: Populism—Canada. | CSH: Alberta—Politics and government—2015-
Classification: LCC FC3676.1 .K46 A67 2024 | DDC 971.23/04092—dc23

We acknowledge the support of the Canada Council for the Arts and the Ontario Arts Council for our publishing program. We also acknowledge the financial support of the Government of Ontario, through the Ontario Book Publishing Tax Credit and Ontario Creates, and the Government of Canada.

Dundurn Press
1382 Queen Street East
Toronto, Ontario, Canada M4L 1C9
dundurn.com, @dundurnpress

For Hiep Bui, Benito Quesada, and Armando Sallegue

CONTENTS

FOREWORD

NOBODY MISSES JASON KENNEY. IF YOU think about it, that's pretty weird. Kenney had all the makings of a political colossus.

He was the Conservative premier of Alberta, no insignificant position. Before that he was an influential federal Cabinet minister who represented a Calgary riding for 20 years, starting when he was only 29. Through seven Canadian general elections, he never faced a challenger who could make him break into even a light sweat. He built a reputation as an unstoppable campaigner obsessed with political strategy and tactics, which, having no spouse or family, was all he ever thought about. So when he announced in 2017 that he was leaving Ottawa for Alberta provincial politics, it was widely assumed it was a bold but calculated step toward the Prime Minister's Office.

Even when criticism of his leadership through the Covid-19 pandemic grew heated from both left and right, no one quite believed the man could be toppled as leader of the ruling United Conservative Party (UCP), which he all but founded in 2017.

When he swept to power with a majority government on April 16, 2019, he was lauded as a saviour by the province's many Conservatives, who had been shocked and appalled by the unexpected majority government won by Rachel Notley's New Democratic Party (NDP) in 2015. To be fair, in some ways Kenney *was* their saviour, although there's little doubt that if he hadn't managed to stitch together the entitled Progressive Conservatives and fractious Wildrosers who split Alberta's conservative vote in 2015, providing an opening for a strong NDP campaign, someone else would have done so before long.

After that victory, Kenney was feted as a Conservative hero, welcome on a talk show or editorial board meeting anywhere in Canada. He had a powerful mandate and a plan to make dramatic, even radical changes in Alberta. There was no one like him on the national scene. Federal Conservative leadership at the time was uninspiring. Disgruntled partisans thought of Kenney, echoing a phrase he once used to describe Saskatchewan premier Brad Wall's role on the Prairies, as the *real* leader of Canada's Conservatives.

Three years later, whipsawed by a bungled pandemic response that satisfied no one and battered by a deeply negative leadership review campaign, Kenney announced his resignation to take effect as soon as a new leader was chosen. He had managed to hang on to the support of only 51.4 percent of the party members who voted. "The result is not what I hoped for or frankly what I expected," he grimly admitted. It was May 18, 2022.

The new leader turned out to be former Wildrose Opposition leader Danielle Smith, and no sooner was she sworn in as premier on October 11, 2022, than Kenney all but disappeared. Since then, there's rarely been a sighting of the man. At times it almost seems as if he never existed.

Oh, sure, now and then there's a news release saying he's been appointed an adviser to a well-known law firm or named to a seat on the board of a big corporation, but it's not as if the guy's being pursued by swarms of paparazzi on Vespas. The only photo of him to surface in the summer of 2023 showed him wearing a scruffy, grizzled beard after agreeing to take on a new role as the "voice of Calgary's tech industry," as the *Calgary Herald* put it. *Some voice!* He hasn't been heard from on the topic since.

If journalists are beating down his door asking for retrospection about his years in power, either in Ottawa or Alberta, he doesn't seem to be responding. Maybe he's writing a book. Who the hell knows? It's as if he's dropped off the edge of the flat earth he inhabited here in Wild Rose Country, and nobody really gives a hoot.

Which, if you ask me, is the weird part. You'd think journalists — at least the few who still have paycheques and modest expense accounts — would be beating down Kenney's door trying to get interviews with him. At least trying to figure out what he does and where he does it, so they could waylay him and try to toss him a question about what went wrong and what he plans to do next.

The Kenney years were tough for all of us. That was the plan, actually; it's just that the hard part was supposed to be austerity, job cuts, wage suppression, privatization, and the continued depredations of neoliberalism. Instead, it was Covid-19, vaccine conspiracy theories, border blockades, and honking trucks flying FUCK TRUDEAU flags. (At least Kenney was spared that fate, although a few latte liberals did drink their $7 designer coffees out of china FUCK KENNEY mugs made by a novelty company in the NDP heartland of Edmonton, Alberta's capital city.) I imagine Kenney is tired after all that. Maybe the journalists are tired, too. The rest of us sure are.

As for the people who once upon a time acted as if they wished they could touch the hem of Kenney's gown and throw their cloaks under his feet, they don't even want to talk about him. Unlike Donald Trump's fans, or Stephen Harper's, there seem to be no nostalgic Alberta Conservatives who look back on the Kenney years and miss the guy. *Jason Who?* Have you ever seen an internet meme showing Kenney's smug mug and asking: *Do you miss me yet?* Not one!

Likewise, you'll never hear progressive types muttering, "Jason Kenney, he seems almost enlightened now." You know, like American liberals used to wonderingly recall George W. Bush as almost rational once Donald Trump was in the White House. Yet even with Danielle Smith and her "Take Back Alberta" sidekicks now driving the UCP clown car, there's precious little lukewarm nostalgia for Kenney on what passes for the left in Alberta.

Moreover, despite the loyalty of Kenney's federal constituents in Calgary, who in those years would have voted for a yellow dog if you'd slapped some Tory blue on its election signs, folks weren't really all that enthusiastic about the man himself. He might have mistaken the reason, but in retrospect his main appeal to federal voters was probably the conservative leaders he served, especially Preston Manning and Stephen Harper.

Despite being a shrewd political tactician and capable and loyal sub-ordinate, a role he played well for Harper in particular, Kenney wasn't really someone the late Ralph Klein's imaginary Albertans, Martha and Henry, or their tattooed and precariously employed offspring, would likely warm to. He was, as a respectable political analyst of my acquaintance privately puts it, *a weirdo.*

Kenney wouldn't be the first weirdo in Canadian politics, of course. Notably, William Lyon Mackenzie King, perhaps the country's most suc-cessful prime minister, was even weirder. Still, that strangely obsessive side of Kenney's character didn't make him into the kind of politician with whom voters imagined they could forge some kind of personal connection. He wasn't a guy, as was often said of Klein, Alberta's premier from 1992 to 2006, with whom most of us would like to have a beer. In fact, Kenney seemed like a guy with whom it would be *no fun at all* to have a beer, any time, or even a shot of cheap Irish whiskey!

He had no spouse and no family of his own. There was no information about whom, other than his mother, he was close to. There was little relatable about the man for those of us who live more normal lives in all their rainbow hues. He exuded no warm fuzzies.

Kenney's obsessive need to defend John A. Macdonald, the deeply flawed Father of Confederation, didn't exactly strike a chord with Albertans. Macdonald turned out to be our shared, drunken, racist, abusive national dad, but Kenney couldn't let him go. When statues of the first prime min-ister were toppled in Montreal and soaked in blood-red paint in Victoria, Kenney wanted to move them all to Edmonton where, presumably, they could be declared essential infrastructure and held safely in the bosom of Canadian conservatism.

Kenney's crankily Dickensian views about pedagogy didn't help, either, especially after he teamed up with a former staffer and little-known his-torian to cook up the ridiculous grade-school social studies curriculum that bedevils the UCP government to this day. Teachers despise it. Many parents are troubled. Parents who aren't troubled are often troubling. Yet Kenney's UCP successors won't let it go. Then there was the stubbornness that gave us "The Best Summer Ever" in 2021, which turned into anything but when Covid bounced back in the fall and nearly collapsed the health-care system.

There was Kenney's overt religiosity as an adult convert to a conservative strain of Roman Catholicism; his cultish devotion to the monarchy, which culminated in him bizarrely live-tweeting from the lineup to view Queen Elizabeth II's coffin in London; his tendency to adopt a professorial mode and deliver boring lectures at news conferences, making us all feel like students forced to stay after class; his contempt for journalists made clear by his frequent assertion that "I refuse to accept the premise of your question"; and that ridiculous big blue Dodge Ram truck, behind the wheel of which he always looked like an undersized phony, even before it leaked out that the instant he was out of town an aide had to slip behind the wheel to actually drive the thing. All of that made him hard to like, let alone love.

You could feel sympathy, even empathy, for the guy, but he wasn't simpatico. You could feel respect for his discipline and determination without sensing a connection. His political talents, in other words, didn't seem to include the normal human kinship through which many flawed politicians can paper over the dangers and unpopularity of the agendas they pursue without making people dislike them personally. Ontario premier Doug Ford and Alberta's Danielle Smith are both politicians with personalities that make it easy to overlook a multitude of sins. Jason Kenney, not so much.

Probably none of this would have mattered, at least not so quickly, had it not been for Covid-19, in which Kenney's political instincts and practical necessity clashed. He could never make up his mind if he was going to go all in for public health or throw caution to the wind and embrace what's come to be known as "free-dumb" — the freedom of the grave for many so that their conspiracy-obsessed neighbours and shirttail relatives could enjoy the "freedom" of antisocial irresponsibility.

In the fullness of time, it seemed, almost everyone came to despise the man. He's probably lucky not to have been run out of Alberta on a rail, covered in hot tar and chicken feathers. Not only are most Albertans happy to wash their hands of him, but they're also delighted to forget as much as possible about the three-and-a-half long years he led the province.

This is a problem, because it's important to put Kenney and what he did, and what he hoped to do, in a proper historical context. This is something political Alberta hasn't been very good at doing in the latter part of the nearly 44 years of Progressive Conservative rule, during the NDP's four years in power, or since, under the UCP.

Which is why this book by Jeremy Appel is so important. It would be easy, given the desire to put Kenney out of our minds, to forget his real policy legacy — decades of steady commitment to destructive neoliberal nostrums in Ottawa and Alberta, a populist pitch that nevertheless held people in contempt if they weren't on the invitation list for private rooftop mid-pandemic patio parties, a profound desire to continue cutting public services and replace them with privatized alternatives that work for elites while the rest of us are damned, and a commitment to the fossil-fuel economy combined with dismissal of the fate of the environment even if the survival of the planet is at stake.

Jeremy Appel, a fine young journalist, may not have written a conventional biography of Jason Kenney. We can safely leave that to some hoary academic in an ivory tower to get around to later. *Kenneyism: Jason Kenney's Pursuit of Power* is a strong *second* draft of history, synthesizing the first reports with solid analysis and entertaining writing to create an account that puts Jason Kenney in his proper place in Alberta history.

David Climenhaga
St. Albert, Alberta
August 2023

PROLOGUE

WHEN I SAW JASON KENNEY AT the annual Conservative Stampede BBQ in July 2022, I witnessed a defeated man. Two months after he announced his intention to step down as leader of the United Conservative Party (UCP) he created, it was unclear whether he was going to show up or not, but he did, sporting a five o'clock shadow, and I almost felt sad for him. I decided I had to get a picture with the man whose rise and fall I witnessed first-hand covering Alberta politics from 2017 to 2022, having written dozens of unflattering columns about him. I wasn't sure if he knew who I was or not, but it did seem as if he was avoiding me. After each handshake with a supporter, or former supporter, he glanced in my direction, then walked the opposite way.

While I was following him around, I saw him speak to a young Conservative family that seemed happy to see him, thanking him for his service. He said something to the effect of "All the time, people come up to me and say, 'Thank you so much for all the important work you've done.'" Again, I *almost* pitied him. Eventually, I got my photo, thanks to one of his handlers I spoke to, who encouraged me to continue following him. When the handler asked my name and I told it to him, he said, "Oh, yeah, I think I've read some of your stuff." I guess he had a good sense of humour. When I finally cornered Kenney, immediately after introducing myself — I didn't even mention my surname — he had an air of "let's get this over with," and

I finally met Jason Kenney at the Calgary Stampede Conservative BBQ in July 2022 after spending the previous five years chronicling his rise and precipitous decline.

we did. Thus ends the one time I met Kenney. Suffice it to say, he didn't answer my requests for an interview.

Kenney's downfall was the end of a long and highly influential political career. It's quite remarkable that after 32 years in public life, from his 1990 appearance on CNN as an "anti-abortion activist" in San Francisco to getting turfed as Alberta's premier in 2022, there hasn't been a book written on the man. Throughout his political career, Kenney has consistently been at the forefront of efforts to shift mainstream Canadian politics rightward, whether as leader of the Canadian Taxpayers Federation, a Reform and Canadian Alliance Member of Parliament (MP), the architect of Prime Minister Stephen Harper's immigrant outreach strategy, a federal Cabinet minister, and Alberta premier. While there have been a couple of essay collections on the policies he pursued as Alberta's premier, and he appears in most books about Harper's time as prime minister, nobody has yet stepped forward to write a cohesive narrative of Kenney's career.

In February 2017, I moved to Alberta from Toronto, where I was born and raised — less than a year after Kenney announced his return to Alberta. His mission was to unite the Wildrose and Progressive Conservative (PC) Parties after spending the past two decades in Ottawa, where he played a key role in accomplishing a similar feat with the Reform Party/Canadian Alliance and federal PCs. Mine was to accept a journalism job after struggling to find one anywhere near home. I arrived in Whitecourt, a small paper-mill town less than a couple hours' drive northwest of Edmonton, where I landed a job at the local *Whitecourt Star* paper, a few months after Kenney accomplished the first part of his plan — winning the PC leadership on the one-issue platform of uniting with the Wildrose.

It was a winter of discontent in Alberta, which Kenney seized on and exacerbated on his path to power. I recall the deep unpopularity of the New Democratic Party (NDP) government in Whitecourt, which had an NDP Member of the Legislative Assembly (MLA), Oneil Carlier, as a result of Wildrose and PC voters dividing the right-wing vote. I remember a Chamber of Commerce forum with Carlier in April 2017 in which he sat at the front of the room at town hall as angry residents berated him over the size of the public sector and the $20 per tonne carbon tax his party imposed at the beginning of the year, which became a convenient punching bag for right-wing local officials. Putting an additional price on carbon-intensive products to create a market-based disincentive for emissions, however, was endorsed by neoliberal guru Milton Friedman as an alternative to directly imposing regulations on polluters.[1] Former Reform Party leader Preston Manning, Kenney's old boss, also endorsed carbon pricing in a November 2014 *Globe and Mail* op-ed.

The NDP government's plan to protect the local woodland caribou population, which would have restricted the number of trees the local forestry industry could chop down, also came under fire at Carlier's town hall. One of the first stories I covered was a visit from Environment Minister Shannon Phillips to sell the caribou conservation plan. For that story, I interviewed someone from the Canadian Parks and Wilderness Society about how the industry's own conservation plans were insufficient, because their goal of extracting as much lumber as they could profit from was fundamentally at odds with protecting local wildlife. I got a call from Ray Hilts of the Alberta Forest Alliance, asking me why I would speak to environmentalists — they're all liars. He became a town councillor later that year. Whitecourt's local lumber industry was a microcosm of the broader extractive industries, namely oil and gas, that Alberta's economic fortunes are so tied to.

It's worth noting that Kenney's PC leadership win occurred not long after a much more seismic event in international conservative politics: the election of Donald Trump as president of the United States. Trump, the billionaire son of a multi-millionaire father, was an unlikely candidate to position himself as the voice of the downtrodden, left-behind masses raging against a corrupt political establishment. Kenney, a career politician in the strictest sense of the term, was a similarly unlikely choice to channel this populist zeitgeist. But it worked for both, albeit temporarily.

In Whitecourt, I saw the success of Kenney's unity pitch when the Wildrose and PCs both voted 95 percent in favour of unity. By the time I arrived seven months later in Medicine Hat, a small city of 65,000 in the province's southeastern "forgotten corner," the UCP leadership race was in full swing. Once Kenney won, under circumstances still the subject of police investigation six years later due to allegations of electoral fraud, it was clear he was going to be the next premier. The vote split on the right that allowed the NDP under Rachel Notley to sneak up the middle and form a majority government in 2015 was no more. I assumed that once he won the 2019 election, Kenney would be premier for as long as he wanted before going back to Ottawa to lead the federal Conservatives.

The *Medicine Hat News* was where I really developed my voice as a writer. I covered Kenney's rise and his attacks on public-sector workers, public education, and the environmentalist movement — the last one of which he approached with an especially vitriolic zeal. I was in a fortunate position that allowed me to deliver blistering criticisms of the government. I was a reporter, yes, who was expected to present the perspectives of others in a relatively neutral, detached way, whatever that means, but I was also permitted to express my view of it all from the opinion page. Medicine Hat was a small enough market that I could say things other people wouldn't have been permitted to with regularity in larger centres, but it was big enough that when I started to develop my own voice as a writer, people started to listen.

About a month into the pandemic, which ultimately led to Kenney's downfall, I got laid off from the *News*, which led me to go it alone as a freelancer. This steered me to Calgary, where I accepted a part-time job covering municipal politics for the *Sprawl*, an online independent media outlet, moving up to the big city in December 2020 — the peak of the second Covid-19 wave — just as Kenney had reluctantly imposed some relatively stringent but nonsensical restrictions. Private gatherings were forbidden, but malls and churches remained open, which is highly symbolic of Kenney's approach to social relations in which individuals exist as part of a collective, either as a means of generating economic activity or participating in traditional social structures. This was ultimately not enough to satiate his hard-right base, which wanted a full return to normalcy regardless of the plague.

While this is a story of Jason Kenney, it's also an account of the success of neoconservative politics in Canada. A pragmatic idealogue, Kenney's talent as a slick political operator made him a leading figure in pushing ideas once considered on the fringes to the forefront of national discussion. But his is also a cautionary tale of hubris in the face of crisis and the perils of a populism from above.

INTRODUCTION:

DEFINING KENNEYISM

NOW THAT KENNEY'S POLITICAL CAREER HAS, at least for the foreseeable future, come to a close, I have no doubt there will be insider accounts of his years in power that attempt to take the reader behind the scenes of the decision-making process behind Kenney's policies. There will also be books that seek to humanize Kenney, separating the man from his politics. This book is neither of those. My goal is to outline what Jason Kenney believes, how he was able to implement those beliefs, their consequences, and Kenney's long-term influence on the conservative movement. Even if I wanted to write an insider account, I wouldn't be able to. Kenney has made a lot of enemies in Alberta in just three years, but few would talk to me for this book. It must be emphasized that those enemies are to Kenney's right politically, meaning their views are still closer to his than to mine.

It was nonetheless helpful to speak to those who were willing to get a better sense of how Kenney operates. Tom Flanagan, former Harper chief of staff and University of Calgary political scientist, has defended forcing Indigenous children into residential schools, citing the "social pathologies" of Indigenous cultures.[1] His expertise in the internal mechanisms of Canadian conservatism, however, were immensely valuable for elucidating the broader movement Kenney was part of. Derek Fildebrandt, who now publishes the far-right *Western Standard* news outlet after his short political career ended in a sea of scandal, was another. I found his insight into why Kenney failed to maintain his political coalition in Alberta, whose right-wing flank Fildebrandt represents, useful in making sense of Kenney's downfall. Rahim Jaffer, who served alongside Kenney as a Reform, Canadian Alliance, and Conservative MP from 1997 to 2008, was of great assistance in describing Kenney's early days in Parliament.

Kenney, I contend, is an emblematic figure in modern right-wing politics who manipulated populist sentiment to implement policies that strengthened elite rule, exclusively benefiting those in positions of authority. That is a consistent thread throughout Kenney's political career. He was by no means the first political leader to pursue this project, but in the Canadian context he was one of the most successful figures to do so. Sean Speer, a conservative political scientist, commentator, and former Harper adviser, correctly called Kenney "one of the most consequential Canada politicians over the past quarter century, and certainly one of the most consequential conservatives."[2] While his career may be over, Kenney's ghost will haunt Canadian politics for the foreseeable future. Before we outline Kenney's place within Canada's broader right-wing political environment, we must first explain what his beliefs are, and in so doing, work toward a formulation of "Kenneyism."

The New Right: Neoliberalism and Neoconservatism

To start, it's important to outline two distinct but interrelated concepts that are often confusingly conflated — neoliberalism and neoconservatism — which are both manifested in Kenney's political approach. The reason these two concepts are often equated is that they frequently cross-pollinate, and few figures provide a better example of their intersection than Kenney. While these two ideologies fall under the umbrella of the "New Right," it's important to emphasize that they're not exclusively confined to explicitly right-wing politics. Neoliberalism, in particular, has been embraced with varying degrees of enthusiasm by all parties. Kenney played an influential role in forging this consensus. This part of the book is more philosophical than the rest, but bear with me. It's important to define the terminology I use throughout.

In short, neoliberalism seeks to limit the state's involvement in the economy, which is regarded as a hindrance toward economic growth. To that end, neoliberals aim to offload state functions onto the private sector through cuts to government funding and taxes, privatization of state assets, and deregulation of the private sector. It's a view that prioritizes individual consumer choices over notions of the collective good. The best thing a government can do, according to this perspective, is get out of the way and allow individuals to make decisions based on their preferences. This libertarian philosophy was most famously summarized by Conservative former U.K. prime minister Margaret Thatcher when she said: "There's no such thing as society. There are individual men and women and there are families. And no government can do anything except through people, and people must look after themselves first. It is our duty to look after ourselves and then, also, to look after our neighbours."[3] This sentiment was succinctly articulated by Kenney when he said in 2017 that "in order to be a compassionate and generous society, you must be a prosperous one first."[4] His stated rejection of the premise that the "state can perfect human nature"[5] is similarly reflective of neoliberal ideology, although as we'll see, there are limits to his distaste for state power.

Neoliberalism is "neo" in the sense that it replaces the progressive liberalism that, inspired by the work of British economist John Maynard Keynes, sought a more active role for the state as a means of stimulating economic growth and limiting the worst excesses of capitalism, namely, poverty. Progressive liberalism was the liberalism of Pierre Elliott Trudeau's Just Society and Franklin Delano Roosevelt's New Deal, but it was part of a broad political consensus that included conservatives such as John Diefenbaker and Richard Nixon, who accepted the state's redistributive function. Neoliberalism, inspired by the work of Austrian economists Friedrich von Hayek and Ludwig von Mises, also established a cross-partisan consensus. Its most enthusiastic adherents were the conservative govern-ments of Ronald Reagan in the United States, Thatcher in the United Kingdom, and Brian Mulroney in Canada, but Bill Clinton, Tony Blair, and Jean Chrétien accepted the premise that the state must be downsized. For neoliberals, the inequities progressive liberals sought to address were not the fault of the market but a combination of insufficient marketization and individual failure.

The "neo" of neoliberalism, however, is a bit of a misnomer, because neoliberalism is, in fact, a return to the pre-progressive classical liberalism of philosophers such as John Locke, who emphasized a need to safeguard individual rights — chief among them, property rights — against state in-trusion. In this view, the state exists solely to mediate between individual disputes through law enforcement. It has no redistributive function. The idea that individuals were separate from the state, and that they had their own "natural rights," as Locke called them, was a radical break with 17th-century political conventions. Neoliberalism was a similarly radical ideology, upending the progressive liberal welfare state in a way similar to how clas-sical liberalism upended the divine right of kings.

The flip side of neoliberalism is neoconservatism. While neoliberalism focuses on the economic sphere, neoconservatism is focused on the social sphere; where neoliberals emphasize individualism, neocons emphasize the collective. Neoconservatism is perhaps best known as a foreign policy doc-trine, which posits that the U.S. Empire isn't just necessary but a right-eous force. It was the driving force behind George W. Bush's ill-fated 2003 invasion of Iraq, which Kenney staunchly supported. This book, for the most part, focuses on the domestic policy realm. Neocon foreign policy, nonetheless, provides an excellent illustration of the ideology's embrace of state power to promote a moral order rooted in tradition, with tradition in the case of the Iraq War being American exceptionalism. The militarism neocons embrace abroad is matched by a tough-on-crime, law-and-order approach at home.

Owing to its embrace of traditional moral systems, neoconservatism offers fertile ground for the religious right, of which Kenney, a zealous Catholic convert, has always been a part. There's a certain theocratic tinge in his politics that sets him apart from many of his contemporaries who share his commitment to the market. "Compartmentalizing my faith into a vacuum-sealed corner of my life is not an option," Kenney told the *Globe and Mail* in February 1999. "It's not an option for any serious person of faith." Catholic teachings, he said elsewhere, inform his opposition to the "moral fashion" of Nazism and communism, which he regards as equally failed attempts at social engineering.[6] Kenney's political orientation is inseparable from his religious convictions. Ultimately, he had to soften his theocratic inclinations for electoral reasons, but this sense of rigid moralism has remained consistent.

In theory, neoliberalism and neoconservatism are at fundamental odds — one is individualist and the other is statist — but in practice there's considerable overlap. Free markets, for example, are a moral value many neocons might use the state to uphold, while policing, with its role in enforcing private property rights, is one of the few state functions a neoliberal would resist offloading to the private sector. Their differences subside in pursuit of establishing "a dominant class power," David Harvey writes in his 2005 book, *A Brief History of Neoliberalism*.

The hollowing out of state institutions under neoliberalism, Harvey adds, creates an opening for neoconservatism, which "has long hovered in the wings as a movement against the moral permissiveness that individualism typically promotes." In other words, neoconservatism provides social glue for piecing together the collectivity torn apart by neoliberalism, providing it with a renewed moral purpose through appeals to patriotism, religion, and tradition. Neoconservatism locks the inequalities created by neoliberalism into place, using what remains of the state to guard against perceived threats to the neoliberal order, by force if necessary. This is why the leading figures of the neoliberal project — Thatcher and Reagan — were also neoconservatives.

The symbiotic relationship between neoliberal economics and neocon sensibility is a defining feature of "Kenneyism," according to researcher John Carlaw, who coined the term in his 2017 Ph.D. thesis, which focused on Kenney's record as citizenship and immigration minister from 2008 to 2014.[7] This book intends to build upon Carlaw's conceptualization. In an interview with me, Carlaw described Kenney as a "movement conservative" engaged in a neocon "ideological battle coupled with a neoliberal approach to economics." Despite never being prime minister, Kenney was one of the most effective emissaries of Reaganism and Thatcherism in Canada.

Kenney, as Alberta premier, provided a clear example of neocon means in pursuit of neoliberal ends, with his "fight-back" strategy against environmentalists, which consisted of a state-sponsored intimidation campaign against those he regarded as a threat to the smooth functioning of the oil and gas industry, which is itself a traditional element of Alberta's political identity. This leads to another aspect of Kenneyism that Carlaw identifies: the demonization of political opponents. Carlaw described steamrolling anyone who stands in the way of the neoliberal order as a "through line" of Kenney's political career in a January 2022 interview with the *Tyee*.

Despite his warranted reputation as a brilliant political tactician, Kenney had an odd inability to answer the most basic critical inquiries. Kenney and his proxies' go-to retort to reporters' pesky questions was to "reject the premise of your question," whether it was the carbon tax he lambasted being used to fund popular infrastructure projects, his race-baiting against South Asian Albertans during the pandemic, banning British parliamentarian George Galloway from entering Canada, a series of questions from the *National Observer* for a profile piece, his seeming reluctance to condemn far-right hate groups, his unwillingness to take responsibility for the province's pandemic failures, and so on. This approach to answering basic critical inquiries is reflective of an authoritarianism that is at the core of Kenney's political project.

Jason Kenney is, however, for the most part, not a hypocrite. Observers commonly refer to apparent inconsistencies in his worldview by contrasting his embrace of free-market economics with his willingness to subsidize the oil and gas industry, or his commitment to deficit reduction with his support for deficit-enhancing tax cuts, or his embrace of established immigrant communities with his draconian refugee policies. But viewed in the context of the New Right project of strengthening existing class structures, these actions aren't contradictory at all. They all serve the same end of increasing the power of those at the top of the economic hierarchy over those who aren't, preventing, as Brooklyn College political scientist Corey Robin put it, "a rotation in the seat of power."[8]

Authoritarian Populism

Offloading state responsibilities onto the private sector, taking them outside the realm of public control, while using the authority of the state to maintain this order, is a fundamentally anti-democratic project. In order for neocon ideologues, like Kenney, to attain power, they need to solicit popular support for their aims, which leads to another concept — populism. Populists speak for the masses alienated by neoliberalism and promise to wrest power from the corrupt elites who have excluded the people from the political process. Populism is ideologically neutral, making it a clever rhetorical strategy for proponents of neoliberalism to deepen the problems they purport to address by shifting blame for the destruction of the social fabric away from businesses and their political enablers and toward something else, whether it's immigrants, big government, criminals, or whatnot.

Jamaican-British social theorist Stuart Hall coined the phrase "authoritarian populism," or "popular authoritarianism," as it's been called elsewhere, to describe Thatcher's ability to create popular consent for her authoritarian project. Rather than construct policies based on the preexisting will of the people, Thatcher fashioned a vision of "the people" that supported her policies as she proceeded to implement them, recruiting seemingly contradictory constituencies into her project, from coal miners to coal mine owners. In doing so, she was able to challenge the old progressive liberal consensus and forge a new "common sense" based on her preferred ideology. Kenney, who once boasted of politicians' "power to create facts" by setting the terms of debate,[9] was an attentive student of Thatcher's. Early in his political career, he learned to speak on behalf of the people standing against "special interests," a term vague enough to define whatever he dislikes — unions, teachers, environmentalists, nurses, refugees — the common thread being those who stand in the way of the neoliberal project.

In helping him forge a new common sense, Kenney had a willing partner in the Canadian media. While the focus of this book isn't media criticism, I do note when media played a role in promoting Kenney's political project by uncritically echoing his talking points, which was evident from his early days with the Canadian Taxpayers Federation (CTF). "[The CTF] play you guys like a finely tuned fiddle," said Paul Taylor, an assistant to Alberta treasurer Jim Dinning when Kenney, as head of the CTF's Alberta wing, was encouraging premier Ralph Klein's neoliberal reforms.[10] The growing concentration of Canadian newspapers in the hands of Postmedia, which in recent years has imposed an explicitly conservative editorial direction on its subsidiaries, and its gutting of local newsrooms, certainly helped Kenney's cause when he returned to Alberta. Reporters, who often did essential work in holding the Kenney government to account, became increasingly over-worked, making it harder for them to cover every story with the attention to detail warranted. Meanwhile, the range of acceptable opinion, as represented by the political punditry, became increasingly uniform in its conservatism. They were Kenney's allies in forging a populist consensus in favour of end-less tar sands extraction, regressive taxes, an assault on public health care and education, and manufacturing a sense of western alienation from the federal government.

Yet the media couldn't protect Kenney from the naked hollowness of his populist appeal, which brought about his demise in Alberta at the hands of his own party. He made a vow to the UCP grassroots he had no intention of keeping — that all policy would be determined by them. This came to a head during the pandemic, but these deficiencies were evident from the outset of his reign. As long as Kenney implemented his neoliberal agenda, his base was willing to overlook his lukewarm commitment to populism. But the pandemic brought into question the feasibility of this economic project, despite Kenney's best efforts to keep business moving as usual, which is when his problems with caucus became exacerbated. He could no longer construct a popular consensus in favour of his agenda, because his agenda became increasingly incoherent, wildly swinging back and forth between inaction and action on pandemic restrictions, unsure of which approach would best serve his long-term project of enforcing neoliberal rigidities.

What to Expect in *Kenneyism*

Kenneyism is roughly chronological, detailing Jason Kenney's political evolution and the policies he pursued throughout his life. The first four chapters detail Kenney's early upbringing through his years as a Harper Cabinet minister. The next seven chapters focus on his efforts to obtain power in Alberta and then on various policy areas of his brief premiership. This lopsided structure, with a disproportionate emphasis on his six-year involvement in Alberta politics, is by design. While Kenney was a highly influential Cabinet minister who was given an unusual amount of free rein by Harper, it was as Alberta premier that he was the chief decision-maker, and where it all went spectacularly wrong for him. His premiership is also what I'm in the best position to make sense of, having covered it as it occurred.

In the first chapter, I discuss Kenney's early political development. I detail his unusual early upbringing, his high school years, which have yet to be examined in detail, and then his conversion to Catholicism and neo-conservatism as an undergraduate in San Francisco. These years provide the underpinnings of his embrace of hierarchy and tradition, which are constants throughout his political career. In Chapter 2, I examine Kenney's time with the CTF, first as the director of its Alberta wing, and then as the executive director of the entire organization, which is where he honed his neoliberal mantra of lowering taxes, lowering debt, and reducing the size of government. This was also where he began speaking about elites and "special interests" on behalf of a vague conception of the masses and became a prominent media voice.

Chapter 3 deals with Kenney's move to electoral politics under the banner of the Reform Party, which allowed him to pursue his economic and religious fundamentalism simultaneously. This chapter examines his role in efforts to expand Reform's appeal, first as a member of the youthful "Snack Pack," and then as a central figure in efforts to pursue unity with the PC Party under the United Alternative banner. During these years, Kenney previewed the ethnocultural outreach strategy he mastered once unity was obtained under the Conservative Party of Canada.

Chapter 4 discusses his central role as Harper's lieutenant for outreach to immigrant communities, resulting in the party expanding the base of its support into electorally important suburban ridings. It also details how this outreach was conditional upon embracing the Harper government's neocon conception of what it means to be Canadian, which Kenney articulated in the updated Canadian citizenship guide. This conditional acceptance was reflected in how Kenney fast-tracked permanent residency for immigrants while at the same time making Canada increasingly unwelcome for those who didn't fit the right economic profile.

Chapter 5 begins with Kenney's return to Alberta after the Conservatives lost the federal election, with the goal of repeating his success in uniting Reform and the PCs for the Wildrose and Alberta PCs. I detail how Kenney was able to tap into Alberta's political culture through the use of long-standing "political codes," which emphasize populism, individualism, and autonomy. While individualism came naturally to him as a dyed-in-the-wool neoliberal, he struggled with the populist and autonomous elements as the very embodiment of the Ottawa elite he raged against.

In Chapter 6, I discuss the early implementation of Kenney's neoliberal policies in Alberta, which served to unite the PC and Wildrose factions of the UCP in common cause. This consisted of tax cuts and deregulation, on the one hand, and using legislation to suppress the labour movement on the other. In an effort to shrink the size of government, he convened a panel to look into Alberta's finances, which was only permitted to examine expenditures, not revenue. Predictably, the panel recommended what Kenney already planned to do — take an axe to the public sector.

Chapter 7 details Kenney's war on the environmentalist movement in the midst of a climate emergency. His so-called fight-back strategy consisted of a government-funded war room to respond to criticisms of the oil sands, and an inquiry into alleged foreign funding of environmentalist groups. The war room quickly became an expensive embarrassment for the government, and the inquiry, after multiple delays, released an inconclusive report. I identify the purpose of these initiatives as casting a shroud of suspicion over environmental activism, which was more effective than their stated goals.

Chapter 8 discusses Kenney's assault on Alberta's public education system, mainly focusing on his decision to completely redo the K–12 curriculum update that had been in the works for more than a decade. His replacement was a disaster, particularly the social studies curriculum, which served to sow confusion in the education system. The curriculum debacle occurred in the context of cutting funding to public education while expanding the reach of publicly funded, privately operated charter schools. The chapter concludes with Kenney's ferocious assault on higher education.

In Chapter 9, I outline Kenney's ideological aversion to harm reduction as a means of addressing the ongoing drug-poisoning crisis, with his efforts to shut down supervised consumption sites while lavishing funds on private, abstinence-only recovery facilities. This juxtaposition reflects Kenney's neocon moralism, in which those who use drugs are sinners who can only be redeemed through dogmatic adherence to abstinence. In this view, any efforts to keep people who use drugs alive through harm-reduction methods enables immoral activity.

Chapter 10 first deals with Kenney's efforts to begin dismantling Alberta's public health-care system before detailing his disastrous pandemic response. Kenney prioritized the smooth functioning of capitalism from the pandemic's outset, as evidenced by his government's efforts to keep the meat-packing industry running steadily, with deadly consequences. This inclination toward maintaining business as usual led him to repeatedly delay imposing pandemic restrictions until it was too late to have maximal impact, reaching a crescendo with his deadly Open for Summer plan in 2021, which he abandoned in the face of record intensive-care unit (ICU) admissions. Kenney's indecision satisfied neither those who supported pandemic restrictions, nor those who advocated a hands-off approach.

In Chapter 11, I discuss Kenney's downfall, which was propelled by the very populist forces he cultivated upon his return to Alberta, who were also frustrated by Kenney's unwillingness to confront the federal government in deed rather than words. They found their champion in former Wildrose leader and talk-show conspiracy theorist Danielle Smith, who promised she would fulfill what Kenney only talked about doing.

The book concludes with an epilogue that ties together the threads defining who Kenney is throughout a political career characterized as much by shrewd political calculation as ideological orientation. I note the continuity of his reverence for symbols of authority, such as the church and monarchy, which upholds the rigid class structure he sought to impose as rooted in a natural hierarchy. He had to make compromises along the way to win elections, but at its core his project is one of snapping the social relations formed by neoliberalism into place. I have no doubt Kenney genuinely believes in his vision.

Kenney is, for all his flaws I hope to highlight, a deep political thinker, which sets him apart from many of his contemporaries, who only know a series of talking points. With this came a certain arrogance. "Jason had this way about him that even though he may be the smartest guy in the room, he would really like to make sure everyone knew this," Rahim Jaffer, his caucus mate of 11 years, told me. Through all his political skullduggery, Kenney has a clear vision of the order he wants to impose on society. He had remarkable success in inching the contours of political debate in his direction, with grave implications for those deemed unworthy.

1

CULTURE WARRIOR

WHILE THIS BOOK ISN'T A CONVENTIONAL biography, it's nonetheless worthwhile to explore Jason Kenney's upbringing. Kenney's early days shaped the contours of his world view, revealing the underpinnings of his reverence for authority, deep-seated religious views, remarkable work ethic, and transformation from a run-of-the-mill Liberal into a fiery right-wing culture warrior. I spoke to a few of his old friends from high school. By all accounts, Jason was a brilliant youngster but a poor student, who took a keen interest in politics from a young age. In 2001, he expressed mystification about his early political development, telling journalist Steve Paikin that his interest "must have been developed in utero."[1] His family had little political involvement, with one notable exception.

Kenney's paternal grandfather is famed jazz musician Herbert Martin Kenney, or Mart, as he was known personally and professionally. Dubbed "Canada's Big Band King," his band, Mart Kenney and His Western Gentlemen, achieved major success in the 1930s and 1940s, getting their start at Vancouver's Alexandra Ballroom before achieving Canada-wide success, being featured regularly on CBC Radio, and touring across the country during the Second World War. Their signature song was a re-interpretation of the 1922 Billy Hill–Larry Yoell waltz, "The West, a Nest and You, Dear"; Mart also wrote a song called "We're Proud of Canada," which was itself a hit. If you go to the Canadian Music Hall of Fame at Calgary's National Music Centre, you will find Mart Kenney's clarinet. When Jason, as Alberta premier, unveiled the government's K–6 draft curriculum in 2021, students were expected to learn about Grandpa Mart in Grade 6 music class.

Jason was born on May 30, 1968, in Oakville, Ontario, a sizable town located halfway between Toronto and Hamilton. A few weeks before Jason's birth, Mart ran for the Liberal nomination in the York North riding in Toronto, losing to Barney Danson, a plastics company executive,[2] who later became Pierre Elliott Trudeau's housing minister. Mart wasn't done with politics. In 1985, he was elected to the town council in Mission, British Columbia, where he and his wife, fellow musician Norma Locke, settled in retirement. Jason cited Mart as a major influence on him, recalling his grandfather's efforts to get him "back into the [Liberal] party of Louis St. Laurent" once Jason's political views shifted rightward.[3]

Jason's father, Martin, born in 1932, attended Oakville's Appleby College, where he excelled in athletics, becoming captain of the private boys' school's varsity football and hockey teams. He then went to Queen's University where he played fullback on the school's Golden Gaels football team. From 1954 to 1962, Martin served as a jet fighter pilot in the Royal Canadian Air Force, assigned to the "Night Hawks" 409 Squadron based at CFB Comox in British Columbia. During the Cold War, Martin was tasked with turning Soviet Buffalo Bombers away in his CF-100 as they tested the capabilities of the joint U.S.-Canadian North American Aerospace Defense Command (NORAD) early-warning system in the North Pacific.

On December 20, 1958, one of Martin's crew members set him up on a blind date after they were forced to land in Vancouver due to inclement weather. The date, which Martin attended in uniform, was with Lynne Tunbridge, the former Strawberry Festival Princess of Mission, British Columbia. A few weeks later, they got married.

Lynne and Martin returned to Oakville in 1962 after Martin accepted a job at Appleby College where he taught history, coached hockey and football, led the school's cadet corps, and was headmaster for its boarding students. In a 2011 *Toronto Star* profile, Jason described his father as a "great raconteur, an extrovert" and his mother as a "formidable, dignified,

A Kenney family photo from 1973 when they lived in Winnipeg. Clockwise from left: David, Martin Sr., Martin Jr., Jason, and Lynne.

hard-working and marvellous lady," citing her work ethic as an inspiration.[4] Martin's 2010 obituary described him as a "master teller of tales, with an occasional tendency to gild the lily," an evident influence on his youngest son.[5]

Jason has two brothers — Martin and David — neither of whom are politically inclined, although both have made the news for very different reasons. The eldest, Martin Jr., is a crusading international anti-fraud lawyer based in the British Virgin Islands. He runs his own firm, Martin Kenney and Co. Solicitors, which employs a team of lawyers, forensic accountants, former Central Intelligence Agency (CIA) and MI6 operatives, retired U.S. Secret Service agents, and a psychiatrist. "Martin embraced the whole approach of my dad: Go hard in everything you did," Jason told the *Toronto Star* for a May 2013 profile on Martin Jr. While Jason was at the Alberta Association of Taxpayers, Martin Jr. cracked his first major case as a young lawyer in New York City, recovering millions of dollars for a Canadian bank by hiring a former CIA agent to pose as a fraudster. The World Bank solicited his services to recover millions of dollars deposed Egyptian dictator Hosni Mubarak held in offshore accounts.[6] Most recently, Martin Jr. helped initiate a lawsuit against Toronto-Dominion (TD) Bank, alleging the financial institution knowingly allowed offshore companies involved in a $7 billion Ponzi scheme to open accounts, which resulted in TD paying a US$1.2 billion settlement in February 2023.

David Kenney is a whole other story. In February 2014, a private inpatient youth recovery centre he ran with his wife, Susan, in Kelowna — the NeurVana Recovery and Wellness Centre — was shut down by the B.C. government for operating without a licence a few months after three girls ran away.[7] David unsuccessfully challenged the closure of the clinic, which charged anywhere from $20,000 to $25,000 for a three-week program using unproven "brainwave optimization technology" to treat mental illness and addiction, in court. Testimony from the proceedings revealed a cultish environment, in which patients had their personal belongings, including prescription medications, stripped from them, and confidential conversations with David were used against them as a means of control. After a stint in the Cayman Islands and an attempt to establish a similar clinic, but for adults, in Barrie, Ontario, he moved to Calgary in late 2021 where he now trains recovery coaches.

From Winnipeg to Wilcox

In 1973, Martin Sr. moved the family to Winnipeg where he was hired as the first male principal for the private all-girls Balmoral Hall, which was in the process of becoming a boarding school. Martin had no daughters or sisters and had never taught girls, but Lynne told him to "just teach them like you teach boys." Tasked with increasing enrollment at the school to a sustainable level, Martin Sr. was "extremely successful," according to a 2001 yearbook celebrating the school's centennial, "bringing back some of the pride in the school." Martin Sr. held a dinner and dancing fundraiser each of the three years he was at the school, starring Grandpa Mart. Jason, then five years old, lived with his siblings and parents on campus. He began his primary education at the girls' school, where he was enrolled in kindergarten and Grade 1.[8]

In Winnipeg, Kenney began to develop a political consciousness at an exceptionally young age against the backdrop of the Watergate scandal. He claims he read the entire front section of the *Winnipeg Free Press* daily by age seven. "My parents must have been thinking, we've got some kind of idiot savant in the house. He can't do math, doesn't have any musical talent. But he talks about American politics," Kenney recalled to Steve Paikin. "Instead of watching cartoons, I was watching the Watergate hearings."[9]

The family left Winnipeg in 1976 after Martin Sr. accepted an offer to serve as president of Athol Murray College of Notre Dame, a co-ed boarding school in Wilcox, Saskatchewan, a town of fewer than 300 people about a 40-minute drive south of Regina or southeast of Moose Jaw. If you blink while driving along Highway 39 from Moose Jaw, you might miss it. When school's in session, the town's population doubles, but every full-time resident has some kind of connection to the school.

Kenney Hall, a multipurpose building with a gymnasium, library, and classrooms named after Martin Sr., is attached to the Duncan J. McNeil Arena, which many NHL players have passed through as Notre Dame Hounds, including two stars of the 2004 Stanley Cup–winning Tampa Bay Lightning — Vincent Lecavalier and Brad Richards, the latter of whom was named playoff MVP that year and won the cup again with the Chicago Blackhawks in 2015 — and Rod Brind'amour, who captained the Carolina Hurricanes when they won the cup for the first time in 2006. The school also has baseball, lacrosse, football, and rugby teams.

Kitty-corner to campus — on the easternmost edge of town — is a big brown house. This is the president's residence, which was first built for the

Kenneys after they lived in the basement of an administrative building for several years. From Grades 2 to 8, Jason went to the now-defunct Wilcox Public School next door, which was previously attended by future federal Liberal Cabinet minister Ralph Goodale,[10] whom Jason would later work for briefly. Lynne worked first as Martin Sr.'s receptionist before moving into administrative roles. After retiring from Notre Dame, Martin Sr. went on to become the headmaster of Emirates International School in Dubai in 1993.

The school's official slogan, "Struggle and Emerge," hints at the harsh disposition of Athol Murray College's namesake, Monsignor Athol Murray, or "Père," as students called him. Murray was described in an April 1980 *Edmonton Journal* article as "a difficult, paradoxical man.... Some called him a bigot. He hated socialism, was often rough and abusive with his students and had the vocabulary of a dock worker. But along with all of this, according to those who knew him, went the soul of a saint and the mind of a Greek philosopher." Murray's pedagogical approach was shaped by Greek philosophy. He believed he could mould students into great intellectuals, athletes, and people of faith through a curriculum that combined equal amounts of academics, athletics, and spirituality.

Murray created Notre Dame College in 1927 out of the St. Augustine's school run by the Sisters of Charity of St. Louis congregation, bringing with him 15 boys from an athletic club he formed in Regina. He found a wealthy benefactor in San Diego Padres' owner Bill Lane, who occasionally came to town to scout baseball players. During the Great Depression, Lane purchased the town's old bank building, which was repurposed into Murray's office and residence, dubbed Lane Hall. Next door, students lived in a series of shacks, which doubled as classrooms, before the modern campus was gradually built. Upon Murray's death in 1975, the Board of Regents brought in Martin Sr., who renamed it after its founder. Murray is buried near the campus entrance, outside St. Augustine's Church, and an adjacent monument to the Abrahamic faiths, the Tower of God.

Politically, Murray sought "to preserve maximum possible individual freedom under divine law," in the words of Murray admirer Ted Byfield,[11] who founded the influential neoconservative *Alberta Report* magazine and was a friend of Jason's. While other pricey private schools "turned out a lot of carbon copies[,] [h]ere we turn out individuals," Murray explained to the *Calgary Herald* in March 1937. "Open-mindedness, that's the spirit of the thing." Yet Murray's open-mindedness was limited. In 1934, he expelled two students for being members of the recently founded Co-operative Commonwealth Federation (CCF), the more left-wing, agrarian forerunner of the NDP, after giving them an ultimatum to leave the party or the school. "All that was done was to point out to the Catholics their duty," he told the *Edmonton Journal* in May 1934. "The Socialist system of thought [is] utterly alien to Catholic thought."

His staunch opposition to anything that smacked of socialism in general, and the CCF in particular, informed his militant stance against the introduction of universal health care in Saskatchewan in 1962 by CCF premier Woodrow Lloyd. "This thing may break into violence and bloodshed any day now, and God help us if it doesn't," Murray told attendees at an anti-Medicare rally,[12] urging them to take up arms.[13] After the Royal Canadian Mounted Police (RCMP) considered arresting Murray for inciting violence, the Catholic Church booted him from Saskatchewan until tensions died down.

Murray wasn't opposed to collectivism per se. "Our philosophy is the idea of the gang," he told the *Edmonton Journal* in February 1937. "Come on gang," Murray reportedly told the students in lieu of a school bell. Although they never met, Jason Kenney was at least somewhat influenced by Murray, whom Kenney called a "great Canadian folk hero."[14] While awaiting the results of his 2022 UCP leadership review, Kenney invoked the spirit of Murray in an interview with the *Calgary Sun*'s Rick Bell: "Fr. Athol Murray used to say: 'Gang, you're either on the building crew or the wrecking crew.' I'm on the building crew, I hope our whole caucus is."[15] Murray's view of the role of the individual as part of a hierarchical collective has clear echoes in Kenney's political evolution.

Jason's political ambitions were fuelled in April 1977 when he was almost nine. Notre Dame held a $100-per-couple fundraising gala at the Saskatchewan Centre of the Arts in Regina, with former conservative prime minister John Diefenbaker as its keynote speaker. In an often-repeated story, Diefenbaker approached Jason, who was wearing a child-sized brown suit and tie, on the couch where he was seated and struck up a conversation with the boy. According to a *Maclean's* profile of Jason when he was head of the Canadian Taxpayers Federation, Diefenbaker asked him if he liked school. Kenney responded he didn't "because it's too easy."[16] According to a Canadian Press wire story from 2019, the former prime minister quizzed Jason about the myth of Jason and the Argonauts, his favourite subjects in school, and future plans. "That 10-minute conversation made an indelible impression on me," Jason told CP, speculating this interaction may have spurred his political ambitions. "That a former prime minister would spend 10 minutes talking to a 10-year-old boy was remarkable to me. I never forgot the kindness that he showed."

Columnist Randy Boswell, writing in *Canada's National Observer*, said Kenney's frequent recounting of this anecdote presents an image "that destiny had a hand in his rise to power, that this was the fulfillment of prophecy." This self-mythologizing isn't unique to Kenney. Bill Clinton's presidential campaign circulated a photo of Clinton meeting President John F. Kennedy as a teenager, and Diefenbaker himself frequently recalled a story of him selling a newspaper to Prime Minister Wilfrid Laurier when he was a teenage paperboy in Saskatoon. But with Kenney's religious convictions, his reading of his encounter with the former prime minister takes on heightened meaning.

Although he served as president of a Catholic school, Martin Sr. was himself Anglican, and Jason was baptized accordingly. But a few years after his run-in with Diefenbaker, Jason visited Westminster Abbey, a B.C. Benedictine monastery, while visiting Grandpa Mart in Mission. He decided then and there he wanted to convert to Catholicism to attend high school at its junior seminary and become a monk. The monastery turned him down, arguing he was too young to make such a drastic decision. Jason eventually converted to Catholicism; he also attended high school in British Columbia, but left halfway for reasons that are obscure.

From Wilcox to Victoria and Back

In 1982, Jason was sent to St. Michael's University School for high school, a private boarding school in a residential area in the east side of Victoria. The campus's buildings, including a non-denominational chapel, form a semi-circle around a massive field where rugby and soccer tournaments are often hosted. With its emphasis on academics, athletics, and faith, and relative seclusion, it's like a larger Notre Dame Academy on the West Coast. Here Jason was reunited with an old family friend from Winnipeg: Gus de Jardin, one of his roommates for two semesters at the boarding school, sleeping on the bunk above him.

I interviewed de Jardin, who hasn't seen Jason in person since he left St. Mike's. He told me over the phone that he remembers Jason as a bookish "fat, giggly kid." De Jardin's father, Gus Sr., was best friends with Martin Sr., who, like him, was an air force veteran. They remained close until Martin Sr. died in 2006. De Jardin's family made the trip to Wilcox to spend Christmas with the Kenneys when they first moved to town and occasionally vacationed together. De Jardin, who now lives in Kelowna, told me Martin and Lynne sent their youngest son to boarding school on the West Coast, rather than have him stay at home to attend Notre Dame, because Jason "was always a mama's boy." They wanted him to become self-reliant. St. Mike's, a former military cadet academy, would have appealed to Martin Sr. as a place to whip his youngest son into shape.

Jason and de Jardin weren't particularly close, but they always got along fine. "The first time I met him, I just remember he was really into reading history books. And my recollection is he's a bit of a loner." De Jardin was always a rebellious type, which left him without much in common with Jason. "You're kind of quirky at that age," said de Jardin, "but Jason was always kind of straight and narrow." Around that time, at age 14, Jason read *The Great Conversation* by Robert Maynard Hutchins, which he later described to the *Toronto Star* as "a fascinating, compelling invitation to read the Western canon of great works."[17] One thing Jason and de Jardin had in common, however, was struggling with math. They had the same tutor, Wild Bill Cochrane, a Second World War veteran who occasionally fell asleep during sessions. "We didn't learn much," said de Jardin.

De Jardin remembers Jason as a staunch monarchist from a young age, a devotion Jason maintains to this day. When Queen Elizabeth II visited Victoria from March 8 to 11, 1983, de Jardin recalls Kenney waking up in the middle of the night to secure a good spot to see the monarch in the flesh at the Inner Harbour where the royal yacht *Britannia* docked, right by the Legislative Assembly of British Columbia. A closer friend from St. Mike's, Simon Jenkins, remembers getting the day off school for the queen's visit. While most students reluctantly went to the harbour because they were bored and had nothing else to do, Jenkins recalls Jason's enthusiasm.

In an October 2022 retrospective interview with conservative online news outlet the *Hub*, Kenney explained his long-standing admiration for the Crown. The stability represented by the monarchy "perfectly reflects the vision of Burkean conservatism, which is a reverence for the received wisdom of the past," he said, referring to Edmund Burke, one of the founders of modern conservative thought. Although he hadn't yet converted to Catholicism, Kenney was similarly enamoured with Pope John Paul II, whom he later cited as a hero. Jenkins recalls Jason's excitement when the pope spoke at BC Place Stadium on his visit to Canada in 1984, Jason having taken the ferry to the Lower Mainland to attend. The blind deference to tradition and authority symbolized by the monarchy and the Vatican no doubt informed Jason's eventual neoconservative turn.

Jenkins, who is a year older than Jason, became close friends with him at St. Mike's after Jason entered Grade 10 and moved into International House, the boarding house for students in Grades 10 to 12. Jenkins, whose parents sent him off to boarding school when they moved to Saudi Arabia, formed a group of outcasts with Kenney, alongside their friends Chris Wynters and Bernie Langille, who didn't fit in with the dominant jock culture permeating St. Mike's. They were instead taken in by mod culture — the anti-hippie counterculture of the 1960s that by the 1980s had been revived in North America, dressing in 1960s-style suits, trench coats, and French berets while riding Chris's and Bernie's Vespas. They would rather "be in Paris on the Left Bank in a café sipping a cappuccino and listening to jazz," as Jenkins put it, than at a stuffy Victoria boarding school. "We didn't go to the officially sanctioned parties," Jenkins told me. "Most of our friends were punk rockers and other misfit nonconformists." After school, they hung out at a restaurant called Pagliacci's in downtown Victoria where all the punks and mods went. The mods listened to bands such as The Who, whose album *Quadrophenia* was made into a 1979 film that presaged the 1980s mod revival, and The Jam, as well as old soul and Motown music from the 1960s.

I found all these details surprising, given the stodgy image Kenney cultivated in later years. "His favourite music is medieval. His idea of a light read is Dostoyevsky. And his hero is the Pope," reads the lead of a June 1997 *Calgary Herald* profile of Kenney. A February 2013 piece in *Maclean's* from Kenney's time as a Cabinet minister described him poring over immigration documents while listening to Gregorian chants and classical music on a stereo. That was always there, "Gregorian chants and that sort of thing," Jenkins said, but Jason was at the same time engaged in a counterculture where he found a community, or "gang," in Père Murray's parlance, of outsiders.

"We used to get beat up all the time for the way we dressed," Jenkins recalls, noting the tension between the mods and metalheads. The gang took a trip to Vancouver to check out its more vibrant mod scene. At a bus stop, Jenkins remembers a driver passing by and shouting the homophobic f-slur at them, to which they responded by giving him the finger. The car stopped, according to Jenkins, did a U-turn, and a man with long hair and an Iron Maiden T-shirt came out of the car to beat them up — "not severely, but Jason got kicked in the ass. It was more like his dignity was hurt." The boys ended up sleeping in downtown Vancouver's Robson Square because they didn't have any money.

In Steve Paikin's book *The Life: The Seductive Call of Politics*, Kenney claims he never had a grand plan to become a politician. "I've read about teenagers, who decided they were going to be prime minister of Canada, who laid out this grand plan and adjusted everything in their life to that plan," he said. "I decided that I never wanted to be that kind of obsessive lifetime politician, for whom the end became so important it justified any means. I was open to the prospect of running for the federal parliament some day, but I was never the kid who had this grand life plan to get elected."[18]

According to de Jardin and Jenkins, that's a lie. Both recall Jason explicitly declaring his desire to become prime minister in high school. "I'm *going* to become prime minister" is how de Jardin remembers it. Jenkins recalls a night when the mods were hanging out at Mount Tolmie, with its panoptical view of the city just northeast of the St. Mike's campus. They were talking about their plans once they graduated, probably drinking a few beers. He isn't sure whether Jason confidently declared he *will* be prime minister, or whether he simply said he wanted to, but the intention was clear. "We all kind of laughed. But no, he was totally serious. He was dead serious."

At the time, Jason, following in Mart's footsteps, became heavily involved with the Liberals. Jenkins vividly remembers Jason, in 1983, telling him to come with him downtown, but wouldn't say why. Their destination was Bastion Square, near the waterfront, about five blocks from their Pagliacci's hangout, where the Liberal Party's Victoria headquarters was. Jason joined the party on the spot. "Lust for power?" a young volunteer asked him kiddingly. "Yes," Jason replied, chuckling.[19] The following year, Jason attended the party's national convention in Halifax, where he was elected to the Young Liberals of Canada's national policy committee — his first of many electoral wins.[20] While Jason often brought up his fateful encounter with John Diefenbaker from his childhood, he was less keen to publicize a one-on-one dinner he had with Prime Minister John Turner when Turner stopped in Victoria during his three-month premiership that summer.

Soon after his date with the short-lived prime minister, Jason was asked not to come back to St. Mike's. While there's speculation this was a result of his engaging in some un-Catholic behaviour, the truth, according to people who knew him, appears to be duller — his grades weren't good enough. He was in Victoria over the summer after Grade 10 because he flunked math. Jason returned to Wilcox to finish high school under Martin Sr.'s watchful eye, living at the president's house, rather than in the dorms. While Jason played some hockey at Notre Dame, he wasn't much of an athlete, so the school set up a debate club for him.

There was some horrific hazing coming from that school's older, more athletic students, involving physical, psychological, and sexual abuse, occurring around the time Jason returned. Kenny Wray, who attended the school from 1984 to 1987, was one of the people who came forward with his accounts of abuse in May 2022. In addition to random beatings, Wray told *CTV News* he was forced to do so-called atlas sit-ups, doing them blindfolded while an older student stuck his buttocks in his face. "It's not a pleasant experience. If they decide to wipe, it's a bonus, I guess, but a lot of times that didn't happen." He was forced to do push-ups, sit-ups, and wall sits until he vomited. However, Wray said his experience at Notre Dame was more positive than negative. I couldn't help but wonder if Martin Sr. had any inkling of what was going on at the school he ran. I reached out to Wray, who said Martin Sr.'s role as president was more of a figurehead position, more concerned with fundraising than any day-to-day operations, so he couldn't have been aware of the abuse.

Wray, who works as a trucker in Olds, a town about an hour's drive north of Calgary, told me he remembers Jason well from his time at Athol Murray College where they were in the same social studies and economics classes. Jason existed outside the predominant athletic culture at Notre Dame, just as he had at St. Mike's, reflected in part by his attire. Whereas most students wore sweats and hoodies, Jason continued to sport his mod suits. "He was businesslike, very professional, even in Grade 12," Wray said, describing a "quiet confidence" Jason possessed that shielded him from the bullying and hazing rampant at Notre Dame. This wasn't because Jason was the son of the school's president, Wray emphasized. His brother, David, who was more of an athlete, was routinely picked on. "When you're at school with a bunch of jocks, whose biggest kick is to pick on each other, and you're sort of an oddball in that you never get picked on, that commands respect."

There's one memory from social studies class that stood out in Wray's mind, which foreshadowed Jason's political career far more than a chance encounter with a former prime minister. For one assignment, they had an elaborate mock Parliament in class, with a sergeant-at-arms and a speaker, and all the mock MPs engaging in debate. Jason, of course, volunteered for the prime minister role. Wray remembers this as the first time he heard this quiet, nerdy kid speak. "He commanded the room and his research was spot on. The opposition couldn't debate, they had nothing with him. It was so amazing to watch him and that was when I gained respect for him.... Everybody was in awe. It was like, 'Holy shit, this guy really knows what to do up there.'" Their teacher, Gerry Scheibel, was equally impressed, telling the students, "This is how it's done, guys. This is exactly how it's done in Parliament."

The year Jason graduated from Notre Dame, he ran to be the Young Liberals' vice-president of national policy. It remains the only time he lost an election in his political career,[21] since he technically won his UCP leadership review by a hair. Over the next few years, he gradually shed his political skin, becoming the neocon we know today. Jenkins, who lost touch with Jason after he left St. Mike's, has remained essentially liberal in his politics. He moved to Seoul, South Korea, for 25 years in 1993, so he only saw Jason's political career take off in fragments, but always wondered what happened to his old friend whom he remembers loathing President Ronald Reagan. "I'd love to get back in touch, have a drink with the guy, and just find out where he's at. Because I haven't changed my world view. But he's changed so much. I just find it fascinating. He's an enigma to me."

The Young Zealot

In 1987, Jason went off to St. Ignatius Institute, a private Jesuit college run out of the University of San Francisco (USF) with a program focused on the great texts of Western civilization. Here his politics began to shift rightward as his religious views grew more extreme. The definitive account of Kenney's student activism during his San Francisco years is journalist Taylor Lambert's two-part "The Young Zealot" story for the *Sprawl*, which details the crusade Jason launched against pro-choice activists and LGBTQ+ people from 1988 to 1990.

In the year before his activism began, Kenney underwent a profound political and eschatological transformation. Kenney said he went to the United States "with all the prejudices of a typical young Canadian," describing his younger self as a "liberal, nationalist, anti-American, knee-jerk supporter of the welfare state."[22] In a 2013 interview with the *Toronto Star*, Kenney said this changed when he "started studying political theory, classical political theory and started reading much more broadly, and realized [his] values were essentially Conservative." His first USF roommate, Marc Pecha, played a major role, with his subscription to the *National Review*, the American neoconservative magazine. "When he wasn't in the room, I'd start peeking at his *National Review* like I was looking at *Playboy*."[23]

A papal visit to San Francisco at the beginning of Kenney's first semester appears to have spurred his long-awaited religious conversion. A September 1987 op-ed he authored in the USF's *Foghorn* student newspaper after seeing Pope John Paul II in the flesh for the second time in three years, with the headline "A View from the Outside," shows Kenney grappling with his changing world view at age 19. While repeatedly emphasizing his outsider status as a non-Catholic, Kenney lambasted a "pick-and-choose brand of American Catholicism," which, he wrote, is rooted in "an obfuscation of the democratic ideal, carrying it into the province of ecclesiastical matters." This "blatant dissent of Papal teaching authority," he continued, is somehow "an insult to those Anglicans and Orthodox who love the Catholic faith, but who are separated from Rome over the single question of the Pope's authority."[24] This argument, of course, doesn't make an iota of sense. Why would an Anglican or Protestant care if the pope's authority, which they by definition don't believe in, is subverted by Catholics? Kenney answered that question definitively later the following year when he officially converted to Catholicism.

The notion that religious authority supersedes democratic principles permeated his student activist years. In his first semester, Kenney was elected freshman class president and to the students' association senate. By the next semester, he attempted to force student senators to say a Catholic prayer before each meeting, which he likened to singing the national anthem before a basketball game — again presenting himself as an objective, non-Catholic outsider. Student government "cannot do work without invoking a higher and proper authority," he told the *Foghorn* in February 1988, adding that it "ought to be a first step to make this a substantive Catholic university."

When the senate voted against his proposal at the urging of the director of the campus ministry, Father Christopher Cartwright, Kenney called the vote a "democratic sham."

While his views began taking on an increasingly theocratic turn, for much of 1988 Kenney remained politically liberal, which might say more about the malleability of a liberalism than it does about Kenney. During the 1988 winter semester, he worked on Al Gore's ill-fated first presidential campaign[25] when the future vice-president placed third in the Democratic primary behind Reverend Jesse Jackson and the winner, Massachusetts governor Michael Dukakis. Over the summer, Jason returned to Saskatchewan to work for Ralph Goodale, the leader of the provincial Liberal Party, who was an MP in Regina from 1974 to 1979, and then again from 1993 to 2019, serving as finance minister in Paul Martin's government from 2004 to 2006.

But by the spring of 1989, Kenney returned to campus as a fully formed right-wing culture warrior, launching twin crusades against free-speech rights for pro-choice advocates on campus and spousal visitation rights for LGBTQ+ people during the AIDS crisis. He began by getting the Women Law Students Association (WLSA) banned from campus for actively supporting abortion rights, which he argued was an affront to the university's Catholic heritage.

On March 27, the association collected signatures for a pro-choice petition while tabling outside Harney Plaza in front of the University Centre. After some students complained, administrators told the group it hadn't done the appropriate paperwork to set up a table. The association was in the process of taking it down when a group of six anti-choice frat boys showed up. "We were just trying to get rid of them," one of the men, David Tognotti, who sat alongside Kenney on the student senate and now works as a director at Google, admitted to the *Foghorn*. "I said something like, 'Whatever you do, don't set your table up here tomorrow.'" Two days later, the senate narrowly approved a motion put forward by Kenney to ban the WLSA from campus, which explicitly cited the association's "promotion of abortion." Kenney framed his position as "an affirmation of the freedom of expression of a Catholic university to stand up for its moral convictions."

The American Civil Liberties Union begged to differ, correctly pointing out that it was the WLSA whose free speech was being brought into question. Kenney became their most aggressive opponent on campus, while the WLSA's Laurie Moore became USF's most prominent pro-choice advocate. But the issue became about more than just abortion — it was about a religious university's ability to dictate which perspectives were permitted on campus. Kenney and Moore had a public debate about the WLSA's banning, which Moore participated in despite not being thrilled with the spectacle. "I remember him being very vociferous and red-faced and angry," she recalled to the *Sprawl*. It was certainly an odd choice for Kenney to agree to participate in a debate he actively sought to suppress, but for him debate was a weapon for vanquishing his opponents, not a consensus-building exercise.

In November 1989, the *Foghorn* ran an op-ed from Kenney, in which he compared allowing pro-choice advocacy on campus to permitting the Ku Klux Klan, pedophiles, "fascist groups," or Satanists to congregate there, which he later acknowledged in the *Sprawl* as a series of "ridiculous analogies and gratuitously offensive language." On the same page of the *Foghorn* was an op-ed from Moore and another student, Shari Eisenberg, who argued this was firmly a matter of free speech. "The freedom to speak and the idea of being a Catholic are not mutually exclusive unless we go back to the time of the Inquisition." Owing to her prominence as a pro-choice voice, anti-choice activists targeted Moore for harassment, filling her mailbox with "horrific dead baby postcards," she told the *Sprawl*.

Due to the ACLU's agitation, the university relented, issuing a new policy that affirmed the right of students to express positions running counter to the teachings of the Catholic Church. Kenney, who assumed leadership of a group called Students United for Life, couldn't let it go. Backed by a unanimous vote from the student senate,[26] which by that point had been stacked with students for the ultraconservative St. Ignatius Institute, and the support of St. Ignatius founder Reverend Joseph Fessio, Kenney wrote a letter to San Francisco archbishop John Quinn in February 1990, demanding the church disown USF for permitting blasphemy on its campus.

By his own admission, Kenney was "playing hardball." This is when the news went national, with CNN separately interviewing Moore and Kenney; in between their interviews was one with Reverend John Clark, USF's vice-president of academic affairs, who bolstered Moore's position that there was no conflict between the Catholic faith and free speech. In his CNN interview, Kenney accused the WLSA of trying to "legalize abortion on demand on this campus," which he said was "destroying the mission and the purpose of this university." The chyron under Kenney's face read: "Jason Kenney, Anti-Abortion Activist."

Archbishop Quinn, after three months of "prayerful consideration," rejected Kenney's request, urging him to appreciate the complexities and contradictions Catholic institutions face in the modern era. A professor in USF's theology department, who attempted to get the student senate impeached for its censorious conduct, accused Kenney of spearheading "a Pearl Harbor–type coup d'état by a fundamentalist junta" that sought to "superimpose a closed-shop, fundamentalist, and authoritarian model of Catholicism." To avoid impeachment, the senate abandoned Kenney's promise to appeal to the Vatican.

While he was attempting to suppress the free-speech rights of pro-choice advocates at USF, Kenney also engaged in the culture war off campus, with the LGBTQ+ community in his crosshairs. The connection between abortion rights and gay rights was acknowledged by supporters and opponents alike. For supporters, both were fundamentally issues of bodily autonomy and self-determination. For opponents, both were attacks on traditional family structures centred around procreation.

In 2000, Kenney boasted to Canadian Alliance supporters that, in addition to directing anti-abortion efforts on campus, he "helped to lead an ultimately successful initiative petition," which led to a referendum abrogating the first domestic partnership law in North America in 1989 in San Francisco. This law, coming amid the AIDS crisis, which at its peak killed more than 1,400 San Franciscans annually, would have allowed gay partners to visit their spouses in the hospital. To agitate against this was exceptionally cruel, but of course Kenney didn't see it that way. His activism, Kenney told his supporters in 2000, brought him "closer to the heart of the church in a spiritual sense."

The passage of the law he helped overturn was the product of a years-long struggle. In 1982, the San Francisco Board of Supervisors, essentially the city's council, voted in favour of extending many of the rights afforded straight married couples to gay people in domestic partnerships. This was vetoed by Mayor Dianne Feinstein, who went on to become a long-serving Democratic senator. Kenney would later use Feinstein's opposition to argue his views weren't so extreme at the time. But with other California cities like Berkeley, also in the Bay Area, and West Hollywood in the Los Angeles area, passing similar legislation in the intervening years, it was almost inevitable that San Francisco, with a gay population of 15 percent, would follow suit. In May 1989, its board did just that.

The religious right was mobilized against the legislation, with a petition spearheaded by fringe Presbyterian Reverend Charles McIllhenny and Rabbi Lionel Feldman collecting 27,000 signatures, triggering a referendum for what became known as Proposition S. In this case, unlike anti-free-speech efforts at USF, the Catholic Church was fully on board, with the petition circulated at parishes across the city through the church's vast network of anti-abortion advocacy groups. The church deliberately sought out Latino community leaders to provide more diverse opposition to Proposition S, according to an August 1989 report in the *San Francisco Bay Times*, an LGBTQ+ newspaper.

In the campaign's dying days, a major earthquake hit San Francisco. While the pro-Proposition S side paused campaigning and urged supporters to donate funds to earthquake relief instead, the opposition had no such inhibition, continuing to fundraise to stop spousal visitation rights. At the same time, the anti-Proposition S campaign rebranded from "Committee Against the Domestic Partners Ordinance" to the more positive sounding "San Franciscans for Common Sense." It also refocused its messaging by emphasizing the purported economic costs of extending spousal benefits to LGBTQ+ partners, rather than moral concerns.

The proposition was defeated in November. Dick Pabich, the campaign manager for the supporting side, noted the "hidden power of church groups to affect an election like this." By the following year, another ballot initiative in favour of the legislation was victorious. But for Kenney, this lesson on the power of mobilizing faith groups in diverse communities, and in using a combination of economistic and moralistic arguments to justify a particular policy aim, was retained.

Kenney downplayed his role in the initiative in response to inquiries from the *Sprawl*, arguing his role was limited to putting up posters. After a visit to San Francisco's GLBT History Museum archives, I concluded his more recent statement is likely closer to the truth. If he was a movement leader, rather than a foot soldier, he would have been quoted in the media, but the archives contained no record whatsoever of his work on the anti-Proposition S campaign. There were just 50 volunteers on the anti-Proposition S campaign, according to reporting in the *Bay Times*. With a team that small, any of them could conceivably claim a leadership role when it suited them. It appears Kenney exaggerated the extent of his involvement for political convenience and then downplayed it for the same purpose at a different time.

In defence of his anti-gay activism, Kenney cited his volunteer work at the Missionaries of Charity Gift of Love AIDS Hospice in San Francisco, an institution that had no affiliation with the LGBTQ+ community. "If the things they say about me are true, then explain to me why a young Jason Kenney spent his time washing bloody sheets at an AIDS hospice in San Francisco in the 1980s," he proclaimed in an interview with conservative *Global News* radio host Charles Adler.[27] Kenney also used this experience to tie his spiritual and economic views together. "There is no government program, and nothing in the market, that can be a substitute for that love and what I witnessed and what changed me," he told at a May 2018 event with Cardus, a conservative Christian think tank.

While there were no doubt gay AIDS patients at the hospice, a small 14-bed facility founded by Mother Teresa's Missionaries of Charity, it wasn't exactly the welcoming environment Kenney depicted. Patients had to observe a 5:00 p.m. curfew, were permitted only two visiting hours per day, and television was banned. "Some patients complained of subtle attempts at religious conversion," the *Los Angeles Times* reported in April 1987. A few years later, nurses and social workers who worked with AIDS patients expressed concern that Gift of Love was discouraging patients from taking pain medications. "Moreover, they say, there is an attitude of discomfort or disapproval that the sisters convey, stemming from the Church's condemnation of homosexual activity," the *Times* noted in a May 1990 article.

Kenney departed USF after the 1990 winter semester without finishing his degree. Like his early departure from St. Mike's, it's unclear exactly why he left. An unsigned November 1990 *Foghorn* editorial referred to Kenney's "academic failure and expulsion," which it argued was unjust, lambasting an academic who referred to Kenney's "one-sided harangues, misrepresentations of Catholic doctrine and journalistic demagoguery."

Kenney did eventually temper his social conservative pronouncements in pursuit of power. But his religious fundamentalism isn't something he "conveniently holds to appeal to a constituency," Cardus executive vice-president Ray Pennings told the *Walrus* in May 2014 when Kenney's career in federal politics was nearing its end. "This is who he is in his bones." If anything, his tolerance of behaviour that fell outside Catholic doctrine was a position of convenience to appeal to a broader electorate. Still, his social conservatism re-emerged throughout his political career to varying degrees.

Many remember Kenney as an Opposition MP saying, "Gays can marry — but not each other,"[28] although those weren't his exact words — it was a headline summarizing his remarks. His actual comments were somehow even more offensive. "Marriage is open to everybody as long as they're a man and a woman. [The law] doesn't say you can't marry if you're a homosexual. The fact is that homosexuals have been married and do marry," he told a Punjabi-language media outlet in 2005. "Marriage is by definition about a potentially procreative relationship. As much as two people of the same sex may love each other, as much as they try ... they don't even have the potential to procreate or raise children." He specifically referenced NDP MPs Svend Robinson, the first openly gay MP, and Libby Davies as people who were once married to a person of the opposite sex. "What on earth is he talking about?" Davies responded. "Why would you marry someone of the opposite sex if you love someone of the same sex?" Kenney replied by scolding Davies to be more "temperate" in her remarks.

The romantic life of Kenney is shrouded in mystery. In January 1999, he and his Reform caucus mate Rob Anders proclaimed themselves celibate to *Ottawa Citizen* reporter Glen MacGregor, and Kenney has never been publicly associated with a romantic partner. This has fuelled rampant speculation about his proclivities, which are ultimately immaterial to his political beliefs and actions. Kenney's views on homosexuality and reproductive rights, as expressed in his early years, are rooted in a fundamentally materialistic view that regards romantic love strictly as a means of procreation, which he attempts to endow with higher meaning through invocations of tradition.

Kenney continued his attacks on LGBTQ+ people through different means when he became Alberta premier in 2019. With the passage of the province's Education Amendment Act, Kenney revoked his NDP predecessors' legislation that prohibited schools from notifying parents when students join a gay-straight alliance club to shield children from potential abuse from homophobic parents. This makes the UCP the first subnational government in Canada to roll back protections for LGBTQ+ people. While Kenney emphasized that parents wouldn't be notified in extreme circumstances in which abuse was likely, his reversal of the NDP's anodyne legislation threw caution to the wind when it came to the rights of LGBTQ+ students.

Using the rhetoric of parental rights, Kenney justified the change. "I don't think it's right to keep secrets from parents about challenges their kids are going through," he told the *Calgary Herald* when he revealed this policy in March 2017, ignoring why LGBTQ+ children might be reluctant to come out to their parents. This notion that schools kept secrets from parents foreshadowed the groomer discourse that became popular in far-right circles a few years later, which accused teachers of grooming kids to be LGBTQ+ behind their parents' backs.

Most recently, in astoundingly tone-deaf remarks, Kenney compared the treatment of people who chose not to be vaccinated for Covid with the stigma AIDS patients faced in the 1980s because they were viewed as "somehow unclean." "It's never OK to treat people like that," he added. Kenney walked his comments back, chalking his indiscretion up to the "pitfalls of improvising an analogy." In a wild understatement, the Radio-Canada report on Kenney's remarks noted his "controversial political history with the gay community."[29] But this history wasn't at all controversial for the people who were targeted by Kenney's anti-LGBTQ+ activism; it was simply cruel.

His moralistic rigidity regarding human sexuality stood in stark contrast with his laissez-faire approach to economics, which demands the state to get out of the way and let individuals make their own decisions — an apparent contradiction at the heart of Kenney's world view that is, in fact, consistent with his broader project of imposing a hierarchical social order. The wealthy are free to make their own decisions about how to spend their money while the rest of us are lectured with moralistic refrains about the need to serve the market through reproduction. When Kenney returned to Canada in 1990, his focus moved to this side of the equation, replacing rigid adherence to Catholic doctrine with an unquestioning support for neoliberal dogma.

2

TAX SLAYER

AFTER HIS SOJOURN IN SAN FRANCISCO, Kenney shifted focus from his social conservative crusader persona to his diehard neoliberal phase, which he approached with equal religious zeal. He did this first as the leader of the Association of Alberta Taxpayers (AAT), and then as executive of its national parent organization, the Canadian Taxpayers Federation (CTF), an outfit characterized by its vociferous opposition to taxes, government spending, and debt. By his own admission, Kenney was a "young ideological firebrand [who] wanted to go 10 out of 10 on every issue all the time" during his CTF days.[1] In his role as an anti-tax lobbyist, Kenney demonstrated an impassioned belief in the power of the free market to solve all problems, and he got results at the provincial, and to a lesser extent, national, levels.

Part of this was a result of his being in the right place at the right time. The 1990s were the era of peak neoliberalism, with governments across the ideological divide focused obsessively on reducing deficits and debt. Writing in December 1993, *Globe and Mail* columnist Kenneth Whyte, a friend of Kenney's, identified "this new vogue for austerity," which he dubbed "hair-shirt" fever — an allusion to the rough shirts made of animal hair religious ascetics wore to punish themselves for their sins that was especially apt in light of Kenney's Catholic zealotry. Within this zeitgeist, Kenney displayed his talents of using the media to bring large portions of the public onside for his austere agenda. He did so with populist flair, juxtaposing taxpayers with government elites who were abusing tax dollars to enrich themselves. Kenney didn't just seek to cut taxes and balance the budget — he sought structural reforms "to reassess the proper function of government." In a 1995 *Maclean's* magazine profile, Kenney remarked on his personal aesthetic tastes, which could be equally applied to his view of government. "As soon as you become an enthusiast of hair shirts," he said, "you'd better not be found buying suits."

Three years after working for future Liberal Cabinet minister Ralph Goodale, and following a brief membership with the Reform Party, Kenney was recruited to lead the AAT by CTF national coordinator Kevin Avram, who was impressed with Kenney's student activism. Avram once compared his organization's anti-tax agitation to "feminist groups that want to empower people." Kenney couldn't have been enthused about that analogy, given his activities in San Francisco, but he would soon become the public face of the organization, proving to be a thorn in the side of Alberta's PC government and the federal Liberals, enthusiastically criss-crossing Alberta and selling memberships,[2] all while being compensated generously for his fundraising efforts.

Kenney used his brief work with Goodale and his longer involvement with the Young Liberals to amplify his non-partisan credentials as CTF leader. At the same time, he argued that, based on this experience, the Liberals have been "co-opted by left-wing elements," which turned the party into a mouthpiece for, a favourite phrase of his, "special interests."[3] After spending the past few years in San Francisco speaking in support of a rigid moral order that must take precedence over individual liberties, chief among them free speech, Kenney now believed that when it came to people deciding what to do with their money, at least those who had the means to do so, individual liberty was paramount. This, as we've already established, wasn't an inconsistency in his world view, because neoconservative moralism provided structure to the otherwise emptiness of neoliberal social relations.

In early 1991, Kenney joined Reform but soon after had to relinquish membership, since the CTF was, at least on paper, non-partisan. However, after building his profile as CTF leader, he returned to Reform to enter the electoral arena. "We're not a redneck organization," Kenney insisted of the CTF. "We've got some folks who are dyed-in-the-wool NDPers as well as people who are further to the right of Atilla the Hun." Yet it was hard to deny an immense overlap between the CTF and the Reform Party, which shared a common enemy — the Liberals and PCs — who were both regarded, not without reason, as two sides of an out-of-touch elite.

The final nail in the PC coffin for many conservatives was the implementation of the Goods and Services Tax (GST) in January 1991. That year, the *Edmonton Journal* spoke to local retiree Joseph Check, who said he had voted PC his entire life, but in 1991 decided to purchase a CTF membership and join Reform. "What the Liberals didn't destroy, Mulroney is doing now," said Check. "It's time that we did something. It's fight-back time!" Kenney channelled the combative spirit from his days at USF to capture this populist anti-tax sentiment espoused by people like Check, who felt under siege by an eastern Canadian establishment that didn't adequately represent their political ideology. They were expressing "western alienation," which has deep roots in Alberta's elite political discourse, dating back well before Pierre Elliott Trudeau or Brian Mulroney.

Robbing Old Ladies

The first cause Kenney pursued with the AAT was the generous pensions offered to Alberta MLAs, which provided the perfect foil in his efforts to gain anti-establishment credentials. Kenney accused Alberta MLAs, the majority of whom were PCs, of forming a "political caste" for themselves, bemoaning that they were "guaranteed a wealthy and happy retirement."[4] The notion that perhaps the Canada Pension Plan should be strengthened so the general population could enjoy the same type of retirement was out of the question. Everyone must suffer collectively, Kenney implied in true ascetic form.

The AAT released a 1991 study claiming Alberta Cabinet ministers had the most generous pensions in the nation based on numbers assuming that they had served in Cabinet for 20 consecutive years. Premier Don Getty accused the CTF of fudging data, calling the AAT's claims "a pile of baloney," a suggestion echoed by a spokesperson for the Speaker of the Legislative Assembly, who called the CTF "out to lunch," pointing out that Getty's first-year pension eligibility was less than half of what Kenney claimed.[5] This only affirmed Kenney's image as fighting for the people against a stodgy, entitled elite. And the media — namely, the *Calgary Herald* and *Edmonton Journal* — assisted this framing by going to the very politicians he accused of being pigs at a trough to respond to his claims, rather than a more impartial expert, who could assess their veracity. Particularly egregious in this regard was *Journal* reporter Joan Crockatt, who reported every Kenney pronouncement as gospel. I suspect it's not coincidental that Crockatt eventually became the Conservative MP for Calgary Centre from 2012 to 2015, serving in the party's Calgary caucus alongside Kenney.

While they preached government frugality, Kenney and the CTF's earnings were far from modest, a contrast that was a perpetual source of criticism throughout his tenure with the CTF, whose sole source of income was selling memberships door-to-door starting at $55 per year. An average contribution of $125 pointed toward supporters' high-income bracket. In July 1991, the Consumers Association of Canada warned that the CTF, which at that point was 5,000 contributors strong, was engaged in some dubious practices. It found that as much as half the proceeds of memberships went back to the canvassers as commission, with an additional 5 percent going to the leaders of each six-member canvass team. "Administration costs shouldn't be as high as 55 percent of the funds being brought in," said Anne Arling, the president of the consumers association's Alberta branch.[6] CTF commissions occurred on a sliding scale, ranging from 36 percent for membership renewals to more than 50 percent for new members. Avram, the CTF's head honcho, was himself on commission, providing a "built-in incentive to pour money into expansion," a sympathetic Kenneth Whyte explained in the *Globe and Mail*.[7] Two years later, the *Edmonton Journal* revealed that when you factor in commissions, bonuses, and managers' compensation, just $18.41 of a $55 membership goes toward actual lobbying efforts. "You can't run an organization like this by passing a KFC bucket around," Kenney explained.[8]

Generous commissions aside, Arling took issue with the CTF, which is a non-profit but not a charity, referring to its memberships as "donations," since it gives the false impression that contributors will receive an income tax deduction. Kenney claimed they referred to contributions as donations so contributors wouldn't have to pay the dreaded GST. But an official with Revenue Canada Excise in Edmonton said most non-profits are exempt from paying GST, suggesting the CTF wanted to give new members the impression their funds would be returned to them in the form of lower taxes. The irony of a taxpayers' advocacy organization using the false prospect of a tax write-off to entice donations shouldn't be lost.

Kenney made it clear that his attacks on government compensation were intended to set the stage for larger cuts to public services. "Unless politicians take the first hits," Kenneth Whyte wrote in the *Globe*, explaining Kenney's thought process, "they won't have credibility when they start making necessary cuts to entitlement programs, public service salaries, the health-care system and so on." Kenney believes "a discouragingly high proportion of taxpayers haven't grasped that making politicians suffer is a prelude to pain all around, not an end in itself," Whyte added.

Early in his tenure as Alberta premier, Kenney pulled the same manoeuvre, with the Legislative Assembly voting unanimously in November 2019 to cut its members' pay by 5 percent and the premier's by 10 percent. An Opposition NDP motion to ensure the salary cut "not be used as rationale to justify any measures to roll back compensation of Alberta's public sector workers" was rejected by Kenney's majority government in a prelude to major cuts to Alberta's public sector.

By the end of 1992, Getty was gone and replaced with former Calgary mayor Ralph Klein, who vowed to eliminate the deficits that had accumulated under Getty's watch, despite having served in Getty's Cabinet. While Klein, a lapsed Liberal like Kenney, shared Kenney's aversion to government debt, he also possessed Getty's impatience with Kenney's antics. In April 1993, he famously berated Kenney for 15 minutes in the Legislative Assembly cafeteria, telling him to "quit robbing the old senior citizens of their money to generate this kind of fear," referring to AAT canvassers' hefty commissions and rumours they targeted seniors' residences. Kenney responded that, unlike taxes, CTF memberships aren't "coerced" from people. "If there's any robbery going on, it's the government's decision to force taxpayers to subsidize completely unreasonable, gold-plated pensions," Kenney said, calling Klein's accusation "grossly misleading and slanderous." Klein apologized for using the word *robbery*, but maintained the CTF's practices were "not entirely ethical." However, he told Kenney to "stay in touch," according to Klein aide Rod Love, who praised the AAT as "one of the more effective lobbies" in Alberta. In the *Globe*, Whyte suggested Klein might have met his match in Kenney, calling Kenney "one of few people in the province as media savvy as Mr. Klein."

Personal animosity aside, Kenney and Klein agreed on far more than they disagreed, but Kenney constantly pushed the premier to take his neo-liberal agenda further. With Klein set on balancing the budget, there were discussions of potentially introducing a provincial sales tax, which during his leadership campaign Klein called the "most unimaginative way of balancing the budget." Kenney, demonstrating his belief in the unimaginable power of free markets, called for a "fundamental expenditure reduction." Mystifying the impact of low taxation, he claimed that "raising taxes does not necessarily balance budgets. There's a very large and intangible economic benefit that occurs to Alberta because of its low taxes relative to the rest of the country."[9] Since it's intangible, there was no need for Kenney to explain what that benefit was and how it might square with his desire for balanced budgets, which became the AAT's white whale during the Klein years. When Klein announced a freeze on education, health care, and municipal funding for his first budget, Kenney said it was a "good start" but didn't go nearly far enough. "The premier's not telling them to tighten their belts, he's just telling them to stop letting it out," he told the *Edmonton Journal*. Kenney expressed similar sentiments toward a pay cut Klein imposed on Cabinet ministers alongside a freeze on MLA salaries, likening the policy to "cosmetic surgery" when "more radical invasive surgery" is needed.[10]

A week after his verbal tussle with Kenney, Klein introduced legislation to cut government pensions by an average of $22,000 for Cabinet ministers and $11,000 for MLAs, in addition to increasing the eligibility age from 55 to 65. Notably, these changes became retroactive, a move Klein had initially scoffed at, arguing it was unethical to claw back what had already been earned. Rather than rejoice at his apparent victory, Kenney scolded the

MLAs who on their way out the door were "whining" about having part of their pensions taken away. "We've lost patience, frankly, with these people. They think we have some kind of ethical obligation to provide them with those benefits. Hogwash."[11]

The following week, Klein announced he would scrap the government pension plan entirely, with MLAs elected before 1989 being able to cash out a diminished pension: "The plan will not be replaced. It will end. There will be no alternative plan. We are out of it, period." Kenney, who never openly advocated for the plan to be eliminated entirely, hailed this "dramatic step" as a "victory for taxpayers," adding that Klein "nicked" his MLAs before realizing "they deserved much more than a nick."[12] Later, when a re-elected Klein brought forward his Deficit Elimination Act, a long-time demand of the AAT, Kenney endorsed a proposal that legislators' pay be docked if they didn't balance the budget. The Opposition Liberals and New Democrats, and three backbench PC MLAs, supported this penalty clause, which an August 1993 *Calgary Herald* editorial correctly identified as "pandering to right-wing conservatives." Having the Liberals and NDP endorse draconian budget reduction measures no doubt helped Kenney burnish his non-partisan image.

Despite earlier musings about freezing spending, Klein's inaugural budget cut funding for 14 of 17 ministries, including a $127 million cut to health-care spending and $154 million cut to family and social services. Although he would have preferred more cuts, Kenney applauded the budget's "general thrust," particularly the government's refusal to increase taxes.[13] Klein, however, did increase user fees, raising health premiums by 11 percent, which Kenney was oddly silent about. This might seem counterintuitive for a taxpayers' advocate, but offloading expenses onto individuals, rather than the collective through taxes, was just what the neoliberal doctor ordered. Klein continued on this path throughout his 14 years in office, brandishing a PAID IN FULL sign at the 2004 Calgary Stampede to announce the province's debt was eliminated. But this was done at great social cost, leaving behind a legacy of thousands of public-sector layoffs, decaying public infrastructure, and underfunded education and health-care systems.

By the time of Klein's maiden budget, the AAT's membership had ballooned to 25,000 members, in no small part due to its aggressive membership drives, populist messaging, and Kenney's media manipulation talents. "The 24-year-old Ontario-born Saskatchewan-raised anti-tax crusader snaps up headlines daily in Alberta's newspapers. His pronouncements on fiscal matters are treated with reverence by pundits," wrote the *Calgary Herald*'s David Climenhaga, who attributed Kenney's success to his "brilliant knack for self-publicity, his quotable quotes and his instant media availability any time of night or day." He also noted Kenney's extraordinary work ethic, often working 80-hour weeks, bouncing from media availabilities in Edmonton to rallies across the province, presaging his attendance of multiple events per day on the ethnocultural community circuit for the federal Conservatives in the aughts.

Climenhaga attended an AAT rally in Okotoks, less than an hour south of Calgary, two days after the budget, where he witnessed Kenney "preaching the gospel of less spending and lower taxes." Kenney warned in an apocalyptic tone that Canada was within a year or two of "total fiscal collapse," which he said was because "you people, the wealth producers, the taxpayers, are cut off by the wealth consumers, the special interest groups, the whole system of politics in Canada." In order to change course, individuals needed to stand up to the "governing elites, who are not really looking out for anybody's interest but their own," presumably by purchasing an AAT membership. "We must accept responsibility!" Throughout his career, Kenney wielded personal responsibility as a bludgeon against those who lacked the resources to take full advantage of the freedom entailed by open markets. For Kenney and the ruling class he served, no personal responsibility was required.

Kenney Goes National

The AAT had supposedly formally disassociated from the CTF in May 1993, but that fall Kenney began being cited in some national stories as the executive director of the CTF. The March/April edition of the CTF's

Taxpayer magazine, which was mailed out to members bimonthly, identified Kenney as the AAT's provincial director and CTF national director. To that effect, Kenney's focus became increasingly national in scope, although he continued to comment on issues in his adopted home province, encouraging Klein to power through with his neoliberal project. "Low taxes mean more jobs, plain and simple," he told the *Globe and Mail* on February 4, 1994, as AAT president, applauding the results of the Alberta Tax Reform Commission, which called for tax cuts once the budget was balanced. That same day in the same newspaper, with his CTF cap on in advance of Liberal finance minister Paul Martin's inaugural budget, Kenney warned that if Martin imposed "significant tax increases," the reportedly 85,000-member CTF would "help organize opposition to it." Then he added, "And we fortunately have the resources to do it."

Kenney stuck to his script during a February 8 debate with Canadian Labour Congress economist Andrew Jackson on CTV's *Canada AM*. Pointing to Canada's mildly progressive income tax system, in which the greater income the greater proportion of taxes were paid, Kenney argued there "is a very large disproportionate burden on the top income earners," which increased taxes on the wealthy would "exacerbate," creating "greater disincentives for people to work, save, and invest." Jackson argued that Canada's tax burden was increasingly borne by the middle class because of all the tax deductions only the wealthy had access to — capital gains, inheritance, and business entertainment expenses. He suggested a fair tax system would close these loopholes and impose a wealth tax. "Obviously, it's only the rich who are getting large inheritances of more than half a million dollars, which most people have suggested as the cut-off for a wealth tax. Most people can't deduct business lunches [or] boxes in the SkyDome. So, there are significant ways in which we can raise taxes at the upper end without that affecting ordinary working people, the middle class, at all."

In response, Kenney insisted "the highest income earners really are not where the revenue is at," arguing that while doubling the marginal tax rate, meaning the tax rate above a certain income threshold, might temporarily help pay off debt service costs, it would "destroy the economy in so doing." Kenney didn't explain how increasing taxes on the wealthy would necessarily lead to economic doom, nor did he directly address Jackson's main argument in favour of a wealth tax. Kenney was tireless in his advocacy of debt reduction, yet rejected out of hand any measures that could reduce the debt without resorting to massive cuts. Despite all his bluster about finances, I suspect Kenney's true motive was political — reducing the capacity of the state while offloading its responsibilities onto private actors. Cutting taxes was simply a means to that end.

Paul Martin's 1994 budget was fairly milquetoast. There were few cuts, the largest consisting of a 4.4 percent reduction in defence spending and a 3 percent cut to cash transfers to the provinces, but even fewer tax increases, the largest of which was a reduction of the business entertainment tax credit to 50 percent from 80 percent. Martin promised deep cuts the following year. He called Kenney "out of the blue," in Kenney's words, before the 1994 budget, and spoke for 20 minutes about ways the government could reduce the deficit without raising taxes.[14] After Martin's first budget, an article in the *Taxpayer* read, in a familiar refrain, "instead of making the tough spending decision necessary … Martin merely tinkered at the edges." The article expressed disappointment that Martin "has not trimmed" $2 billion in education and welfare funding, "but simply offloaded it onto provincial counterparts." The piece quoted Kenney's tepid approval of cuts to Unemployment Insurance and foreign aid, as well as a two-year extension of a public-sector wage freeze the Liberals inherited from the PCs. "More are needed," he said characteristically.

In April 1994, the gap between the restraint the CTF urged governments to exercise and its much laxer approach toward private entities like itself came into focus again. "One of Alberta's best-known opponents of deficit funding is staring at some red ink of its own," reported Jim Cunningham at the *Calgary Herald*. The CTF, whose provincial wing was "leading the cheers for the Klein government's deficit-slashing budget," was short $60,000 on its $3 million budget, Cunningham noted. Kenney insisted this wasn't a deficit, because he claimed the CTF would be in a surplus position by the end of June. "We have never run a deficit and we have a policy for the very reason that it would be hypocrisy for us to do so." This was handled quite cleverly by Kenney, who acknowledged poor optics while denying it was actually what it looked like. "Hold me accountable," he told Cunningham. "We need it around here." As a result of this non-deficit, which he attributed to the CTF's expansion into Ontario and winter weather on the Prairies, Kenney had his pay docked 6 percent. What appeared hypocritical was consistent with the CTF's advocacy that the public balance its budgets through reducing expenditures while private entities were free to operate as they wanted.

It was much harder for Kenney to rebut hypocrisy charges after he asked to be reimbursed $1,500 in travel expenses for flying from Edmonton to Ottawa to appear before a parliamentary finance committee hearing in November 1994. Again, he pleaded this would be hypocrisy if it was what it appeared to be, but, conveniently, it wasn't. "If I had ever thought that submitting an expense claim when invited to appear before a committee is somehow asking for a subsidy, well, we never would have done it and we won't in the future," he told the Canadian Press in a piece headlined "Top Tax Fighter Asks Ottawa to Pick Up His Expenses." The problem was, according to committee officials who turned down his reimbursement request, he wasn't invited. Kenney then claimed Reform MP Ray Speaker invited him to appear, a claim Speaker denied. "I didn't go out and phone him and say come and make a presentation," Speaker said. "It wasn't on my request — it was his." Inviting yourself to a committee hearing to expound on how government spending is out of control and then asking for the government to subsidize your appearance takes an extraordinary amount of audacity. The advocacy of subsidies for me but not for thee reveals the facade of the CTF's concern about government compensation, which, as Kenney freely admitted, was a pretext to impose larger austerity on the broader public.

The goal of the committee was to advise Martin on how to cut the deficit to $25 billion by 1997 from $42 billion in 1994. Bob White of the Canadian Labour Congress urged the government to implement a wealth tax on incomes over $1 million and a 30 percent estate tax on those worth over $1 million, which he said would enable the government to reduce the deficit without slashing spending. Acknowledging the deficit, and the interest payments associated with it, was a pressing issue. Canadian Auto Workers president Buzz Hargrove suggested the government lower interest rates and increase taxes on those who made more than $100,000, rather than cut spending. Public Service Alliance of Canada president Daryl Bean said "society would benefit from increased social expenditures, not less," which *Calgary Herald* reporter Sheldon Alberts, who now does public relations for the billionaire Walton family, likened to telling the government to end "its overspending by spending more money," in another example of media parroting CTF framing. "No, that's not a typographical error. And it wasn't a joke," Alberts editorialized,[15] leaving out the part in which Bean called on the government to eliminate tax loopholes, cut waste, stop contracting out government work, and enhance collection of outstanding taxes, which he estimated would save $15 billion.

Alberts then, of course, quoted Kenney. "We're disturbed to see that so many of the traditional interest groups still don't understand ... [Canadians] are prepared to make some sacrifices." Kenney didn't specify which Canadians, nor did Alberts appear to have asked him to. Kenney's arguments were bolstered by the Canadian Chamber of Commerce, who said the government needed to cut spending steeper in the upcoming budget, except for business subsidies, which should be phased out in an orderly fashion, with the goal of completely eliminating the deficit by 1997. The International Monetary Fund (IMF), too, called for the Feds "to plan on the basis of a more ambitious medium-term target in the 1995–96 budget, with a view to accelerating fiscal consolidation in the next few years."[16] While the chamber and the IMF naturally held more sway than the CTF and similarly minded groups, such as conservative-lobbying outfit National Citizens Coalition and neoliberal think tank Fraser Institute, it's undeniable that the CTF under Kenney's watch became a formidable force, playing a significant role in shaping the parameters of debate in favour of austerity, buttressed by amplification from a credulous press.

Manufactured Tax Revolt

The CTF held a series of anti-tax rallies in February 1995 leading up to the federal budget in 20 cities across Canada, which were sponsored by the conservative *Sun* tabloid chain and at least some, most notably for an allegedly non-partisan organization, by the Reform Party. The federation also purchased ads in both national newspapers — the *Financial Post* and *Globe and Mail* — to promote the events and circulated an anti-tax petition that garnered 230,000 signatures. Alberta Federation of Labour president Linda Karpowich expressed frustration with the media attention the CTF was getting. "Jason gets 1,600 people to a rally in Edmonton and the media calls it a tax revolt," Karpowich told *Maclean's*. "We get 10,000 people outside the Legislative Assembly rallying against Alberta government cuts, but that's not called a revolt."[17] Indeed, the attendance at rallies elsewhere — 2,000 in Pickering, Ontario; 1,500 in Vancouver; 700 in Saskatoon; 400 in Winnipeg; 500 in Lethbridge; 150 in London, Ontario; and an embarrassing 200 in Ottawa — suggest this movement might not have been the "grassroots anti-tax rebellion" or "great tax revolution"[18] depicted in the media. But, attendance numbers aside, Kenney flexed his populist muscles at these events. "Tonight, the taxpayers are telling the government that we're taking control of the spending agenda. That means no new taxes. Not on jobs. Not on people. Not on anything," he said to chants of "No More Taxes!" at the Edmonton demonstration.[19] It was a simple message, and while it might not have galvanized masses of people across the country to turn out to CTF rallies, people in power were certainly paying attention, although not to the extent Kenney wanted.

Prime Minister Jean Chrétien promised a "tough budget," and Martin delivered. "Our reduction in government expenditures are unprecedented in modern Canadian history," Martin boasted in the House of Commons on the eve of the 1995 budget. It included an 8.8 percent, or $10.4 billion, cut to program spending over two years and 45,000 civil servant layoffs over three years, but Martin vowed not to stop cutting "until the deficit is erased."[20] Martin also announced the creation of the Canada Social Transfer, which combined welfare, education, and health transfer payments to the provinces and cut them by $7 billion over two years. Martin didn't increase income taxes, although he boosted the gas tax by 1.5 cents per litre, tobacco taxes by 60 cents per carton, and a special tax on large corporations by 13.5 percent. The spending cuts far outweighed revenue increases.

The austerity measures in the 1995 budget were of historic proportions, the effects of which are still felt almost three decades later. "Former Tory prime minister Brian Mulroney took a pickaxe to the welfare state. The federal Liberals under Prime Minister Jean Chrétien and his finance minister, Paul Martin, were using dynamite," opined the *Toronto Star*'s Thomas Walkom, who warned the 1995 budget will "fundamentally change the role of the state in Canada and in so doing to dramatically alter the balance between individual and collective action."[21] In *Maclean's*, Peter Newman wrote that Martin's budget "signals a new psychological mood [and a] dramatic shift in the Canadian character." While the Liberals previously succeeded electorally by adopting NDP ideas, the party was now "getting their ideas from the Reform Party of Canada, and just like the old days, are carrying Reform supporters along with their rented ideology."[22] Yet the CTF's attitude toward this historically austere budget was summarized in a *Taxpayer* headline: "Budget '95 — The Same Old Tune."

Meanwhile, Kenney set his sights on the generous pension plan for MPs, attempting a repeat of his success in Alberta. Chrétien announced reforms to federal MPs' pensions the week before the 1995 budget, most notably establishing 55 as the minimum age for collecting the pension, but not retroactively, which Kenney decried in the pages of the *Taxpayer* as "weak" and reflective of an "appalling lack of leadership." The Reform Party, in lockstep with the CTF agenda, responded by announcing that most of its caucus agreed to opt out of receiving the pension altogether; they were soon joined by a smattering of Bloc Québécois and Liberal MPs. In a stunt presaging the hijinks to come when Kenney became a Reform MP, the CTF placed 242 pink plastic pigs on the lawn of Parliament Hill as a statement against the pension plan, with each pig representing a politician at the trough. An hour after the stunt, Kenney was invited to speak before a Commons committee discussing the pension issue, from which he had initially been barred.

There was a clear element of hypocrisy with Martin pledging cuts to public pensions while largely leaving government pensions intact. This out-of-touch Liberal elitism certainly fuelled Reform support. But there was plenty of apparent hypocrisy to go around. The Reform caucus members made a big show of reducing their pay by 10 percent when they were first elected in 1993, but after opting out of the pension, most of them asked for their pay to return to normal. Reform MP Stephen Harper captured the prevailing sentiment in caucus when he said it was unfair to have MPs "entirely fund their own retirement and then also take a pay cut."[23] What did these Reformers expect would happen to their finances once they opted out of the pension? The ostensible inconsistency, on which Kenney was uncharacteristically silent, was ignored in the media outside a single Canadian Press wire story. But for Kenney and his Reform allies, it was never about pensions; it was about having a pretext to downsize the state's ability to care for its citizens.

In late 1996, Kenney announced he was stepping down as the CTF executive director to seek the Reform nomination in Calgary Southeast, running to replace incumbent MP Jan Brown, who left the Reform caucus to sit as an independent after criticizing extremist elements in the party. Launching his campaign, he set the tone by slamming Brown the apostate for "behaving as though she's never met a microphone she didn't love"[24] — incredibly rich coming from the director of the CTF. Brown ended up running as a PC in Reform leader Preston Manning's Calgary Southwest riding where she was predictably trounced. In an interview with the right-wing *Alberta Report* magazine, Kenney suggested he grew tired of beating the same drum for the past several years, expressing a desire to expand the scope of his advocacy "beyond taxing and spending which are of deep importance to me" to incorporate "things like the family, and criminal justice, even foreign affairs and human rights."

Reform was a natural fit for Kenney. In his CTF and AAT days, Kenney expressed a single-minded commitment to deficit and debt reduction while, most importantly, cutting taxes. These two stated objectives were inherently at odds but made much more sense in the context of neoliberalism, where the welfare state was the ultimate enemy. If Kenney came out and said he wanted to kick people off their social supports, his support base would be limited to diehard ideologues. Framing the issue as one of taxation and debt, and adding in some populist flair about how politicians were excessively compensated, obscured the larger goal of reducing the state's capacity to provide for the most vulnerable.

The Chrétien government made cut after cut, but it was never enough for the CTF, who constantly pushed it to move harder and faster. Yes, the national debt, thanks to the free spending and tax cutting of the 1980s, had grown increasingly unsustainable, with interest payments eating up increasing funds that could go toward social programs. Yet there were alternatives to the cuts Chrétien and Martin pursued. They could have, as labour leaders suggested, shifted the tax burden upward, generating billions in revenue and sparing Canadians the worst of their cuts. The Liberals, however, made a conscious decision to adopt a watered-down version of the CTF agenda. Reform, by contrast, went full tilt, proposing an attack on the social safety net so radical that it was denounced by Canadian Federation of Independent Business president John Bulloch as "robbing Canadians' piggy bank to pay off the government's credit card."[25]

Kenney running for office was inevitable, given his ambition and involvement in party politics from a tender age. While Klein more or less adopted the CTF agenda wholesale, Chrétien and Martin proved more cautious. It only made sense for Kenney to challenge them on their own terrain. Despite boasting that the CTF accomplished more than any elected official could, the truth was there was only so much Kenney could do with his oversized media presence and thousands of riled-up CTF patrons. He had to take his politics to the next level, and Reform provided the ideal venue in his efforts to push Canadian politics farther rightward, not just on economic issues but larger questions concerning the state's role in society. In order to implement this agenda, Reform had to expand its support to a degree where it could form government, which proved challenging. A youthful Kenney was a central figure in efforts to broaden Reform's base and make its agenda palatable to the broader Canadian public without losing its ideological edge.

3

THE SNACK PACK

IN MAY 1996, AS KENNEY WAS mulling over his entrance into electoral politics, he attended the "Winds of Change" conference in Calgary, which was centred around divisions within Canada's conservative movement the Reform Party would have to confront to win power. It came at a tough time for the Reform — just weeks after Nanaimo-Cowichan MP Bob Ringma called homosexuality "repugnant" in an interview in which he defended businesses' right to fire Black or LGBTQ+ employees if their presence cost them business, and Athabasca MP David Chatters said LGBTQ+ people shouldn't "openly promote" their sexuality if they wanted to avoid discrimination. It was clear Reform needed a rebrand. The conference was co-hosted by two people who went on to become influential figures in right-wing politics in the United States and Canada — future George W. Bush speechwriter David Frum, son of CBC journalist Barbara Frum and sister of future senator Linda; and Ezra Levant, who, before becoming a far-right influencer as the founder of *Rebel News*, was a major figure in mainstream Canadian conservative politics and media.

Frum wrote the conference's manifesto,[1] which easily could have been written by Kenney, with its bleak warning that Canada and all its untapped potential "is in trouble," before outlining a path to redemption through adherence to a unifying ideology. It described a country that lacked a moral purpose, "crushed under debt and taxes [and] demoralized by perverse social policies." It lambasted a federal government committed to "reactionary liberalism: a doctrine without ideas or principles." The right, Frum contended, had never been a stronger force "in the realm of ideas," but the division between the PCs and Reform put the prospect of a conservative government out of reach for the foreseeable future. This conservative federal government would be one that "cherishes our free-market economy instead of treating it as a goose to be plucked; that respects Canadians' moral convictions, rather than seeing our convictions as superstitions to be remodelled by Ottawa social engineers." In order to bring this project to fruition, the manifesto concluded, right wingers across Canada need to unite under a shared set of principles.

The 65 delegates reportedly in attendance made for an influential cast, including Reform MPs Stephen Harper and Ray Speaker; Rod Love, chief of staff to Alberta premier Ralph Klein; Klein Cabinet members Jim Dinning and Stockwell Day; and Stephen Greene, Reform Party leader Preston Manning's chief of staff. The only journalists invited to the conference were those sympathetic to the cause — *Saturday Night* magazine editor Kenneth Whyte, *Financial Post* editor Diane Francis, *Calgary Sun* columnist Paul Jackson, *Calgary Herald* columnist Peter Stickland, and the *Alberta Report*'s father-son duo of Ted and Link Byfield — on the condition they participate in the event as part of the conservative movement and didn't report what participants said.

The conference was faced with "two utterly contradictory visions," one unnamed delegate told the *Globe and Mail* a week before it took place. "One is to be ideologically pure, and the other is to form a national government. Either objective on its own is rational, but together they are irrational." This tension was a persistent thread throughout the existence of Reform and then its Canadian Alliance successor. While many politicians have their visions for how society should function, they must water them down to some extent and meet voters where they are in pursuit of power — the ultimate goal of electoral politics. The question is how much of this vision can be implemented while remaining a viable electoral force.

Another major challenge was the fact the Liberals' commitment to neo-liberalism largely took economics out of the equation, exposing an additional fault line among Reformers. "With the battle for government fiscal prudence largely won in Canada, the two factions on the right — economic libertarians and social conservatives — have found they hold significantly different visions of the ideal society," an *Alberta Report* story with no byline read. At the conference, resolutions calling for balanced budgets, tax cuts, and cutting the public sector down to size passed unanimously; but motions involving social issues, such as abolishing employment equity initiatives, preserving the "natural family," and tough-on-crime policies, though ultimately adopted, were far more contentious.

Perhaps nobody embodied these contradictions more than Kenney, who in his years on the Opposition benches became a central figure in juggling efforts to unite Canadian right wingers while presenting the party as a palatable alternative to perpetual Liberal rule. His role in efforts to unite Reformers and Tories was a crucial asset when Kenney returned to Alberta in 2016 to merge the provincial PC and Wildrose Parties. On the first day of Winds of Change, Kenney told the *Calgary Herald* that Canadian conservatives need to look southward for a winning strategy. "There is a movement consciousness in the United States among conservatives. You can go from your social conservatives, to your economic libertarians, to your country club Republicans to your Oklahoma rednecks," he said. "This is simply not the case in Canada." Kenney found his movement in Reform. He and three other Alberta-based Reformers in their twenties — Rahim Jaffer, 25; Rob Anders, 24; and the aforementioned Levant, 24 — formed the so-called Snack Pack, which was regarded as an asset in Reform's efforts to broaden its appeal to a younger, more diverse electorate, while attempting to paper over its membership's ideological differences.

Ric Dolphin, writing in the *Edmonton Journal*, called the Snack Pack a "fraternity-like amalgam of young neo-con Reformers, who met to play pool, drink beer, smoke cigars, talk enthusiastically about Ayn Rand and Margaret Thatcher and eat big breakfasts."[2] The name was a riff on the so-called Rat Pack of Liberal MPs — Sheila Copps, Don Boudria, Brian Tobin, and John Nunziata — which grabbed headlines as a thorn in the side of

Brian Mulroney, the final PC prime minister. It was also a self-deprecating reference to the members' girth. "When we show up at an all-you-can-eat buffet, people get a little worried," Kenney joked to a *Calgary Herald* food reporter writing a piece on the pack's barbecuing tips.[3]

Herald columnist Don Martin declared Kenney the "unofficial leader" of the group, who at 28 was the eldest of the pack. While Jaffer was a libertarian, Kenney was a "far-right social and fiscal conservative," Anders was somewhere in between, and Levant "defies conventional labelling," Martin explained.[4] Levant, the behind-the-scenes operator of the bunch, was "good buddies" with Kenney and talked to him about where Kenney should run when Kenney decided to leave the CTF.[5] He played a more active role in Anders's and Jaffer's campaigns

Levant's philosophy might have been best been summed up in a 1989 *Herald* piece quoting the "best and brightest" Calgary high school graduates: "There are so many opportunities, the thing to do is to grab them" — and grab them he did. At the University of Calgary, Levant was active in campus life, serving on the debate team alongside future Calgary mayor Naheed Nenshi while participating in Reform's campus club.

During his first year in law school at the University of Alberta in 1993, Levant received national attention for his bombast. He wrote a letter to the editor of the law school's *Canons of Construction* newspaper, calling efforts to hire more Indigenous and female faculty a form of bigotry. "Racists today don't burn crosses or wear swastikas. Get with it, they've gone nineties," he stated in the deliberately provocative, pugnacious tone that became his trademark. This earned him a reprimand from the associate dean, which in turn landed him an *Edmonton Journal* guest column where he compared affirmative action to the Nazis' Nuremberg Laws,[6] CBC appearances, a profile in the *Globe and Mail*, and eventually a syndicated *Sun* column. Levant's abrasiveness and media savvy were valuable assets in Reform's efforts to attract young people to the movement by cultivating a conservative counterculture. However, the result of these efforts varied.

The 1997 Election and Its Aftermath

If Reform was serious about forming government, it was clear it would need a major breakthrough in the 1997 election, specifically in Ontario. "This is do or die for Reform," Kenney confessed to the *Herald*'s Don Martin in between knocking on doors in the Calgary Southeast riding. Considerations of uniting the PCs and Reform were at this point out of the question. Reform would either replace the PCs as the "national party of Canadian conservatism," Kenney explained, or be reduced to a "regional rump party" of western Canadian grievances.[7] Naturally, with his CTF experience, Kenney was assigned to Reform leader Manning's "tax-buster" team, where he catered his message to youth. When incumbent prime minister Jean Chrétien announced his intention to increase CPP premiums, Kenney called the policy an "intergenerational rip-off," which forced young people to pay for their parents' pensions.

Kenney first met Rahim Jaffer at a Canadian Taxpayers Federation rally in Edmonton when Kenney was the executive director and Jaffer was one of the speakers. Of the Snack Packers, Kenney is the only one Jaffer is still in touch with, Jaffer told me over a cup of coffee at the restaurant he owns in Edmonton's Old Strathcona neighbourhood where Kenney occasionally went to catch up with his old friend when he was premier. Jaffer and Kenney were always aligned on economic issues, with their shared desire to see taxes as low as possible and for government to be run more like a business, but they had their disagreements on social policy, particularly on matters of church and state. "Those earlier days were a really unique time," Jaffer, who represented Edmonton-Strathcona in the House of Commons from 1997 to 2008, said, describing a spirit of conviviality within Reform. Paradoxically, as the party widened its support and came closer to power, the space for internal debate became increasingly constrained. "At the end of my time, I noticed things were getting very partisan."

Jaffer, the first Muslim MP elected in Canada, was seen as a key figure in getting a younger, more diverse group of people involved with the party, giving "Reform an important new weapon in the struggle for nationwide acceptance," columnist Colby Cosh opined in a January 1997 *Alberta Report* piece. Jaffer, an Ismaili Muslim, told me he was always uneasy about being seen as an emissary for the broader Muslim community, which was heightened in the days after 9/11. "I was never super-religious. I had so much respect for our community and all other religious communities, but I just felt it was an odd thing for me to do," he said.

However, Jaffer did face racism from certain elements within the party. Margaret Rusch, campaign manager for his nomination opponent David Fletcher, called him a "boy with off-colour skin" who should be tested for "exotic foreign diseases." What Rutsch regarded with disdain, Levant saw as an opportunity to expand the party's base. "Look at the demographics here," Levant said at Jaffer's nomination. "Have you ever seen so many interesting-looking people voting Reform?" Ultimately, Jaffer said, Rusch became an active member of their constituency association.

While matters of race and religion made him somewhat uneasy, Jaffer was more comfortable embracing his role as a youth ambassador. "You go to campus clubs to speak and they would naturally connect with you, because here's somebody who's not 50, 60 years old. I was in my early-20s at that time, and so the campus clubs were the same age practically," he said. All four Snack Packers cut their teeth in campus politics. In the early days of his candidacy, Rob Anders described the hostile environment he faced as a campus conservative. "We had garbage thrown at us when we tried to speak. It was very hostile," he told the *Calgary Herald* in December 1996.

For the 1997 election, Anders won the nomination in the Crowfoot riding formerly represented by Stephen Harper, who switched roles with Anders by temporarily quitting politics to work for the National Citizens Coalition (NCC) where Anders had worked prior to entering politics. Like Kenney, Anders was a movement man. During the 1994 U.S. congressional election, Anders was reportedly paid to heckle the Democratic opponent of hard-right Oklahoma Republican senator James Inhofe while wearing a Pinocchio nose.[8] Anders served as the director of the NCC-affiliated Canadians Against Forced Unionism, which attempted to lobby the Klein government in Alberta to impose U.S.-style right-to-work laws.

During the 1997 campaign, Anders received jeers at a local candidates' forum for suggesting most women would choose to stay at home with their children if they had the economic flexibility to do so.[9] While he shared Kenney's social conservative leanings, Anders's unabashed populism proved to be a point of contrast. "Vote for the person who will vote as you would, who has the same moral compass as you do," Anders said. "Every politician has a sense of what has to be done. The question is whether things are done as the voters want them done, or as the politician wants them done."[10]

Kenney certainly engaged in populist rhetoric, but his commitment was half-hearted. Preston Manning had a policy forcing members to sign a form declaring they would vote according to the will of their constituents, even if it contradicted their deeply held values. Kenney, owing to his anti-abortion proclivities, refused to sign the form. "Democracy is predicated on the inviolable dignity of the human person. No democratic majority, no parliamentary majority, no majority of constituents can alienate inalienable rights," he told journalist Steve Paikin. Manning, who had billed Kenney as a "star" candidate, caved and let him run.[11] Paikin presents this as demonstrating Kenney's extraordinary commitment to his principles, ignoring a tension between neoconservatism and democracy, in which neocon moralism won.

When it served his desired outcomes, Kenney was quite content with Reform's direct-democracy initiatives. He advocated a national referendum on abortion rights on moral and practical grounds. Such a referendum "would open the issue up to serious, decisive debate for the first time," he told the *Alberta Report*. "Whether we like it or not, we won't be able to legislate protection of human life by divine fiat, or the wave of some cleric's wand. So how do we do it? Parliament has failed. We should try the people."[12] Proposing plebiscites was a convenient means of squaring Reform's social conservative wing with its more libertarian elements.

While Reform grappled with the tensions embodied by a figure like Kenney, the PCs under leader Jean Charest took a hard-right pivot in a blatant effort to recapture Tories who had moved into the Reform fold. Charest advocated a 10 percent income tax cut accompanied by a 24 percent slash to employment insurance premiums that would be funded with $12 billion in reductions to the public sector over three years. The PCs also attempted to outdo Reform as proponents of harsh criminal justice measures, proposing to lower the age of criminal responsibility from 12 to 10 and calling for the abolition of the Liberals' long-gun registry. University of Calgary political scientist Tom Flanagan, who alongside colleagues Ted Morton, Reiner Knopff, and Barry Cooper, was part of the "Calgary School" of academics whose writings and political activism helped shape the Reform movement, suggested the PC pivot was "a possible first step towards convergence of the two parties," allowing remaining differences to "be resolved on some incremental basis."[13]

Kenney's response to the PC platform was instructive. First, he tied Reform's sweeping tax cuts, including a $3,000 to $5,000 child-care tax deduction for those with kids under 13, to its family values credentials. "We're trying to say in our platform to Canadians that their top priority is their families, and the government will honour that," he said. "The Tories, well, it's just not a priority for them."[14] At the same time, in an apparent effort to guide disaffected Liberals away from the Tories and into the Reform fold, Kenney attacked the Tories' tax proposals for occurring before the country's finances were in the black. "In terms of the sequence, the Liberals and Reform are fairly much in line with one another. It's the Tories who are offside public opinion in their proposal to cut taxes before the budget is balanced," he told the *StarPhoenix* in Saskatoon. Elsewhere he likened the PC's tax-cut talk, with characteristic wit, to "hearing a vampire talk about becoming a vegetarian."[15]

During the campaign, Reform overplayed its hand nationally with an ad targeting Charest, Chrétien, Bloc Québécois leader Gilles Duceppe, and Quebec premier Lucien Bouchard for being Québécois, insinuating the province played too prominent a role in federal politics. This negative advertising sharply contrasted with Manning's assertion that "this strong wind coming out of the West is a warm wind, and is a positive wind, one that ought to be beneficial to the country as a whole."[16] Kenney wisely stayed out of the Quebec discourse during the campaign, focusing instead on issues closer to his heart, namely, reducing the state's size and scope and opening his arms to the family values crowd.

While Reform gained 10 seats in the 1997 election and achieved Official Opposition status, the needed breakthrough in eastern Canada didn't occur;

the party didn't win a single seat east of Manitoba. It was, however, a good night for the Snack Pack. In Calgary Southeast, Kenney beat the PCs' Carol Kraychy by nearly 14,000 votes. In Crowfoot, Anders beat Liberal Dave Bronconnier, who later became Calgary's mayor, by more than 9,500 votes. Jaffer's race in Edmonton-Strathcona was closer, but he still defeated the Liberal challenger by almost 3,000 votes.

Although Kenney began his career lambasting government fat cats for their generous perks — primarily pensions, but other allowances, as well — he began to sing a different tune almost immediately after taking office. "It's a dilemma," he told the *Calgary Herald* in June 1997. "I'd like to take French classes in Ottawa and that's one of the perks of MPs, and some people might criticize me for taking advantage of that. But I think it's a legitimate perk." So, too, did Manning, who received a $20,000 raise as the new Leader of Opposition. Defending Manning, Kenney said he never opposed the salaries of the prime minister, Cabinet members, or Leader of Opposition. Anders, however, was more conflicted, acknowledging it's "a tough call" and saying, "there's only so long you can go on as a martyr."[17] Manning began taking a chauffeur-driven car and moved into the Official Opposition residence at Stornoway, both of which he previously dismissed as needless perks, apparently contradicting his commitment to "fiscal responsibility in the broadest sense of the word."[18] In other words, Reform became part of the Ottawa establishment it purported to oppose, or "Ottawashed," in Kenney's words.[19]

Ezra Levant, who promised "aggressive, guerilla warfare"[20] against the elites, was now a special aide to Manning, advising the party's Question Period performance and embracing theatrics by telling members to "think Hollywood." Manning appointed Levant manager of the party's Senate reform campaign — a long-standing objective of Reform, which proposed a "Triple E" solution to make it an effective elected body with equal representation from each province. After Ontario senator Andrew Thompson was caught soaking up the sun at a Mexican beach while the Senate was in session, Levant had the idea of sending Reform supporters wearing sombreros to the Senate dressed as a mariachi band to stage a "welcome-back" party for Thompson where they handed out burritos. Unconfined by parliamentary decorum, he teamed up with Stockwell Day's son, Logan, to heckle senators, daring them to "step down and run like a man," in the younger Day's words. This was all good fun, but it fuelled perceptions that Reform was unserious, something it was trying to shake.

Unite the Right

It was exceedingly obvious there would need to be some sort of rapprochement between the PCs and Reform if they were ever to remove the Liberals from power, as the 1996 Winds of Change event highlighted. The question was what form this would take. *Alberta Report* publisher Ted Byfield, conceding the impossibility of Reform breaking through in seat-rich Ontario and Quebec, suggested a counterintuitive push to "Disunite the Right," in which the Tories and Reform would enter an informal coalition, with the PCs running candidates in eastern Canada and Reform running in its western heartland. "There's not enough room for two national conservative parties," Byfield wrote.[21]

The Tory leadership of Jean Charest was regarded as a major impediment to conservative unity. Charest held an apparent personal animosity for Preston Manning from the ads targeting Québécois politicians, including himself, during the 1997 campaign. This stumbling block was removed when Charest announced his intention in March 1998 to run for the leadership of the neoliberal, federalist Quebec Liberals. He used the announcement as an opportunity to call for right wingers to return to the PC fold. Manning wasted no time in announcing his desire to establish a "United Alternative" to the Liberals, which was approved at the party convention in London, Ontario, that spring with 91.3 percent support.

A major shortcoming of the United Alternative (UA), which Kenney was tapped to lead, was its insistence that any unity occur under the Reform banner. Kenney demonstrated the plan's limits when he said "everything will be on the table but the basic [Reform] party principles."[22] Laying bare what sort of principles Kenney had in mind, party members approved a resolution at a convention for a "family-values" test to be imposed on any policy decision. The resolution's text was vague, but Calgary delegate James Istvanffy made his interpretation clear: "Governments should not give spousal benefits to people who commit acts that many Canadians find immoral, such as a sodomy."[23] At the same time as Reform was extending an open invitation to disaffected members of other parties to join, it passed a resolution reminding them why they might want to think twice. To attain unity with more moderate voices, these views needed to be either stamped out or toned down. With Kenney's deep-seated beliefs, he was eventually forced to do the latter.

In September, Reform established a steering committee chaired by Kenney, Alberta treasurer Stockwell Day, and Ontario transport minister Tony Clement. On paper, this was one Reformer and two Tories, but Day and Clement were part of PC governments that fitted well with Reform's neoliberal wing, and Day was at least as extreme in his socially conservative positions as Kenney. The committee itself notably included federal PCs Peter White, who served as Prime Minister Brian Mulroney's principal secretary; Toronto lawyer Bob Dechert, with his notable fundraising prowess; and Saskatchewan Party founder Don Morgan, who said he'd never voted Reform before, suggesting the dial was slowly moving in a merger's direction.

The next PC leader, Joe Clark, who was previously prime minister for less than a year in 1979 and 1980, poured cold water on the idea of merging with Reform, calling the United Alternative an "attempt at survival, a lifebuoy they are tossing out to try and keep themselves afloat."[24] Clark was riding high on the defection of MP Jim Silye to the PCs from Reform, as well as charges of hypocrisy against four Reform MPs who sought to opt into the pension plan they ran against. The PC leader's assessment that Reform was talking about unity to distract from internal discord was correct. "It's a means of taking all the dissent and differences on other issues and trying to focus their energy towards some other goal."[25] Kenney's cutting response: "We never counted on support from old-establishment red Tories from the 1970s to begin with." Ralph Klein adviser Rod Love, who sat on the United Alternative steering committee, was much more diplomatic, telling Clark the PCs must "adapt or perish."[26]

The UA passed with 60.5 percent support at Reform's June 1999 convention, although fewer than half of party members voted, setting the stage for a

UA convention in January 2000. What seemed like a convincing victory on paper risked splitting the right into three parties. With a significant minority opposed, one diehard Reformer, Bruce Stubbs, cautioned that the ensuing struggle over the party's future "won't be pretty." Cypress-Grasslands MP Lee Morrison, who was the leading UA opponent in caucus, said the results mean "no major, major disembowelment of the party is possible." Conceding to the reality of a split right-wing vote, Morrison suggested collaborating with the PCs on a riding-by-riding basis, but Clark soon made official his opposition to any form of alliance with Reform.

In the midst of October's Tory convention in Toronto, Clark published a six-page open letter inviting the 60 percent of Reformers who wanted unity to join the PCs, striking a conciliatory tone in applauding Reform for providing a "wake-up call" for the Tory establishment.[27] "The major division now is not between Reform and the PCs. It is within Reform itself," Clark said at the convention.[28] Although Reform was divided, the PCs suffered a dramatic loss of membership, falling from 90,000 during its 1998 leadership election to 18,682 in 1999, whereas Reform's membership remained consistent at 64,000. The people behind the PCs' answer to the UA, the Canadian Alternative, recommended selling multi-year memberships to lock party members in and stem its slide into irrelevance.[29] Across the street from the Tory convention, the UA unveiled its platform for unity, which called for balanced budget legislation, mandatory annual debt payments, and sweeping income and corporate tax cuts, although it intentionally didn't provide any specifics, with the implication that those would be hammered out by the membership.

While 40 percent of Reformers voted against unity, the remaining PCs were nearly unanimous in opposition, with 95 percent of convention delegates endorsing a motion forcing the party to run candidates in all 301 ridings, compelling conservatives to choose between the UA and PCs. Delegates also defeated motions calling for expanding free trade, and an emphasis on low taxes, debt reduction, and balanced budgets, paving the way for neoliberals to turn to the UA, which advocated all of the above. While Charest ran as Reform light, it was clear Clark would run as Liberal light, as he had in 1979, which UA supporters were eager to capitalize on.

From Reform to Alliance

With formal conservative unity off the table, Reform continued to press for a broader tent, deciding a new party with a new name might be a sound starting point. But without any co-operation from the Tories, the party would be Reform in all but name. "Manning is stuck between a party he wants to leave behind and a movement that has no immediate future," read a 1999 *Globe and Mail* editorial. Even before Reform approved the UA, Manning's suitability as leader for a party with a more national scope was questioned. "When you break it all down, the problem is Preston," former MP Ed Harper, who was the only elected Reformer in Ontario, said bluntly.[30] Stockwell Day — who unlike Manning is bilingual — began preparing to run for the leadership of a new party when he stepped down from the UA steering committee in February 1999 and immediately received the praise of his boss, Ralph Klein. A couple of months later, Day headlined a fundraiser for Tony Clement, who remained on the UA committee with Kenney, in Brampton, Ontario, drawing 1,500 attendees and raising $100,000 for Clement. Federal PC organizer and UA booster Kevyn Nightingale said Day's recent introduction of a flat tax in Alberta "makes a lot of us salivate."[31]

Day and Kenney were kindred spirits, with their shared commitment to the harshest forms of neoliberal austerity and the state's role in promoting moral values. In fact, the social conservatism of Day, an ordained pastor like Manning, went even further than Kenney's. At the 1995 Alberta PC convention, Day pursued a vote on defunding abortion, which was narrowly defeated after Klein urged members to vote it down, understanding the negative impact it would have on perceptions of the PCs outside religious fundamentalist circles. Day called being gay a "mental disorder," advocated conversion therapy, and attempted to have *Of Mice and Men* banned from a school library for obscenity. He was sued for libel by a Red Deer lawyer who defended a person accused of possessing child sexual abuse images in court after Day alleged the lawyer supported the legalization of child pornography. The Alberta government spent $792,064.40 to settle out of court.[32]

The PCs' refusal to co-operate with Manning's unity plans, combined with Day's looming challenge to his leadership, likely produced the neocon rhetoric emanating from Manning in his response to the Liberals' 1999 Speech from the Throne. In a 105-minute harangue, Manning proclaimed "the highest moral responsibilities of the state" to be imposing "just laws" promoting the "maintenance of public order." The state's "most important social responsibility," he added, "is the protection and nurturing of the family," which Manning declared "the most important organizational unit of society," with its foundation being the marriage of a man and woman. He demanded the Liberals summon the "moral nerve" to protect "the right of the unborn" by overriding the Supreme Court if necessary. Kenney applauded Manning's "courage" in addressing social conservative shibboleths, arguing this approach wouldn't contradict its outreach efforts. "I don't know any fiscal conservatives who also don't happen to believe that marriage is a union between a man and a woman."[33]

Impressed as he might have been with Manning's neocon pivot, it wasn't enough to secure Kenney's support in the leadership race that ensued in January 2000 after UA conference delegates agreed to rebrand Reform as the Canadian Conservative Reform Alliance party, or Canadian Alliance for short. After its acronym (CCRAP) became the subject of ridicule, the party's name was shuffled around to the Canadian Reform Conservative Alliance. Its policies were standard Reform party fare, with two notable exceptions — for the first time, in a sign of moderation, the party accepted official bilingualism, and in a sign of its continued commitment to neoliberal doctrine, endorsed a 17 percent flat tax. Not long after the convention, a group of people who met there launched a "Draft Stockwell Day" campaign. In February 2000, the University of Calgary Reform club, which at the time included future federal Conservative leader Pierre Poilievre, revealed to *Calgary Herald* reporter Howard May, who was in the midst of scabbing during the paper's long strike, that Kenney would be Day's campaign manager.

Day's campaign was officially launched on March 28 in Red Deer where Kenney touted Day's experience at actually implementing the tax cuts Manning only ever had the chance to muse about. Despite his ambition to expand the Alliance's reach to Ontario, Day made it clear he would not be toning his neocon inclinations down. "Politically correct is not cowering in fear because you are speaking up for your constituents," he said to chants of "Go Stock Go" and "Amen." Day used the recent conviction of serial rapist and murderer Paul Bernardo to advocate for a harsh criminal justice agenda, arguing Bernardo shouldn't have the right to appeal his conviction.[34] The next day, the campaign appeared in Toronto where Day was met with protests for his anti-gay, anti-abortion, and pro-death penalty stances.

The first leadership race for a party specifically oriented around unity was used to highlight its divisions. Nowhere was this clearer than with the Snack Pack, whose apparent demise made headlines. Joining Kenney in his allegiance to Day was self-proclaimed "Stockaholic" Levant; Anders supported Manning, whom he likened to George Washington;[35] and Jaffer backed Tom Long, an Ontario political strategist credited as the brains behind Conservative premier Mike Harris's back-to-back majority governments, whom he saw as the party's best chance of building support in Ontario. "Perhaps we can revive our social activity after it's over," Kenney said. "It's just that we're all individuals. It's just not a pack mentality."[36] Jaffer told me that after the leadership race, this was essentially what happened, with their social circle expanding as they gained experience to include veteran MPs, such as Monte Solberg. Anders, whom Jaffer described to me as an "odd duck," however, drifted away.

In the leadership race, Kenney was motivated by a desire to win, and in Day found a candidate who not only shared his moralistic worldview but also looked electable. It was thought that Day's charisma, combined with his tax-cutting, deficit-busting prowess, could provide cover for an emboldened religious right. In May 2000, Kenney was received enthusiastically as a proxy for the Day campaign as a headline speaker at the third annual anti-choice March for Life in Ottawa. Karen Murawsky of the Campaign Life Coalition told the *National Post* that under Day's leadership the Alliance was a "pro-life party." Kari Simpson of the ultraconservative Citizens Research Initiative, whose fundraising abilities were highly regarded, applauded Day's "record of standing up for marriage [and] strong family values." Asked about Day's support from the religious right, Kenney said coyly: "We welcome the support of people for whatever reason."[37]

One Day supporter, Roy Beyer of the Canada Family Action Coalition, attacked Tom Long for having "homosexual activists" on his team. Kenney denounced his remarks and said Beyer wasn't associated with the campaign in any official capacity, pivoting to how the campaign included "everybody from socially conservative Muslims, Jews and Christians to gay libertarians and Quebec nationalists," previewing the multicultural outreach strategy he would master once the united conservatives formed government. Stephen Harper, still in political exile at the NCC, warned these sorts of outbursts from supporters like Beyer posed a major stumbling block toward the Alliance's appeal in Ontario. "You can't expect to build a coalition to advance conservatism if you start saying everyone must agree on a certain social or religious view," Harper, who endorsed Long's leadership bid, told the *National Post*. "The growth of such a party will be pretty negligible."[38]

Once elected leader, Day picked his battles for the sake of attaining power. He appointed Kenney finance critic in a shuffle that otherwise largely left Manning's shadow Cabinet intact, indicating broad tax cuts were a high priority. For the religious right, he posed federal tax credits for people who sent their children to religious schools. "We touched a nerve with that," Kenney boasted. "The ethnic religious communities have heard Liberal rhetoric about diversity and pluralism for decades. But it's the Canadian Alliance that is getting serious about giving them what they want to protect culture, education and faith." *Canadian Jewish News* reporter Ron Csillag noted that, in doing so, the Alliance "tapped into a growing moral conservatism in this country."[39]

Elsewhere, Day was more cautious on both fiscal and social issues. While offering sweeping tax cuts, the flat tax was not on the agenda for the early 2000 election, which Prime Minister Jean Chrétien launched on a Sunday, knowing Day refused to work on the Lord's Day. That left Kenney and co-campaign chair Peter White to kick off the Alliance campaign in the leader's stead. When Day was asked in the midst of the campaign about the B.C. government making the morning-after pill available without prescription, he was notably circumspect. "That's something we haven't taken a position on ... no MP, including myself, has a private agenda related to this issue," he told the CBC while at the same time dog-whistling to the religious right by expressing concern that medical officials might have "abbreviated any of the usual, fairly lengthy testing periods for a pill that is obviously that strong."[40] It was no doubt a delicate balancing act. The very people he cultivated to win the Alliance leadership needed to have their expectations tempered for the sake of winning the election.

Suffice to say, Day wasn't victorious, with the Liberals increasing their majority to 171 seats from 155, and the Alliance's seat count rising just six seats from Reform's 1997 performance, including two in Ontario. Bemoaning the vote split on the right, Day said in his concession speech, "it is clear the message to us is: Not yet. Not this time."[41] There wouldn't be a next time for Day; as soon as the electoral smoke cleared, the knives came out. "He won the leadership on his capacity to do what Preston [Manning] was unable to do, which is to make a breakthrough in Ontario. He should be judged on the expectation he created," observed former Reform pollster Andre Turcotte.[42] Ian McClelland, an Alberta PC MLA and former Reform MP who spearheaded efforts to have Harper return to politics, told the *National Post* the Alliance was a failed political experiment. "It's over for Stockwell Day and it is over for the party. The Canadian Alliance, in my opinion, as a political vehicle capable of exerting leadership authority in the country, is over. It is finished. It is dead. There is no future."[43] Attempting to unite conservatives without the participation of the country's other right-leaning party proved a fruitless endeavour.

Day announced a leadership race to determine his fate at the Alliance's helm; Kenney remained a staunch supporter, arguing "people have lost sight of" Day's talents.[44] Harper entered the race in December 2001, promising to eschew the support of the religious right while allowing them to express themselves. "I, as leader, am not going to focus this party on the abortion issue or on the leader's personal moral and religious views. That's a fundamental decision the party is going to have to make."[45] He also vowed not to back a merger with the PCs until Joe Clark was removed as leader, calling Clark's old-school Red Toryism "completely incompatible with this party."[46] Harper easily won on the leadership race's first ballot with 55 percent support, earning nearly 16,000 more votes than Day. A victorious Harper set his sight on securing a seat in Parliament, ultimately forcing an obstinate Ezra Levant to step aside as the Alliance candidate in Calgary Southwest, despite Levant having won the nomination for the by-election triggered by Manning's retirement. Working on Levant's campaign was fellow Stockaholic Pierre Poilievre.[47]

Tom Flanagan, the University of Calgary professor who was a key player in Reform's early days, managed Harper's leadership campaign, which was the first time he encountered Kenney in person. After Day's devastating defeat, he told me, Kenney needed some time to cool off before being "gradually reabsorbed back into caucus activities." Flanagan, who served as Harper's chief of staff in his first year as Opposition leader, said Kenney was largely out of the picture as Harper sought to rebuild the party after Day's tumultuous leadership. "There was probably initially some distrust between him and Harper. They had been friendly before that, but [because of] Jason managing Day's campaign, there was some coolness there for a while," Flanagan recalled. "But Jason is too valuable a player to be left sitting on the sidelines."

When Harper unveiled his inaugural shadow Cabinet in April 2002, he gave Day the foreign affairs portfolio, much to the dismay of Muslim and Arab groups, who deplored Day's hardline views on Israel. Kenney was stripped of his finance critic role and designated for a "special assignment." Of the apparent demotion, Kenney said, "I'm not sore. I'll be a team player. Stephen and I are quite happy to go forward on that basis."[48] Placing Day in the foreign affairs role was a clever way for Harper to largely muzzle him on contentious social issues while putting him to use as a mouthpiece for their shared neocon foreign policy perspective. As the United States launched its Shock and Awe campaign against Iraq the following year, Harper and Day co-authored a *Wall Street Journal* op-ed endorsing the American invasion of Iraq while bemoaning Jean Chrétien's lack of support, headlined "Canadians Stand with You." Jaffer told me there were internal debates about the extent to which the Alliance should support U.S. foreign policy in the Middle East after 9/11, with some questioning whether it was in Canada's national interest, but these disagreements were never expressed publicly.

Kenney, who was later assigned to the Canada-U.S. relations portfolio, shared Day's and Harper's foreign policy views, which saw U.S. power as not just a force for stability but as a moral necessity. The week after their *Wall Streeet Journal* op-ed, Kenney appeared at a pro-war rally at the University of Calgary organized by Ezra Levant, which was attended by 1,000 people, just two dozen of whom were students, where he expressed shame that the Canadian government didn't endorse U.S. president George W. Bush's war. "In the last couple of weeks, for the first time I was not proud to be a Canadian … not proud of what Jean Chrétien did to undo 130 years of Canadian history," Kenney said. "Jean Chrétien has no right to undermine the history, the tradition of our country."[49] Support for Bush's war was one point of agreement the Alliance shared with the man who was about to become the new PC leader.

United at Last

The long-elusive journey to unite conservatives under one party appeared to be at yet another impasse when Peter MacKay was elected Joe Clark's successor as PC leader in June 2003 with a far less convincing mandate than Harper's. In order to win, MacKay made an agreement with leadership rival David Orchard to not pursue a merger with the Alliance as a condition for Orchard's support, but MacKay quickly began walking back that vow. The first indication was MacKay's endorsement of tacit co-operation with the Alliance, in the form of an agreement not to openly attack each other, which was a significant departure from Charest and Clark. MacKay publicly stood steadfast against the notion of any formal arrangement, let alone a merger, until the *Globe and Mail* revealed on its September 18, 2003, front page that the two parties were in the "final phase" of secret unity talks.

Much to the chagrin of Orchard and Clark, MacKay and Harper announced on October 16 an agreement to create the Conservative Party of Canada (CPC), one reportedly helped along by mining magnate Peter Munk. In December, 96 percent of Alliance members and 90 percent of Tories endorsed the merger, a week before former finance minister and perpetual Chrétien rival Paul Martin became prime minister. In the ensuing CPC leadership race, which MacKay didn't contest, Kenney endorsed Harper, acknowledging there was no social conservative with Day's credentials in this race. Kenney didn't play a significant role in the campaign, which Harper won decisively in March 2004, defeating rivals Belinda Stronach and Tony Clement on the first ballot.

Martin, battered by revelations that the Liberal government provided $100 million to government-friendly advertising firms with little to show for their work — the so-called sponsorship scandal — dropped the writ on the federal election a couple of months after Harper's win. Canada appeared on track to elect an avowedly right-wing government for the first time since 1988. Kenney, who was by then promoted to finance critic and questioned Martin and his inner circle relentlessly about the sponsorship scandal in the House of Commons, was ready to fight.

When Ralph Goodale suggested people in western Canada vote Liberal if they wanted a say in the government, Kenney accused his old boss of running a "campaign of fear and intimidation."[50] The next day, Kenney, without a hint of irony, warned that Canada wasn't doing enough for the War on Terror, invoking the "nightmare scenario [of] a sequel to 9/11," and the risk to the economy if a Canadian was linked to this entirely hypothetical attack.[51] At an all-candidates forum at a Calgary charter school, Kenney told Grade 4 and 5 students that Canada needed to boost its defence budget "so we can protect ourselves against countries with terrorists."[52] Kenney was put on the defensive when remarks at an anti-abortion rally comparing abortion to child abuse and slavery were uncovered, with the Liberals citing him as an example of CPC extremism on social issues.

On election day, the Grits were reduced to a minority government — Canada's first since Joe Clark became prime minister in 1979. The CPC's vote share of 30 percent stayed the same from 2000, but this time it was spread more efficiently. The CPC's failures in Ontario were in part attributed to the Liberals' strength in ethnic ridings surrounding Toronto, an issue Kenney would seek to redress in due course. At Harper's campaign headquarters, Kenney went to each of his colleagues one by one and urged them to keep their remarks "moderate."[53] The Liberal government could fall at any time, and the Conservatives were well placed to take power for the first time in a generation; they couldn't risk being painted as a bunch of extremists when the next election came.

About 18 months later, Martin's minority government collapsed. Tom Flanagan was brought back to run the CPC war room, which was the only time he worked directly with Kenney. "He had a lot of good ideas for rapid response and the ability to carry them out. And then as an MP, he also had a public persona, so we could send him out to make public statements," Flanagan recalled, calling Kenney a great "team player" who was willing to be blunt with Harper on electoral strategy. "He just had tremendous energy."

The CPC won a minority government, essentially swapping seat counts and popular vote with the Liberals while remaining shut out of Toronto, Montreal, and Vancouver. It was clear Kenney's tenacious efforts at conservative unity over the past decade had begun paying dividends. The CPC was able to bring together libertarians and the religious right, neoliberals and neoconservatives, western Reform populists and eastern establishment Tories, united in pursuit of power. He would again attempt the feat of reconciling two estranged conservative factions when he returned to Alberta to merge the urban PCs and rural Wildrose.

For the CPC, 2006 was a time of renewal. Rob Anders, who wore a FREE TIBET shirt to a Chinese New Year celebration in 2000 and called Nelson Mandela a terrorist long after it was fashionable to do so, acknowledged he had to tone the antics down on the government benches. "When you're in opposition, part of your job is to garner attention. On the government side, you have to guard against answers that are too flippant." Now that his friends were in charge, Ezra Levant agreed it was time for them to get serious. "That's the difference between winning, and being the NDP of the right. How much of your idealism can you maintain while executing the discipline of power?"[54] Levant himself, of course, had no such inhibitions.

The CPC could only go so far with its agenda as a minority government; they needed a majority. In that respect, they still faced the same dilemma the Reformers did in the Snack Pack days — how to bring new constituencies into the Conservative fold. But the Day campaign showed Kenney it was possible to mobilize socially conservative elements within various ethnocultural communities to electoral advantage, providing a trial run for the outreach strategy he perfected during the Harper years. Inviting diverse communities into the Conservative fold, however, came with strings attached.

4

WEAPONIZED IMMIGRANTS

ON A BRISK AUTUMN DAY IN October 1994, Jason Kenney approached Stephen Harper at Ottawa's Royal Oak Pub on Bank Street. Harper was at the time a newly elected Reform MP, while Kenney had recently assumed leadership of the Canadian Taxpayers Federation. But their conversation that day would shape the strategy that would propel them to power under the Conservative Party of Canada banner. The regional divide between Reform and the Progressive Conservatives had already become apparent, but Kenney convinced Harper there was another issue the conservative movement had to address. "Even with a united right," Kenney said, "conservatism has peaked. Votes are becoming stagnant." The only way for conservatives to win power was by crossing the "final frontier" of attracting immigrant voters. "Look at demographic trends — it's the future. Immigrants have the same values as us, we have to talk to them, to convince them." Harper wasn't sure this was worth the effort. After all, the Liberals, with their full-throated embrace of multiculturalism, were dominant with new Canadians; he didn't see that changing any time soon.

After Harper formed his first government in 2006, he met Kenney at an Ottawa hotel. Harper asked, "Do you remember the conversation we had in October 1994?" Kenney remembered it vividly. "Prove to me that I was wrong," Harper urged him.[1] While Kenney, whom the *Calgary*

Herald described as Harper's "fully bilingual pitbull," was initially left out of Cabinet,[2] Harper appointed him his parliamentary secretary, with a specific focus on multiculturalism. From this perch, Kenney would further Conservative efforts to build a bridge to immigrant communities; he showed up at cultural events to court right-wing elements within those communities by emphasizing his party's commitment to lower taxes, family values, and tough-on-crime policies. His approach was flexibly pragmatic in its electoral considerations but served clear ideological ends with the set of policies he was selling.

Conservative strategist and University of Calgary academic Tom Flanagan noted the social conservatism of many newcomers, which was often rooted in religion, jibed well with Conservative values. "Many immigrants look like Conservative core voters, except that they may have a different skin colour and mother tongue," Flanagan wrote in a June 2011 article for *Policy Options*. Kenney called immigrant communities the "personification of Margaret Thatcher's aspirational class," with their "massive work ethic ... striving to get their small business going, strong family values, respect for tradition."

Kenney drew new Canadians into the Conservative fold through a superficial commitment to diversity, which provided cover for the party's vision of Canadian nationalism that emphasized tradition, deference to authority, neoliberal individualism, and a sense of cultural superiority. John Carlaw, whom we met in the Introduction with his formulation of "Kenneyism," described this approach as "neoconservative multiculturalism," which he expressed as "both a hollowing out of the anti-racist potentials of multiculturalism discourses and policies as well as shifting the concept in more conservative directions."[3]

Tasked with getting immigrants "tuned into our frequency,"[4] Kenney acknowledged his outreach efforts were more about showing up than anything more substantial. Not long after he was appointed Harper's parliamentary secretary, he spoke to a South Korean immigrant physician at a Vancouver event who derided Conservatives as racist and anti-immigrant. Kenney responded by invoking Prime Minister John Diefenbaker's elimination of racial discrimination in immigration in 1962. Be that as it may, the doctor pointed out, it's the Liberals and NDP who showed up to cultural events and were a strong presence in immigrant community media. "It woke me up," Kenney told *Maclean's*. "I understood that I would have to be everywhere at all times. Personal contact is crucial for new immigrants."[5]

Kenney's habit of jetting from various ethnocultural community events — at one point averaging six appearances per day[6] — led to him being dubbed "Minister for Curry in a Hurry" by caucus mate Rahim Jaffer — himself a Ugandan émigré. This approach was widely credited with winning the Conservatives enough seats in the suburban ridings surrounding Toronto and Vancouver to form a majority government in 2011. Kenney's approach focused on branding the Conservatives as a pro-immigrant party, rattling off clichés about hard work, family values, and public safety to put a friendly face on the same old neocon agenda. The party's policies changed less than its demeanour, which provided a veneer of inclusivity for a political project that was at its root exclusionary.

Journalist Yasha Levine describes how the United States uses "immigrant groups — and their ethnic, national, and religious identities — as a geopolitical weapon."[7] He's specifically referring to U.S. authorities inflaming right-wing nationalist sentiment among exiles from the Communist Bloc to serve its foreign policy objectives. Immigrants who support these policy aims are embraced while those who don't are left to fend with everyone else in the neoliberal state. Levine focuses on U.S. foreign policy, but the same dynamic exists elsewhere and can be wielded in support of domestic policy goals as much as foreign, or both, in the case of citizenship and immigration policy.

As minister, Kenney increased the country's annual immigration target to 280,000 from 250,000 but changed the configuration of immigrants welcomed to Canada, focusing more on economic than humanitarian factors while aiming to crack down on what he claimed were rampant abuses of the system. These policies made immigration easier for those who could provide economic value while closing the doors on the most vulnerable from abroad. It was a project that was welcoming if you shared the right views, but otherwise exclusionary. "The invitation was a conditional one," Carlaw told me in an interview. "If you accept the neoconservative sensibility, you're welcomed into the Conservatives' political coalition. If not, then you could face a much harsher approach." For Kenney, the conditional acceptance of immigrants was a weapon to be applied for both electoral and ideological ends.

As Flanagan noted, the Conservative approach to recruiting immigrant communities was an effort to create a "minimum winning coalition," which would allow the government to broaden its support enough to win a majority, but not so much that they would have to contend with competing interests. By the party's own admission, 20 percent of the "ethnic vote" was inaccessible due to what it called "foreign policy issues" — namely, the government's support for any and every Israeli action, which alienated many Arab and Muslim voters.[8]

I came into my political consciousness during the Harper years. I regarded the Harper government, and Kenney in particular, as cruel, vindictive, and regressive, but lacked an understanding of the broader ideological project its agenda served and Kenney's shrewdness in bringing it to fruition. As a Jewish teen, I couldn't help but notice elements of the community embracing the Harper project wholesale based on his staunch support of Israel. Harper's approach to the most conservative elements of the Jewish community was part of a broader strategy that was just as inviting for some as it was disciplinary for others.

On the disciplinary side, Kenney eliminated a two-year $447,297 grant to the Canadian Arab Federation (CAF) for its immigrant resettlement program, which taught language and job-hunting skills to newcomers. This came after its president, Khaled Mouammar, called Kenney a "professional whore" for his wholehearted support for Israel during its 2008 attack on Gaza and 2006 invasion of Lebanon. While Mouammar's remarks were no doubt uncouth, they were borne out of a valid frustration with the government's refusal to meet with his organization or the Canadian Islamic Congress in its first three years in power, while it was at the same time adopting an obstinately pro-Israel orientation. Using Israel as a conditional wedge for inclusion didn't just impact Arabs or Muslims — 95 percent of those enrolled in the CAF's programming for newcomers weren't Arab. The Harper government also cut funding to Christian aid group Kairos, which Kenney declared anti-Semitic based solely on its Israel criticisms. This wasn't the only condition for the Harper government's embrace of immigrant communities, but it was a blatant one.

The anti-immigrant sentiment that plagued the old Reform Party, which cautioned in 1988 against efforts to "radically or suddenly alter the ethnic makeup of Canada,"[9] was channelled toward opprobrium for immigrant communities who weren't deemed useful to the neocon cause, chief among them failed refugee claimants, who were portrayed as liars and cheats. Kenney made life more difficult for refugees and asylum seekers, conflating them with criminality and deceit in the public consciousness while using state power to keep increasing numbers of them out. The unique personal circumstances that led them to apply "improperly" for refugee status were simply ignored, allowing Kenney to draw a contrast between good, lawful immigrants who could be incorporated into his neocon project and the rest, who would be dealt with by the harsh hand of the state.

Curry in a Hurry

In the early days of Harper's first minority government, the Conservatives pursued some long-overdue symbolic gestures that served to burnish their image in immigrant communities. Kenney, alongside Heritage Minister Bev Oda, was sent on a tour of Vancouver, Winnipeg, Toronto, Ottawa, Montreal, and Halifax to consult with Chinese Canadians on redress for Canada's head tax policy. This policy charged Chinese immigrants a $500 fee from 1885 to 1923 before the Chinese Exclusion Act prohibited the immigration of Chinese people altogether until it was revoked in 1947. Harper provided an official apology in the House of Commons and offered compensation of up to $20,000 for those people or their spouses who had had to pay the head tax. By 2006, there were just 29 people alive who had had to pay the tax and 250 to 300 of their widows.

Kenney was a hit with conservative elements of the Chinese-Canadian community, some members of which called him "Smiling Buddha" for his sunny demeanour and portly figure. The Conservatives were assisted in their outreach efforts to this community by the Chinese-Canadian Conservative

Kenney marches in the Lunar New Year Parade in Vancouver as citizenship and immigration minister in January 2012.

Association (CCCA), but their relationship was a one-way street, with the CCCA carrying out the party's agenda within the community. "There is so much control by (Tory party) headquarters that it is insulting," one disgruntled CCCA member told the *Toronto Star* on the condition of anonymity. The more left-leaning Chinese Canadian National Council did much of the heavy lifting in getting the government to apologize for the head tax, efforts which predated the Harper government, but they were cast aside for a more pliable community group.

In a gesture toward the large Indo-Canadian community, on May 2, 2006, the government announced an inquiry into the 1985 Air India bombing, the worst terrorist attack in Canadian history, which killed 329 people, most of whom were Canadian citizens. The day after the inquiry announcement, the Harper government cut the landing fee for new immigrants in half to $490 from $975, offering partial rebates for those who had already paid the $975 but had yet to obtain permanent residency. This fee had been criticized in some quarters as a neo-head tax when it was introduced in 1995 by Prime Minister Jean Chrétien. Lowering it was a relatively inexpensive way for the Harper Conservatives to burnish their pro-immigrant image while correctly and subtly identifying the Liberals' superficial commitment to inclusion. However, the Conservatives later tripled the fee for obtaining citizenship to $300 from $100, sending a clear message about the economic class of immigrants it sought.[10]

That summer, Harper became the first prime minister to hold a business roundtable specifically with Indo-Canadian leaders. Aditya Jha, co-founder and CEO of software developer Osellus, said Harper's presence "busts the prevailing political myth that Indo-Canadians are a Liberal voting block. Many in the community are Conservative-minded, but they have not been engaged or cajoled by this party before." Jha was referring not to the Indo-Canadian community writ large but to the economic elites of the Indo-Canadian community he represented, who were naturally amenable to the Conservatives' neoliberal economic project. Harper said this meeting was necessary, because if he had gone "through traditional government channels to meet with business leaders of Toronto, to be blunt with you, most of the people I'll end up meeting with will be old-stock Canadians … not necessarily business leaders from more recent immigrant communities, some of whom run multi-billion dollar operations."[11] Courting elements of immigrant communities was just as ideological as it was electoral, bringing wealthy elites in lockstep with his agenda.

So impressed was Harper with Kenney's role in wooing immigrant communities that he promoted him to secretary of state for multiculturalism and Canadian identity less than a year into the government's tenure. Kenney's outreach efforts continued apace with other ethnocultural communities in the leadup to the 2008 election.

At a gathering at the Polish National Union of Canada building in Toronto's west end, Kenney expressed interest in creating a monument to victims of communism that would appeal to conservative-minded members of the Polish, Czech, Ukrainian, Hungarian, Tibetan, Cuban, Latvian, Lithuanian, and Korean communities while also showcasing the Conservatives' vehement opposition to communist ideology. Zuzana Hahn, the Czech-born coordinator of the monument project, said

Kenney's presence was a great asset to the Conservatives, given the emotional resonance of anti-communist sentiment. Kenney was sold on the idea months earlier when he visited a statue of a man crucified with a hammer and sickle at a Scarborough park privately owned by Toronto's Czech and Slovak communities, and decided they must build something similar in Ottawa. As of this writing, the Memorial to Victims of Communism is still under construction after repeated cost increases, relocations, and redesigns. In a July 2021 *CBC News* story, journalist Taylor Noakes revealed that the monument received several donations dedicated to Nazi collaborators who are venerated in some Eastern European diaspora communities as nationalist heroes.

In a further gesture to an anti-communist Eastern European community in May 2008, Canada became the first country in the world after Ukraine to recognize the Ukrainian famines of 1932 to 1933, or Holodomor, as Ukrainians refer to them, as a genocide, although the applicability of genocide has been subject to much scholarly debate about whether the starvation was intentional. Kenney also encouraged Harper to drop visa requirements for people visiting from ex-communist countries, whose Canadian relatives represent millions of votes. From 2007 to 2008, these restrictions were abandoned for visitors from Poland, Slovakia, Lithuania, Hungary, Czech Republic, Estonia, and Latvia.

Kenney was remarkably upfront about the electoral calculus behind the party's efforts to solicit the support of ethnic communities, which cleverly blunted appearances of cynicism. An event the party hosted on the outskirts of Toronto — near Highway 401 and Dixon Road — was "symbolic" of the Conservatives' efforts to win more seats in the racially and religiously diverse suburbs of Toronto, he acknowledged. "It's no secret that in order to win a majority, we need to do well in the metro belt around the GTA, and in Toronto itself, and we're making every honest effort to do so."[12] Left unsaid by Kenney was the ideological project these efforts served to bolster.

Redefining Canadian Citizenship

The 2008 election, occurring under the backdrop of a global financial crisis, saw the Conservatives win a stronger minority despite a historically low 59 percent turnout. With the party winning 10 additional seats in Ontario, Kenney's outreach efforts had begun to bear fruit. While Harper had long sought to rebuild Brian Mulroney's PC coalition of western populists, eastern establishment Tories, and soft Quebec nationalists, the third pillar proved elusive. With an inability to break through in Quebec combined with steady gains in Ontario, Harper began to accept that Kenney had indeed proved him wrong. The path to a majority government wasn't through Quebec, as it had been historically, but through building support in the immigrant and seat-rich Toronto and Vancouver suburbs.

Kenney was rewarded for his efforts with an appointment as minister of citizenship, immigration and multiculturalism. While he served other Cabinet positions in the Harper government, this portfolio was where he had by far the greatest impact, reshaping Canada's immigration policies with a vision of citizenship rooted in an individual's "duty to integrate." "We don't need the state to promote diversity," he told the *Globe and Mail* in March 2009. The responsibility was on newcomers themselves to become part of the Canadian nationalist project, but the state would provide the ideological framework under which they could be accepted. It would be hard work for immigrants to purge themselves of their cultural sins and develop a sense of Canadian identity, Kenney promised. "Canada isn't a hotel," he proclaimed.[13]

One manifestation of this philosophy was his insistence that immigrants be fluent in either English or French before they could obtain citizenship. He expressed this concern through an anecdote of a woman he encountered at the Indian consulate who had been a Canadian citizen for 12 years and was attempting to sponsor her husband to come to Canada but couldn't conduct the immigration interview in one of the official languages. "It made me wonder — is this an isolated example? Regrettably, I don't think it's isolated enough."[14] Critics observed that language fluency wasn't necessarily an indicator of good citizenship. People could be active in their communities without being fluent in English or French, and plenty of people who were fluent in either official language engaged in anti-social behaviour. For Kenney, that was immaterial, because his conception of citizenship was fundamentally conformist in nature, made explicit in his approach to rewriting the Canadian citizenship guide.

Andrew Griffith, who served as a general director in the Ministry of Multiculturalism while Kenney was a secretary of state and then minister, noted in an interview Kenney's tendency to base policy on anecdote, but wouldn't cast judgment on this approach. "I have a bias toward data, toward more academic research. But what I learned personally is that you can't discount the value of anecdotes. A good anecdote tells you that maybe there's a blind spot here, and you should dig into that," he told me. After years of working under Liberal and more centrist PC governments, Harper's team certainly had a "harder ideological edge" than bureaucrats were used to, Griffith explained, calling Kenney a "very activist minister" who "basically renewed every area of policy of the department." In the bureaucracy, director general is a mid-level position below the deputy minister and associate deputy ministers but above directors.

I found Griffith to be a true bureaucrat, reluctant to cast aspersions on his political bosses while demonstrating a keen understanding of the internal logic behind the political decisions he was tasked with implementing. I got little sense of where he personally stood on any of the issues we discussed. "The bureaucracy needs to learn how to serve. Challenge some of the specifics of what's proposed but accept that there's an error that needs to be looked at and addressed," he explained. The role of bureaucrats isn't to make policy but to smooth out its implementation.

One of Kenney's major projects in his early days as minister was to update the citizenship guide, which is used to help newcomers prepare for the citizenship test. In April 2009, Kenney announced the ministry's plans to rewrite the guide, the most recent iteration of which was introduced by the Liberals in 1997. Calling that guide "ridiculous," he said its content is "indicative of a completely insipid view of Canada." The minister bemoaned how the 47-page document had two pages on the virtues of recycling, but "not one single sentence on Canadian military history," nor "does it indicate what the poppy represents as a Canadian symbol." He promised the new guide would address the "challenges of integration" but would be "in no way a small-c conservative, partisan or ideological project."[15] The ensuing guide would be all three.

Kenney brought in his trusted adviser Chris Champion to help him redefine what it means to be Canadian. Champion was Griffith's "main interlocutor on the citizenship file," with whom he would "clash ... based on ideas, concepts [and] ideology to a certain extent." But Griffith, in true bureaucrat fashion, said these clashes "resulted in a richer discussion" than would have occurred otherwise.

The degree of Champion's involvement was unprecedented in Griffith's experience. In one incident, the ministry staff produced a draft citizenship guide that wasn't to Champion's liking, so the adviser wrote his own draft, which according to Griffith was unheard of. "We never give the pen to a staffer," but the bureaucrats accepted this was the "only way we're going to move forward." A two-hour meeting followed where Griffith went through Champion's draft line by line and critiqued the language the staffer used. "It didn't change his view," said Griffith. "It is one of those discussions that we were both trying to be frank, we were both trying to understand each other, and in so doing, move the file forward."

Released in November 2009, the new 62-page guide, *Discover Canada: The Rights and Responsibilities of Citizenship*, was much more philosophical than its predecessor. Kenney said his vision for the guide was one that emphasizes Canadian "history, values and institutions."[16] It was crucial, he said, for the guide to inform newcomers that in addition to rights, Canadians also have obligations toward the state, namely, "to know who we are, from where we came, what values define us and to live in accordance with those values."[17] The weighty subject matter of the new citizenship guide created an additional, implicit educational barrier for newcomers while ensuring that those who passed the test were sufficiently indoctrinated in a specific vision of Canadian identity.

The guide was highly nationalistic with its glorification of the Canadian military, highlighting the "enormity of sacrifices made by our men and women in uniform," Kenney explained. He said this was far more important to newcomers to know than learning "that potash is an important industry in New Brunswick." Noting that military service wasn't mandatory, the guide said it was nonetheless "a noble way to contribute to Canada and an excellent career choice," where newcomers could gain "valuable experience, skills and contacts," pointing them toward the website for enlisting in Canadian Forces. Reading like a military recruitment ad, this portion suggested a way for immigrants to be accepted into the country by demonstrating unquestioning loyalty.

Kenney's passionate monarchism also shone throughout the document. Monarchist League of Canada chairman Robert Finch told the *Ottawa Citizen* in November 2009 that he was "thrilled with the prominent place given to the Crown" in the updated guide. Queen Elizabeth's photo appears three times throughout the booklet: on the second page alongside the Oath of Citizenship sworn to the monarchy; in the "rights and responsibilities" section, which has an image of her signing the 1982 Constitution Act; and in the section on Canada's government structure, which emphasizes she is the official Head of State.

While an emphasis on the military and monarchy demonstrated a reverence for tradition and authority central to Kenneyism, most criticism focused on its depiction of social issues. The guide had no mention of LGBTQ+ rights beyond the caption of a photo of Olympic gold medal swimmer Mark Tewksbury, which described him as a "prominent activist for gay and lesbian Canadians." That's because Kenney, whose opposition to LGBTQ+ rights dates back to his student activism days, intervened to remove reference to the 1969 decriminalization of homosexuality and 2005 legalization of gay marriage, as well as a section noting protection from discrimination based on sexual orientation. "We can't mention every legal decision, every policy of the Government of Canada," Kenney explained.[18] An early 2011 update to the guide, however, added "recognition that gay and lesbian Canadians enjoy the full protection of and equal treatment under the law, including access to civil marriage."[19]

Despite downplaying LGBTQ+ rights, the document was sure to emphasize gender equality as a means of promoting a femonationalist perspective emphasizing the superiority of Canadian values. It referenced "barbaric cultural practices that tolerate spousal abuse, honour killings, female genital mutilation or other gender-based violence." This section included a photo of a woman in a hijab.[20] For Kenney, it was important to emphasize the limits of Canadian tolerance. "Multiculturalism doesn't mean that anything goes," he said, referring to a "culturally rooted abuse of women."[21] Griffith, who was broadly sympathetic to Kenney's integrative approach to multiculturalism, said the "barbaric cultural practices" phrasing was Champion's idea, which Griffith characterized as a major error. "You can say the same thing without a dog whistle."

Yet this dog whistle against certain immigrant communities was the point, reflecting a disciplinary approach to multiculturalism. The forms of gendered violence outlined in the guide of course warrant the harshest form of condemnation on their own terms. Tying these practices into culture, however, reflected an us-versus-them mentality that immigrants were forced to embrace as a condition of citizenship. Combined with the glorification of Canadian militarism and the British Crown, the updated guide reflected a form of Western world chauvinism that sought to cleanse immigrants of their alleged cultural sins.

Deportees

At the same time Kenney was updating Canada's citizenship guide to reflect a particular vision of Canadianness, he pursued immigration policies that opened the door to a highly specific set of newcomers. In order to maintain high levels of immigration, Kenney said, immigration policy must be "geared to our economic interest."[22] He sought "high-value innovators" who could be "the next Bill Gates or the next Steve Jobs"[23] while engaging in increasingly harsh policies of deportation for those who didn't fit this mould. One of his first actions as minister was to fast-track permanent resident status for immigrants who worked in 38 skilled job categories deemed high-demand. The contrast with Kenney's vilification of asylum-seeking "queue jumpers" perfectly illustrates his conditional welcoming to newcomers deemed productive combined with harshness towards those he regarded as a drain on the system. That many of these skilled immigrants were likely to settle in the electorally important Toronto suburbs revealed an intersection between electoral calculation and ideology.

Workers who weren't employed in the 38 prescribed fields, which included health care, oil and gas, skilled trades, and finance, had their immigration applications automatically denied. Kenney emphasized that those who were rejected were welcome to come to Canada as temporary foreign workers, where they would face restrictions on where they could work and for how long. This rejection of permanent residency for broad swaths of the workforce, most of whom were racialized, kept them "precarious and exploitable … flexible and expendable," making them easy prey for capitalist interests, activist and author Harsha Walia wrote in a 2015 retrospective of the Harper years for the Canadian Centre for Policy Alternatives.

In her 2021 book *Border and Rule: Global Migration, Capitalism, and the Rise of Racist Nationalism*, Walia detailed how immigration policy is used to uphold neoliberal class structures internationally. "While borders are hierarchically organized and permeable for white expats, a handpicked immigrant diaspora, and the rich investor class," Walia writes, "they form a fortress against the millions of 'deportspora,' who are shut out, immobilized and expelled."[24] In this view, migrant worker programs, such as Canada's Temporary Foreign Workers Program, are "carceral regimes" that create a "state-sanctioned pool of unfree, indentured labourers" who exist as a permanent underclass deprived of rights.[25] Walia played an active role opposing Kenney's immigration and citizenship agenda as a member of the activist collective No One Is Illegal.

Not long after inviting foreigners who didn't fit his skilled worker criteria to come to the country as temporary workers, Kenney began cracking down on those who overstayed their welcome. In what was at the time the largest immigration raid in Canadian history, 120 temporary foreign workers in the Bradford West Gwillimbury area, about an hour's drive north of Toronto, were detained and deported for overstaying their visas or working for employers other than those they were assigned to. This figure included 40 Thai migrant workers who were paid $8.50 per hour to round up poultry for slaughter — a dollar less than Ontario's minimum wage. The Thai government at the time was engaged in the violent suppression of protests against its autocratic rule, which led Canadian foreign affairs officials to warn visitors to exert "extreme caution" if they visited. Marco Luciano of migrant advocacy group Migrante noted how these workers, many of whom didn't have lawyers and couldn't speak English, were now deprived of income and forced back to a volatile situation at home, leading to increased anxiety about their precarity.[26]

No One Is Illegal's Toronto chapter organized a rally in May 2009 attended by 800 people, despite rain, protesting the migrant worker deportations. In addition to the Thai workers, migrant labourers from China, Vietnam, Laos, and Mexico were deported in the raids. At the protest, Chris Ramsaroop, an organizer with Justicia for Migrant Workers, told the *Toronto Star* that many of those deported were victims of unscrupulous recruiters who misled them about how much money they would earn, forcing the workers into debt, which led them to seek employment elsewhere.

The raids in Bradford were followed by similar ones against temporary foreign workers at greenhouses in Leamington, a 45-minute drive southeast of Windsor. In late May, nine Mexican women who were working at the Lakeside Greenhouse were detained, and in June, six people were apprehended at another greenhouse, three of whom were Mexican. Between 2006 and 2011, Canadian border officials completed 83,382 deportations. To facilitate these forced removals, staffing at the Canadian Border Services Agency increased by 54.6 percent, representing 5,200 new employees from 2006 to 2012 — the single largest increase in public sector jobs in that period.[27]

Kenney brought forward reforms to the Temporary Foreign Worker program in October 2009, which were ostensibly designed to protect workers, but, in fact, made them more vulnerable to deportation. It imposed a two-year ban on employers who were found to have failed to live up to wage or working condition standards, with a blacklist of companies posted on the ministry's website. But it also placed further restrictions on workers themselves, allowing them to work for up to four years in Canada before banning them for six years. In doing so, Kenney provided these workers with a bare minimum of protection, just enough to keep them disposable while presenting a compassionate facade.

Critics such as Clarizze Truscott, a Filipina immigrant volunteer with the Alberta-based Citizens Concerned for Temporary Foreign Workers, noted that temporary foreign workers were unlikely to take the risk of reporting their employer to the authorities. The solution to the problem, she said, was to give migrant workers the opportunity to become permanent residents, rather than treating them as "second-class citizens,"[28] a sentiment echoed in statements from the labour movement and other civil society groups. "After living and working in Canada, these vulnerable migrants should have access to a path to citizenship and a right to permanent residency, not a pink slip and a deportation order," said United Food and Commercial Workers (UFCW) national president Wayne Hanley.[29] A letter to Harper and Kenney signed by various civil society actors, including UFCW, Canadian Arab Federation, No One Is Illegal (Toronto), the Chinese Canadian National Council, Canadian Union of Public Employees, Migrante Ontario, and Justice for Migrant Workers, argued Kenney's reforms maintained an exclusionary structure where increasing numbers of newcomers were precluded from citizenship while being exploited as a source of cheap labour.

Kenney's approach toward refugees was similarly lacking in nuance, which only grew more aggressive once the Conservatives secured a majority government. In a revealing exchange, Kenney met in Quebec City with a few of the 300 Rohingya refugees the government committed to resettling in Canada, who asked how they could bring their families over. "We have a reunification program and you will be in a good position to help your family if you settle here and integrate well into your new country," Kenney replied, suggesting they get jobs and learn English or French.[30] The burden was placed on refugees to demonstrate their utility to Canada as a condition for reuniting with their loved ones and being accepted as Canadians.

The earlier removal of visa requirements from former communist Eastern European countries urged by Kenney led to a wave of asylum applications for people from the Czech Republic, increasing to 853 asylum claims in 2008 from 78 in 2007, consisting primarily of Roma people fleeing violence from neo-Nazis. Kenney noted that the Czech Republic was the only country of those European nations who had had their visa requirements waived that had produced a spike of asylum seekers, without questioning why that might be. "It's hard to believe that the Czech Republic is an island of persecution in Europe," Kenney said, painting these asylum seekers with the broad brush of "false refugee claimants."[31] At the same time, a U.S. crackdown on undocumented workers led to a major increase in Haitian and Mexican asylum seekers in Canada. Kenney's response was to reimpose visa restrictions on Czech and Mexican visitors.

As the rationale for reimposing visas on Mexicans, Kenney said that the Immigration and Refugee Board (IRB) only accepted 11 percent of Mexican asylum requests. But this appeared to be a case of the board applying overly restrictive criteria rather than an overabundance of claims. The Plaza Ortega family, who fled violence from drug cartels in Mexico with two children in 2006, was deported from the Vancouver suburb of Burnaby in April 2009 because immigration officials concluded they could simply move to another part of Mexico. A couple of months later, a pregnant 24-year-old woman who was rejected twice for asylum in Canada — in 2004 and 2008 — was murdered by drug traffickers in Mexico after deportation. The board argued she would be safe in Mexico. After her death, her mother and sister, who had attempted to seek asylum with her, were given a temporary visa to return to Canada, but only after paying their $3,200 deportation fee. In an October 2009 interview with the *Toronto Star*, the mother noted how it took her daughter's murder for Canadian officials to believe the family was, in fact, in danger. This, she said, was too steep a price for acceptance.

Clearly, the refugee system was broken, which Kenney acknowledged. There was a growing backlog of asylum claimants — from 20,000 before the Conservatives took power to 60,823 by June 2009. But refugee advocates pointed out that this was a problem of the government's own choosing. The IRB had 37 vacancies that had yet to be filled as of mid-2009. The IRB played an important role in hearing asylum claims, determining their validity, and hearing initial appeals. Failed applicants who wanted to appeal a second time had to do so in federal court. Kenney filled the IRB vacancies through late 2009 and early 2010, but obstinately maintained the issue was too many applicants abusing the system. As the 2011 election approached, he shifted toward publicly accusing judges of not issuing deportations quickly enough.

At a February 2011 gathering of Western University law students in London, Ontario, Kenney complained that the "integrity of the decisions made by my department is being questioned too often without sufficient justification" by judges ignoring the "spirit of what we're trying to do." The government, Kenney claimed, simply sought a "constructive dialogue between the legislative branch and the judiciary." Immigration lawyer Lorne Waldman said Kenney's comments betrayed ignorance of the need for the judiciary to act as a check on government power. "I don't think the role of the court is to have a dialogue with anyone. The role of the court is to interpret and apply the law."[32] It's hard to believe Kenney didn't understand this. Rather, his outburst showed that all his veneration of Canadian institutions was just window dressing for his goal of using the immigration system to fulfill a corporate agenda. Once these institutions got in the way of that goal, Kenney transformed into a raging populist of convenience. Kenney's office proudly posted a link to a *Globe and Mail* story covering the event to his website but removed all the quotes critical of his remarks.

The following month, Opposition politicians called for Kenney's resignation after his office sent out a partisan fundraising letter on government letterhead previewing his approach to immigrant outreach for the upcoming election. The letter was intended for Conservative riding associations but was accidently sent to NDP MP Linda Duncan, rather than Conservative MP John Duncan.[33] The missive detailed the Conservatives' efforts to target "very ethnic" voters in the Greater Toronto Area through immigrant media outlets, asking recipients to help raise $200,000 for this strategy. Kenney staffer Kasra Nejatian, an Iranian exile with a maple leaf tattoo, took the fall for the letter, resigning, while claiming it was his idea alone to use parliamentary letterhead and the phrase "very ethnic."

The strategy outlined in the letter was precisely the Conservatives' approach to the May 2011 election. Harper sent Kenney on the road, rather than keep him in the Ottawa war room, as he had in 2006 and 2008. Kenney boasted to journalist Paul Wells that he was "finding new frontiers" in immigrant-oriented news outlets from Punjabi talk radio, with its "huge advertisers [and] cutthroat competition," to the Chinese-Canadian newspaper *Ming Pao*.[34] Wells described the seductive logic of branching out to immigrant-centred media: "*Star* readers also read the *Globe* or the *Post*, listened to the CBC or to satellite radio, maybe checked out some blogs they liked. *Ming Pao* readers read *Ming Pao*. If they like what they read about the Harper government, they increasingly voted Conservative."[35]

Harper was re-elected with the first Conservative majority government since 1988, in part due to a uniquely dismal performance from Liberal leader Michael Ignatieff, who was supplanted as Leader of Opposition by NDP leader Jack Layton. Vote splitting between the Liberals and NDP certainly helped in closer races, but Kenney's ethnocultural outreach strategy proved decisive. The Conservatives gained 13 seats, nine of which were in the "905" ridings surrounding Toronto, which University of Toronto political scientist Stephen Clarkson attributed to a "very sophisticated targeting of areas and groups."[36] Armed with a majority, Kenney's hands were freed to pursue an even more aggressive approach toward migrants, refugees, and others deemed unworthy of Canadian citizenship.

"Bogus" Refugees and "Safe" Countries

Within weeks of the election, Kenney brought Kasra Nejatian back into the fold, promoting him to director of communications, which gestured that the new majority government would no longer be constrained by optics of ethics and propriety. This lax attitude toward his friend who engaged in dishonest conduct would be matched by an increasingly bellicose approach to those suspected of abusing the immigration system. Rather than hypocrisy, this dichotomy demonstrated an ideology centred around power and control, with Nejatian serving as a case study in conditional acceptance.

Declaring "citizenship [wasn't] for sale," Kenney announced an immigration fraud tip line in September 2011. Three months later, the government announced with great bluster it would strip 2,100 immigrants of citizenship for suspected fraud while investigating 4,400 permanent residents. As a result of the scrutiny, Kenney boasted, 1,400 people had given up their efforts to obtain permanent resident status. "This is by far — by many orders of magnitude — the largest enforcement action ever taken in the history of Canadian citizenship," Kenney proclaimed.[37] From 1977 to 2010, by comparison, just 63 people had their citizenship revoked.[38]

It appeared Kenney was engaging in some major hyperbole. Eighteen months after its launch, the tip line had received 22,000 calls, which resulted in 132 tips serious enough to warrant referral to investigators — a rate of 0.06 percent — and a dozen citizenships revoked.[39] These numbers suggest not only that the problem may not have been as urgent as Kenney portrayed but also that his rhetoric was driving people to make unfounded claims of immigration fraud about their neighbours, with blatant racial overtones. Kenney was undeterred, arguing there was a mass of people "who lied or cheated to obtain Canadian citizenship."[40] By his admission, many of the people who obtained citizenship fraudulently were victims of "crooked immigration consultants," yet he constantly conflated the issues of supply and demand in service of his disciplinary approach to immigration policy.

Tightening the screws on family reunification, Kenney announced in late 2011 that he was putting a sponsorship program for parents and grandparents to obtain permanent residence on hiatus, replacing it with a "super visa" program allowing parents and grandparents to visit Canada two years at a time for up to 10 years. The visa, which itself cost just $150, was conditional upon the families purchasing private health insurance for the newcomers, which cost around $3,300. "This is so expensive that only the rich need to apply," declared Felix Zhang of the advocacy group Sponsor Our Parents.[41] In practice, Harsha Walia noted, this policy transformed reunification into a "privilege for the wealthy and those from western countries, preventing thousands of low-income racialized children from meeting their grandparents. It also further entrenches poverty for low-income immigrant families who are unable to afford child care and have typically relied on grandparents to perform child care and domestic labour."[42]

The following year, Kenney imposed a probationary period forcing spouses who came to Canada to live together for two years before the sponsored spouse was eligible for permanent residency. This policy had a stated exception for abuse and neglect. But, like the Temporary Foreign Worker program, it was hard to imagine a newcomer taking the risk of informing the authorities on the person who brought them into the country, in effect trapping largely racialized newcomers in abusive relationships. As usual, Kenney insisted this policy was necessary to punish "fraudsters who lie and cheat to jump the queue."[43]

While he imposed roadblocks for family reunification, Kenney fast-tracked permanent resident status for thousands of individual university and college students through the Canada Experience Class Program. The temporary foreign workers were technically included in the program, but its condition of English or French proficiency revealed a slant toward those who could afford post-secondary education as international students. As an example of one of the program's beneficiaries, a November 2011 *Globe and Mail* article quoted Goomaral Chukhalkhuu, the daughter of a Mongolian diplomat who managed small businesses for Royal Bank of Canada. Kenney noted the program was intended for those the "best and brightest ... in what is increasingly a global marketplace for human capital," providing yet another example of Kenney opening Canada's doors increasingly to the wealthy and connected.

The centrepiece of the majority Harper government's refugee policy was the 2012 Protecting Canada's Immigration Act. The legislation gave Kenney the power to unilaterally declare certain countries "safe,"[44] which fast-tracked asylum hearings for claimants from these countries and eliminated their right to appeal at the IRB. They still had the right to appeal in federal court but would have to leave Canada within a year of the IRB's decision regardless. To justify these measures, Kenney raised again the spectre of "bogus refugee claims ... from democratic countries that respect human rights,"[45] all of which happened to be geopolitical allies.

Kenney's rhetoric had a multifaceted impact, Debbie Douglas, the long-time director of the Ontario Council of Agencies Serving Immigrants (OCASI), told me. For one, it put pressure on judges, politicizing the IRB system, since the government was funding its functions. "When you have a minister who is demonizing and who is basically sending the message that we want the system to reduce the number of claimants, the system then begins to reduce the number of claimants." It also made Canadians as a whole less welcoming of immigrants and refugees, who — they were constantly being told — were abusing the system. And this, of course, made failed asylum seekers, who were depicted as cheats and freeloaders, less safe by forcing them into the underground economy if they wanted to avoid deportation while exercising their right to appeal.

Under the guise of combating human trafficking, the legislation allowed the minister to unilaterally declare non-citizens "irregular arrivals," precluding them from obtaining permanent resident status, sponsoring relatives, or acquiring travel documents for five years, even if their claims were accepted. It allowed for them to be detained for up to two weeks without review, and then six months after, separating claimants from their children who might have accompanied them. This was the government's apparent response to two boats carrying a total of 568 Tamil asylum seekers that arrived on the shore of Vancouver Island in 2009 and 2010 after the Sri Lankan government's brutal crackdown on the Liberation Tigers of Tamil Eelam, which the Harper government listed as a terrorist organization. Upon their arrival, Harper depicted the Tamil migrants as either potential terrorists or potentially hapless victims of human trafficking. There was no consideration of the risks they took to start new lives in Canada.

In a scathing critique of the refugee reform legislation published in the *Toronto Star* in February 2012, University of Toronto law professors Lorne Waldman and Audrey Macklin noted Kenney's conflation of rejected asylum claims with malice, accusing him of trying to "make reality bend to his vision." They wrote: "Kenney's system-abusing bogus refugees include those fleeing discrimination, oppression and hardship not quite horrific enough to satisfy the standards required by the jurisprudence defining and applying the refugee definition." The safe country provision formally presumed refugee claimants from Canadian allies were fraudulent, ignoring the circumstances that led people to claim asylum in the first place. The legislation empowered the state to deny claimants a fair hearing, incarcerate them, separate families for extended periods of time, "and hang the threat of deportation over their heads for many more years."

Douglas of OCASI said Kenney fundamentally misrepresented Canada's refugee system, making it sound as if anyone could come to Canada and receive asylum, no questions asked. "Kenney's legacy," she said, "was to demonize and to completely misrepresent our asylum claimants system. People don't just come in and get handed permanent resident status. They have to jump through hoops, they have to prove that they're in need of protection." Furthermore, they had to report their claims in detail, and any deviations from those claims when they appeared before the IRB were scrutinized and often resulted in refusals based on technicalities. This served as a valuable pretext to exclude newcomers who didn't fit Kenney's mould.

Twenty-five of the 27 countries Kenney declared safe, or "designated countries of origin," in December 2012 were European, which notably included the Czech Republic, Hungary, and Slovakia. These three countries included substantial Roma populations who were being targeted by far-right forces. In Hungary, Kenney spent $3,000 to erect billboards in Miskolc, home to many Roma refugees, telling them they weren't welcome in Canada. "Those people who make a claim without sound reasons will be processed faster and removed faster," it boasted. Gyula Gulyas, a Roma Hungarian who fled to Canada after he and his family in Miskolc were threatened and beaten to intimidate them into voting for the ruling FIDESZ party, said the ad campaign was dumping fuel on the far-right xenophobic fire, sending a clear message that Roma Hungarians were unwelcome anywhere. "Nobody wants us or protects us."[46] Kenney eventually added an additional 17 countries to the list of designated countries.

The Centre for Israel and Jewish Affairs (CIJA), which supplanted the more centrist Canadian Jewish Congress and shared the Harper government's extreme pro-Israel orientation, rejected suggestions that the safe country edict was in any way comparable to the policies that kept Jewish refugees out of Canada during the Second World War. CIJA exemplified the type of ethnocultural organization welcomed into the Conservative fold, which they reciprocated. Gina Csanyi-Robah of Toronto's Roma Community Centre, by contrast, expressed outrage at the suggestion Hungary was safe for Roma people: "Everyone who spends 10 minutes on the Internet knows that's not true."[47] The new policy had its intended impact. In its first seven weeks in force, asylum claims were reduced by 70 percent, with claims from fleeing Hungarians down 98 percent.

The contrast couldn't have been sharper with a Canadian ad campaign in Silicon Valley, which sought to lure start-up workers from India who couldn't get their visas renewed in the United States. H-1B PROBLEMS? PIVOT TO CANADA, read a billboard advertising Canada's "start-up visa" program, which sought to fast-track permanent residency status for up to 2,750 entrepreneurs annually who had the backing of venture capital firms. Asylum seekers and temporary foreign workers who overstayed their welcome were subject to increasingly rapid deportation orders while tech bros who overstayed their U.S. visas were invited to the Canadian fold.

This punishment-and-reward approach to immigration necessitated increased executive power for Kenney so he could decide who got invited and who had to leave. Kenney gave himself the ability to ban people from entering Canada based on sweeping "public policy considerations" with the crudely named Faster Deportation of Foreign Criminals Act. The same legislation allowed him to deport permanent residents convicted of crimes who were spending more than six months in jail, regardless of how long they had been in the country, their prospects for rehabilitation, or the nature of their crimes.

In one of his most brazen acts as minister, Kenney cut $100 million in federal health benefits for refugee applicants, including dental care, eye care, and most prescription drugs, forcing the provinces or private practices to pay the difference if they wanted to maintain funding. Kenney was quick to claim that refugees continued receiving the most basic health coverage to protect the broader public, arguing in an *Ottawa Citizen* op-ed that he was merely preventing "bogus refugees" from receiving "at taxpayer expense, enhanced services such as eye and dental coverage that are unavailable to many Canadians." Using the well-worn xenophobic trope that foreigners were vectors of disease, Kenney said, "perhaps most importantly, all asylum claimants are provided, free of charge, a medical exam which screens all claimants for disease," which he added was "more preventive health care than most Canadians receive on a regular basis."

Dr. Mark Tyndall, an emergency room physician in Ottawa, accused Kenney of "pitting those who are dissatisfied with their own health coverage against refugees," identifying the cuts an assault on the health-care system writ large.[48] Tyndall was among the physicians who protested against these changes that hindered their ability to provide care to their most vulnerable patients. Some, such as Toronto's Dr. David Wong, defied the government, absorbing the cost of providing this care. In doing so, Wong prevented failed Colombian asylum seeker Daniel Garcia Rodriguez, who had fled violence from paramilitaries, from permanently losing his vision from a chronic retinal detachment. Rejected Roma asylum seeker Ladislav Kina ended up paying $200 in cash for his weekly heart treatments while he appealed the IRB's decision, despite having arrived in Canada prior to the December 2012 cut-off date, because the new rules were so convoluted. Doctors had difficulty understanding who was covered and who wasn't, so some asylum seekers ended up paying unnecessarily for treatments.

After making life increasingly unbearable for refugee claimants, Kenney unveiled a program to match immigrants with employers in January 2013, which he linked to a "dating site," with prospective immigrants posting their profiles online so employers or the government serving their interests can "fish out of that pool." Foreigners would now have to be invited by employers to apply for permanent residence, representing a significant break with the historic first-come, first-served approach to immigration. Canada's immigration system was contracted out to the private sector, with Kenney serving as what *Toronto Star* columnist Haroon Siddiqui called the "chief headhunter for business."[49]

It made perfect sense then, that Kenney's next role would be as minister of employment and social development, which Harper shuffled him into in July 2013. Kenney's work at citizenship and immigration was transformational, wielding the prospect of acceptance over newcomers' heads in a way that provided a multicultural sheen for policies that at their core served business interests. At the same time, he brought well-heeled immigrants into the Conservative tent, weaponizing liberal rhetoric of diversity to enfold immigrants in support of his fundamentally authoritarian project.

While the contrast between his harsh treatment of refugees and embrace of certain immigrant groups might appear contradictory, it was anything but. Selective inclusion allowed Kenney to strengthen pre-existing power relations. Ethnocultural groups who didn't serve that purpose were either marginalized or found themselves under attack; those who were willing to support Harper's broader agenda were embraced. In doing so, Harper and Kenney were able to establish a reactionary rainbow coalition based on a shared exclusionary vision of Canadianness.

All Kenney's talk about Canadian values and their fundamental superiority boomeranged at his party during the 2015 election campaign, demonstrating the limits of this conditional acceptance. The Conservatives went too far in pursuing their neocon agenda. They advocated a "barbaric cultural practices" snitch line and were forced to defend their 2011 ban on Muslim women wearing niqabs at citizenship ceremonies. Harper's talk of "old-stock Canadians" and Kenney's hamfistedness toward refugees became perceived as increasingly cruel at the height of the Syrian refugee crisis. Justin Trudeau was able to win back the very suburban immigrant communities Kenney spent so much time and effort cultivating, reviving the Liberals from their third-party status to win a majority government in 2015. Trudeau eliminated some of the worst excesses of Kenney's time as citizenship and immigration minister, such as the designated countries of origin list and cuts to refugee health care, both of which the Supreme Court ruled unconstitutional. Yet the RCMP continued to arrest irregular arrivals, the hyper-nationalist citizenship guide was untouched, and the immigration system serving the interests of employers was maintained.

Months before the Liberals won the federal election, the NDP won its first-ever mandate in Kenney's adopted home province, which provided an opportunity for Kenney. The Alberta NDP victory resulted from a split conservative vote that resembled the Reform/PC divide a younger Kenney played an active role in resolving. After the disappointment of the federal election, Kenney, who spent just a few days per month in Calgary as a federal Cabinet minister, made the fateful decision to return to Alberta to unite the right a second time. As Alberta premier, he would be untethered by the need to attract Ontario swing voters, allowing him to use the Wild Rose province as a testing ground for his ideological inclinations.

5

BIG BLUE PICKUP TRUCK

IT WAS A SURREAL SCENE AT United Conservative Party headquarters on April 16, 2019, when Jason Kenney stormed to victory over Rachel Notley's NDP. After the results were tallied, he was driven in a blue Dodge Ram 1500 pickup, his so-called Unity Truck, which he had spent the past three years criss-crossing the province in, into the event centre, giving supporters high-fives and waving at the audience on the vehicle's path to the stage while his official campaign theme song, "Strong and Free" by Alec Harrison and Julianna Hindesmith, played on the loudspeakers. Watching his victory party from the *Medicine Hat News* newsroom, it felt as if I was watching World Wrestling Entertainment, and Kenney's combative victory speech fuelled that perception.

It started off innocently enough. "To all of those Albertans who are struggling, to the unemployed, to those who have given up, to small business owners hanging on, to young people who got their degrees and their diplomas but can't find work, to those who have lost their homes and their hope after years of economic decline and stagnation, to them we send this message — help is on the way and hope is on the horizon." But it took an increasingly pugnacious turn when he identified the alleged culprit of these disenchanted people's woes. He described an Alberta that had been "blocked in and pinned down" by outside forces — namely, "foreign-funded special interests" — that were using the guise of environmentalism to sabotage Alberta's energy industry. Albertans had been duped, and the federal government "has made a bad situation much worse," he said, pausing mid-sentence for a chuckle while the audience booed. When he talked about Prime Minister Justin Trudeau's cancellation of the Energy East pipeline, which was opposed by its supposed beneficiary, Quebec, he was interrupted by chants of "Build that pipe." Kenney corrected them. "Folks, we should have never ended up with the faint hope of one pipeline; it's 'Build *those* pipes.' Tonight, Albertans have accepted that we will no longer passively accept the campaign of defamation against the industry that has helped create one of the most prosperous and generous societies on earth." But, he added, "this is not just about our shared prosperity, it's also a moral cause." Addressing the supposed cabal of environmentalists, he said: "Your days of pushing around Alberta with impunity just ended…. Today we Albertans begin to fight back!"

I remember my then colleague, Scott Schmidt, turning to me and saying something along the lines of: "Have you ever heard a victory speech this angry and aggrieved?" Indeed, Kenney's win was a culmination of three years of work trying to bring together Alberta's divided right-wing, merging its PC and Wildrose factions into the UCP — an outgrowth of his earlier work on the federal scene with the United Alternative initiative, as detailed in Chapter 3. Surely, the tone of his election night victory speech should have been jovial, and there was definitely some of that in his address. But in uniting the right in Alberta, he cultivated forces that didn't simply want to cut taxes and keep business running as usual, as his conservative predecessors had done. They wanted to tear down Alberta's relationship with the rest of Canada. It was what Kenney later referred to derisively as "populism with a snarl,"[1] but he amplified this sense of aggrievance at every turn to build consensus for his efforts to turn Alberta into a neoliberal testing lab.

An Alberta politician promising to keep Albertans secure from a purportedly overbearing federal government stymying Alberta's greatness isn't unique. In fact, it has deep roots within Alberta's political culture. But the viciousness and dogmatism with which Kenney pursued this vendetta put him in a league of his own. He constructed an authoritarian populist vision of Alberta that gave him temporary success before the forces he harnessed got out of his control.

Alberta's Political Code

In his book *Code Politics: Campaigns and Culture on the Canadian Prairies*, University of Alberta political scientist Jared Wesley examines the distinct elite discourse that shapes the political culture of Canada's three Prairie provinces — Alberta, Saskatchewan, and Manitoba. He does so by examining the way successful politicians in each province have historically communicated to voters in campaign literature. "One of the main tasks of political elites is manipulating political discourse to enhance and maintain their authority," Wesley writes. This is done by establishing "a set of shared symbols around which to build social cohesion and popular allegiance."[2] The broader political culture in each province — Alberta's free-market conservatism, Saskatchewan's social democratic collectivism, and Manitoba's mushy middle between the two — is transmitted to citizens through a distinct set of codes, which exist in various configurations across time and partisan lines.

Alberta's code emphasizes freedom, whereas Saskatchewan's focuses on collective security and Manitoba's on moderation. Alberta's code has three main expressions: populism, which is oriented around "freedom from government overreach"; individualism, which emphasizes the "primacy of the individual as the core unit of society"; and provincial autonomy, which is expressed as alienation from the centres of Canadian power and a desire for Alberta to chart its own path. In this light, the Alberta government "serves as the defender of provincial interests against external, oppressive forces, be they the federal government, a socialist menace, or any other Big Shot foe of the Alberta community," Wesley writes.[3] The code is the common thread through most of the Social Credit and PC governments that dominated Alberta from 1935 to 2015, tying together Social Credit premier William "Bible Bill" Aberhart's railing against eastern banking interests; Social Creditor Ernest Manning, father of Reform Party founder Preston, promoting unmitigated free enterprise as a foil to communism; and PC premier Ralph Klein's targeting of government debt. Even Peter Lougheed, who used Alberta's oil and gas revenues to expand the province's social safety net, articulated his vision as a form of "free enterprise that cares" while emphasizing notions of self-reliance and securing Alberta's autonomy. Ed Stelmach, whose policies were all over the map, provided an exception to the rule, suggesting that by his time in power, the PCs were experiencing an identity crisis.

This is the legacy Kenney inherited. But when Kenney accepted the nomination of his Frankenstein party on October 28, 2017, Wesley noticed something that set Kenney apart from his predecessors. In his victory speech, Kenney identified the UCP's goal as forming a "government focused on prosperity so that we have the means to be a compassionate and generous society." The codes were the same, with prosperity representing the fruits of unbridled individualism, but the emphasis changed. He returned to this theme later in the speech, saying his goal "has always been about uniting Albertans who understand the traditional values that have animated this province since its beginning; those who understand that in order to be a compassionate and generous society, you must be a prosperous one first." Wesley calls this Kenney's "prosperity-first" mentality, which he describes as a uniquely blunt articulation of Kenney's neoliberal leanings.[4]

As we saw in his 2019 victory speech, Kenney depicted himself as the guardian of Alberta's interests against the federal government in the same way his predecessors had. But prosperity was in the driver's seat, appearing five times in the UCP platform for the 2019 election. His platform slogan of "Jobs, Economy, Pipeline" was similarly oriented around this theme. Placing individual prosperity at the forefront also contributed to Kenney's uniquely belligerent tone toward those who stood in its way. Labour leaders were crooked union bosses, environmentalists were foreign-funded radicals, teachers were indoctrinating children, and harm-reduction advocates were enabling addicts to poison themselves — all were declared enemies of prosperity, and by proxy, the state. The Covid pandemic pushed this approach to its limits, demonstrating the folly of putting prosperity at the forefront of a social vision.

Prosperity politics have deep roots in Alberta's political culture, as well; in a sense, Kenney's reign marked a return to the unmitigated individualism preached by Ernest Manning in the mid-20th century, but with a more authoritarian bent. Although Kenney, as we've seen, is a devout Catholic, his propensity-first mentality was grown out of Alberta's evangelical Protestant soil. In *God's Province: Evangelical Christianity, Political Thought, and Conservatism in Alberta*, another University of Alberta political scientist, Clark Banack, argues that a highly individualistic Americanized evangelical Protestantism was a "key force" in shaping attitudes toward the state and responsibility of individuals among Alberta political elites,[5] including United Farmers of Alberta president Henry Wise Wood, whose party governed Alberta from 1921 to 1935; Aberhart; and both Mannings. Whatever their differences, they all believed in the "moral and intellectual capacity of common individuals and their corresponding right to be free," in contrast to the more European, communitarian form of evangelism predominant elsewhere in Canada.[6] This individualist gospel informed Alberta's secular political code.

While Kenney could harp about the virtues of individualism all day, going after the federal government, which he spent nine years serving in, wasn't a natural fit. It was what he had to do, however, if he wanted to forge a popular consensus for the rest of his agenda from above. There was growing discontent in Alberta, embodied by increasing separatist sentiment, dubbed "Wexit," which shared its British namesake's distrust of elite institutions. This was no doubt an uncomfortable match for Kenney, with his adoration of traditional authority embodied by the Crown and the Vatican. But in Alberta's case, this discontent centred around economic, rather than cultural, issues, which gave him an opening with his prosperity doctrine.

The seeds of the recent appeal to Alberta sovereignty were planted in the so-called Firewall Letter, published in 2001 in the *National Post* and signed by a number of Kenney confidants — Harper, who was out of elected politics at the time; former Stockwell Day adviser Ken Boessenkool, who later emerged as a Kenney critic; CTF director Andrew Crooks; and Calgary School academics Tom Flanagan, Rainer Knopff, and Ted Morton. Addressed to then premier Ralph Klein, the letter called on him to "build firewalls around Alberta, to limit the extent to which an aggressive and hostile federal government can encroach upon legitimate provincial jurisdiction." Its agenda was wide-ranging and would sound familiar to anyone who followed the Kenney years, calling on the province to assume control over policing, pensions, health care, income taxes, and Senate appointments. Notably, it also asked Klein to "take all possible political and legal measures to reduce the financial drain on Alberta caused by Canada's tax-and-transfer system," in part referring to the equalization program, which redistributed income tax revenues to poorer provinces to ensure each province was able to deliver the same level of social services.

Harper, once in government, wrote the updated equalization formula that continued to incense Alberta sovereigntists. Kenney, on the other hand, who played no role in writing the Firewall Letter but was part of the Harper government, had to deal with its consequences when he returned to Alberta in 2016. He said all the right things, lashing out at alleged federal overreach in an effort to channel the anger of Wexiteers into his larger political project, but at the end of the day he was just another Ottawa elite.

Alberta's Divided Right

The Wildrose Party was founded in the midst of Ed Stelmach's chaotic premiership by disgruntled conservatives who saw his government as spending too lavishly while failing to confront the federal government. While it wasn't expressed in these terms, their criticisms of Stelmach were rooted in his perceived violation of key features of Alberta's political code. In September 2009, its leader Paul Hinman, who's now an avowed Alberta separatist, seized on this bubbling anger with Stelmach and captured the party's first seat in the Calgary-Glenmore by-election. A month later, right-wing *Calgary Herald* columnist and failed Calgary Board of Education trustee Danielle Smith captured the party's leadership, presiding over its unprecedented growth.

While polls indicated she would soundly defeat PC premier Alison Redford in the 2012 election, Smith's campaign was undone, in part, by her refusal to condemn candidate Allan Hunsperger, who was revealed to have written a year earlier that LGBTQ+ people were destined to "suffer the rest of eternity in the lake of fire." Redford's PCs were returned to power with a majority government while the Wildrose became the Official Opposition for the first time. In an early effort to unite the right, in December 2014, Smith crossed the floor with eight of her MLAs to join the PC government of Jim Prentice, who had replaced a scandal-plagued Redford months earlier, neutering the Wildrose Opposition, which was left with five MLAs. The floor-crossing debacle was an unmitigated failure for Smith, who didn't even have the opportunity to run for the PCs in the 2015 election after losing the nomination for her Highwood riding. The handful of her fellow floor-crossers who ran in the election were all defeated.

The NDP's victory over the two conservative parties in May 2015, who combined got significantly more votes than the NDP, underscored the need for conservatives to join forces, as they had federally. While the NDP garnered a historic 40 percent of the vote, the PCs received 28 percent and the Wildrose got 25 percent. But, due to the vagaries of a first-past-the-post electoral system, a reinvigorated Wildrose under the leadership of Brian Jean remained the Official Opposition. The Conservative Party of Canada's defeat in the federal election five months later heightened a sense of urgency among Alberta conservatives about the need to elect a counterweight to Liberal prime minister Justin Trudeau. It also provided an opportunity for a federal Conservative from Alberta to swoop into the province and take charge.

Speculation was rampant that Kenney would enter the federal Conservative leadership race to succeed Stephen Harper, which, he told *Maclean's* columnist Jason Markusoff, was his original inclination, yet he was also being pressured from the other side to repeat the feat of uniting the federal Canadian Alliance and PCs at the provincial level. The vacant PC leadership provided an opening. "One night in May 2016," Markusoff wrote, "Kenney, unemployed and with no partner to nag him to kill the lights, stayed up past dawn in his condo. He crafted a 25-page memo to himself about how to retake Alberta, become leader of a dilapidated PC party, forge a merger with Wildrose, secure leadership of that new party and then keep marching onwards, right at Premier Rachel Notley."[7] Although he would have taken a significant pay cut no longer being in Cabinet, Kenney was still gainfully employed as an MP. Nevertheless, Markusoff's broader point remains true — Kenney was putting his lifelong political ambitions on the line. Compounding his challenge was the fact that the Alberta PCs voted against uniting with the Wildrose at its convention earlier in May.

Keith Brownsey, a political scientist at Mount Royal University, told me Kenney's decision to unite the right in Alberta, rather than remain in Ottawa, was a "fatal miscalculation." Brownsey said, "If he had stayed in Ottawa, been bored for a couple of years on the backbenches, he would have become leader of that party," and likely prime minister. Kenney never intended to be premier for long. He confessed in an October 2022 retrospective interview with the *Hub* that his plan was to govern for four years, get re-elected, and then step down within a couple of years to make way for a successor. Kenney didn't say what he would have done after, but the implication was clear — he had his eye on the ultimate prize, fulfilling the goal he had boasted about in high school. Before he could do that, he thought he could burnish his right-wing résumé by getting rid of Alberta's NDP government.

Kenney changed as a person when he returned to Alberta. He became more conniving. The gregarious figure who had jetted from ethnic community event to ethnic community event had seemingly been replaced by a ruthless, calculated politician intent on winning at all costs. Kenney, who was known for his keen attention to policy detail, ran for the PCs on a one-word platform: "Unity." He put on a cowboy hat and sought to embody the populist spirit of Bible Bill and Ralph Klein updated for the age of Wexit. But, ultimately, this isn't who Kenney is. This was a man so deeply ideological that he refused to sign a pledge to vote as his constituents wanted when he ran for Reform in 1997. His supporters in Alberta were willing to overlook his populist deficiencies because of his proven track record of uniting disparate conservative factions and creating a winning coalition. But within a few years, this goodwill would evaporate completely.

Kenney had his plan ready to go, but he needed a partner on the Wildrose side of the ledger. That person was at first newly elected hotshot MLA Derek

Fildebrandt, who became the most outspoken booster of Kenney's plan to unite the right in the Wildrose caucus before his brief political career flamed out spectacularly. Fildebrandt co-authored an open letter with Brian Jean calling for a "united conservative party" around the time Kenney pulled his fateful all-nighter. While they depicted a united front at the time, Jean wanted unity to occur within the Wildrose; Fildebrandt was more flexible.

Like Kenney, Fildebrandt cut his teeth at the CTF at a young age, which was where he and Kenney first got to know each other while Kenney was in the federal Cabinet. "I'd meet him at the odd function and he was always really personable, it was always very good to have a drink with the guy. He was charming ... and made one feel listened to," he told me. Fildebrandt, who now identifies as an Alberta separatist, tore up his federal Conservative membership after the Harper government "bailed out the auto companies and started engaging in pretty open Keynesianism" in response to the 2008 financial crisis, but he always considered Kenney "one of the good guys" in Harper's government, and given their CTF connection, a "role model."

In June 2016, at a party at Calgary energy executive Michael Binnion's home, Kenney told Tom Flanagan about his scheme to run for the PCs on an explicit promise to unite the right. "At first I thought he was crazy," Flanagan told me. "I said, 'Jason, this can't possibly work.' But the more he went on about it, the more I became convinced that maybe it could work." Flanagan always suspected Stephen Harper played a role in crafting the plan, because Harper was "in a class by himself as a strategist," but Flanagan, who had a falling out with Harper while Harper was prime minister for reasons that remain obscure to him, said he has no evidence this was the case. This speculation isn't as far-fetched as it might sound. The *National Post* reported in May 2016 that after Notley won, Harper floated the idea of creating a provincial wing of the federal Conservative party in the event the PCs and Wildrose couldn't get their acts together but gave up on it after he lost the 2015 election.

While Flanagan was initially skeptical, once Kenney announced his intentions, he wrote a *Globe and Mail* op-ed expressing confidence in Kenney's "audacious" plan, noting that in all the other western provinces, conservatives had coalesced around a single alternative to the NDP — the B.C.

Liberals (now B.C. United), the Saskatchewan Party, and the Manitoba PCs. One person who wasn't sold on Kenney's plan was Danielle Smith. She warned that it would be a difficult task uniting the largely rural Wildrose and mostly urban PC constituencies, a weakness in Kenney's coalition she deftly exploited six years later.

Hostile Takeover

In July 2016, Kenney announced he would run for the PC leadership. He applauded himself for resigning as an MP before seeking provincial leadership, but he didn't quite do that. Kenney announced he would return to Ottawa in September to say goodbye to his colleagues, meaning he would continue to collect an MP's salary, for which he was condemned by the CTF. Compounding his rocky start, Kenney used his official MP webpage, which was supposed to be non-partisan, to boost his PC campaign. In the days before announcing his selfless desire to step down from Parliament in three months while he sought the nomination, he had already begun his travelling road show, stopping in Edmonton, Calgary, and Red Deer, and set up a for-profit corporation called Unite Alberta to fund his expenses, which lacked the rigorous reporting requirements of a non-profit while allowing him to raise money before the campaign officially kicked off in October.[8]

On August 1, Kenney drove up to the official kickoff of his "Unity Tour" in a big blue Dodge Ram 1500 pickup truck, matching the colour of Alberta's flag, six of which flew beside his podium at the announcement. He outlined his ambitious endeavour to visit all 87 constituencies in Alberta before the PC leadership election in November, beginning with a two-week trek across small towns in northern Alberta. To burnish the grassroots image he sought to project, Kenney said he intended to crash with supporters, "who are going to be generous enough to open up their homes to a free boarder for a night or two," along the way. Asked about his choice of vehicle, Kenney quipped: "I'm going to be getting all around Alberta all year, including the wintertime, so I figured my Dodge Ram would do the job better than a Prius."[9] It's hard to deny the symbolism of a pickup truck roaming across

Kenney greets security during the Westerner Days Parade in Red Deer in July 2018, with his blue Dodge Ram 1500 "Unity Truck" seen in the background.

rural Alberta, with the image it conjures of self-reliance and autonomy in getting to where you want to go.[10] It didn't hurt that auto dealerships proved to be some of Kenney's most enthusiastic backers.

Channelling the right-wing populist playbook of Donald Trump and Brexit, Kenney said that the working class was being left behind by the NDP. "The kind of blue-collar NDP spirit that Brian Mason once represented isn't the spirit animating this current NDP government, this ideological government that is undermining the basis of prosperity and union jobs that is the energy industry," Kenney said, referring to MLA and former NDP leader Mason's previous career as a bus driver. "I'm confident we can build a big tent coalition that includes a lot of traditional New Democrats." Mason shot back: "As spokesperson for Brian Mason–types everywhere, we're dying to know, 'When will Mr. Kenney stop campaigning on the taxpayer dime?'"[11]

Kenney initially faced five opponents on his path to the PC leadership — former Cabinet minister Donna Kennedy-Glans, Calgary-North West MLA Sandra Jansen, former Cabinet minister Stephen Khan,

Lloydminster-Vermillion MLA Richard Starke, and lawyer Byron Nelson. But on November 9, the day after Trump's presidential victory, both female candidates — Kennedy-Glans and Jansen — dropped out of the race. While Kennedy-Glans said there simply wasn't a constituency for her old-school Toryism in the party anymore, Jansen cited misogynistic abuse she received from Kenney supporters while trying to get her nomination papers signed at the party's convention the previous week in Red Deer, as well as online harassment. "Insults were scrawled on my nomination forms. Volunteers from another campaign chased me up and down the hall," shouting epithets, Jansen said. Less than two weeks later, Jansen crossed the floor to the NDP, calling the prospect of a Kenney-led province "frightening" because of his "Trump-style politics," while astutely noting the NDP were now the party of the centre.

In classic Kenney fashion, he disavowed "any disrespectful conduct or language directed at anybody in public service" while claiming he, too, was a victim. "During the course of this weekend, I had people who don't agree with me pushing their fingers in my chest or hollering expletives at me," he said. "Unfortunately, some of that goes with when people get in a political context. Sometimes people don't control their emotions. I don't condone that for a second, but I'm saying I myself have faced disrespectful behaviour."[12] In late January 2017, Stephen Khan dropped out of the race, calling the contest a "destructive circus" and noting the increasing Islamophobic and racist vitriol he was receiving from new members Kenney attracted to the campaign. "The Kenney people are as intelligent as they are diabolical," he told *Edmonton Journal* columnist Paula Simons. Khan endorsed Richard Starke, who only then recognized how "nasty" and substance-free the leadership campaign was.

Kenney's platform was hyper-focused on the unity question, but he couldn't help but attack Notley's carbon tax, which was for him the perfect embodiment of Notley being in cahoots with Justin Trudeau and foreign-funded environmentalists. At an anti-carbon tax rally hosted by his old friend, Ezra Levant, protestors began chanting "Lock her up" at the mention of Notley. Kenney wasn't there, and he denounced the rhetoric, as did Brian Jean, but neither took responsibility for portraying Notley's policies as not just misguided but a threat to Alberta's autonomy. That was because the people at the rally were precisely those they needed to mobilize to take control of the province's conservative machinery and defeat Notley.

Kenney dog-whistled to them and then beat them back when they went too far, ultimately demonstrating he wasn't really of their kind but was using them to further his political machinations. In his final speech to PC members before the leadership vote, Kenney hit all the right buttons of Alberta's political code. He said the province was under "assault" from its own government. The NDP, he said, was motivated by a "resentment of success. A distrust of enterprise. A mistaken belief that the powerful state is a greater force for good than strong families and free women and men."

Meanwhile, Derek Fildebrandt went all-in on unity. "I'm willing to put everything I've accomplished in politics on the line for this," he told Whitecourt country music station XM 105 in December 2016. Brian Jean, who told a gathering in his Fort McMurray home base that the "best way for Jason Kenney to unite the right would be to come join the Wildrose,"[13] was still reluctant. But then Fildebrandt's fundraising numbers came in. In 2016, his riding association raised more than any other with $25,247.[14] In late January 2017, just days after the numbers came out, Jean changed his tune, telling *Calgary Sun* columnist Rick Bell that he was now in favour of merging the PCs and Wildrose if Wildrose members supported the measure in a vote.

The PC leadership race wasn't close. Kenney won on March 18, 2017, with 75 percent of the vote, giving him a massive mandate to pursue unity. He declared his victory "springtime in Alberta" and the "beginning of the end of this disastrous socialist government," further describing the NDP as "tax-hiking, job-killing, debt-loving, mean-spirited, [and] incompetent." In May, he and Jean announced they reached a tentative agreement on a merger to form the UCP, which required a 50-percent-plus-one vote on the PC side and 75 percent support from the Wildrose. Two months later, both parties endorsed a merger with 95 percent support. Before the unity votes, Doug Schweitzer, a Calgary lawyer who organized Jim Prentice's successful 2014 PC leadership campaign, announced his intention to challenge Kenney and Jean for the leadership.

On August 1, 2017, the one-year anniversary of his Unity Tour, Kenney announced the "grassroots guarantee" outside Blackfoot Diner in Calgary, promising a bottom-up approach to policy-making, in which constituency associations would bring resolutions endorsed at the local level to the convention. These would be voted on by the party membership, with the results automatically accepted by the leadership. Just as his PC platform was focused solely on the unity question, Kenney's UCP leadership campaign would be similarly policy-free, hitting the populist button by deferring all these questions to the party membership. "Jason's 'new' grassroots guarantee is simply a sad attempt to turn this leadership race into a campaign of rhetoric over substance," Schweitzer correctly noted. Kenney's decision to again run on a lack of policy turned the UCP leadership race into a Seinfeldian race about nothing.

In lieu of actual policy commitments, Kenney still hammered on the major theme of an Alberta under siege by outside interests who were getting in the way of its prosperity. When B.C. premier John Horgan vowed to block the construction of the Trans Mountain Pipeline expansion, which would triple the amount of Alberta crude shipped to the B.C. Lower Mainland, Kenney promised "there will be repercussions." When asked what these would be, he simply said, "Stay tuned."[15]

Kenney's decision to defer policy decisions to the party's grassroots eventually returned to haunt him, as it became increasingly clear that his electoral prospects came first. By the time of the UCP's inaugural policy convention in May 2018 in Red Deer, Kenney, secure in his leadership, arrogantly proclaimed about a resolution requiring schools to notify parents when their child joined a gay-straight alliance: "Guess what — I'm the leader and I get to interpret the resolution and its relevance to party policy … I hold the pen." Yet this policy was implemented when Kenney came to power, demonstrating an uneasy tension with the party's grassroots that could implode given the right circumstances.

The Kamikaze Mission

Early on in his unity efforts, Kenney's campaign showed a flagrant disregard for rules, which only grew more brazen. Shortly after Jansen and Kennedy-Glans dropped out of the PC race, Kenney's campaign was dinged $5,000 by the PC Association of Alberta for setting up a hospitality suite outside the delegate selection meeting for the Edmonton-Ellerslie riding. Leadership candidates weren't permitted to be in the vicinity of selection meetings for fear they might unduly influence the process. When the Kenney campaign was asked to leave, organizer Allan Hallman confidently remarked they could pay whatever fines they faced.[16]

While we learned about the extent of Kenney's rule-bending from diligent reporting in the Alberta media, he was greatly assisted in his electoral efforts by the province's partisan punditry. When *Calgary Herald* columnist Licia Corbella was exposed as a card-carrying UCP member, despite portraying herself as a neutral observer, 13 of the columns she wrote from May 2017 to May 2018 praising the party and Kenney were wiped from the *Herald*'s website.[17] In one of them, published on August 5, 2017, in which she applauded the "top-notch" cast of candidates in her party, Corbella introduced Albertans to former Wildrose president Jeff Callaway, who lost the Calgary–North West race as a Wildrose candidate in 2015 to Sandra Jansen. "I don't want to let all of my tricks out of the bag yet, but I've got some pretty bold, visionary ideas," Callaway told Corbella. Callaway, who officially announced his candidacy five days later to little fanfare, served as Kenney's attack dog, going after Brian Jean for the six-figure deficit their former party accrued under Jean's leadership, while Kenney appeared to stay above the fray, allowing the front-runner to focus on building an authoritarian populist consensus. This dynamic was by design.

Callaway campaign organizer Wendy Adam privately admitted that Callaway's role was "to say things about Brian Jean that Jason Kenney cannot." UCP member Mark Hudson, who recorded the conversation and leaked it, asked if the campaign was a "kamikaze run," which Adam affirmed.[18] The extensive coordination between the Callaway and Kenney campaigns became known as the "kamikaze scandal." Callaway campaign manager Cameron Davies sent the candidate's campaign kickoff speech, the date he planned on dropping out, his concession speech, and anti-Jean talking points to Kenney staffer Matt Wolf, who would become one of Kenney's most obnoxious online defenders, for approval. Wolf, in turn, provided the Callaway campaign with attack videos, graphics, and talking points to use against Jean. Hardyal "Happy" Mann, a key organizer in the Punjabi community, said Kenney's camp pressured him into making an illegal $9,000 donation of somebody else's money to the kamikaze candidate.[19] Callaway dropped out of the race on October 4 and promptly endorsed Kenney. The kamikaze scandal resulted in the elections commissioner levying thousands of dollars in fines for illegal donations to the Callaway campaign funnelled through straw donors, including Mann, Callaway himself, Davies, and Calgary businessman Robyn Lore, who wired a mysterious $60,000 to Davies's bank account.[20]

Fildebrandt was the first choice to serve as Kenney's pitbull, but he claims he simply wasn't interested. "If I ran for something, I wanted to win," Fildebrandt told me, adding his view that the kamikaze campaign was "not nice politics but it's fair game." Others, such as Mount Royal University political scientist Duane Bratt, have suggested Fildebrandt was a willing participant, but that a series of scandals, which began the day before Callaway's campaign kicked off and slowly dripped out throughout the rest of 2017, precluded his involvement.[21] He was caught renting out his government-subsidized Edmonton apartment on Airbnb, double-dipping on meal expenses, and leaving the scene of a fender bender.[22] He left the UCP, and after pleading guilty to illegally hunting deer on private property in February 2018, Kenney made it clear he wasn't welcome back.[23] Fildebrandt, however, maintains Kenney had already made up his mind in late 2017 when he encouraged Brian Jean supporter Leela Aheer to run in the Chestermere-Strathcona riding and then blocked Fildebrandt from challenging her for the nomination. "We never spoke again," Fildebrandt said.

As the leadership vote approached, the Jean and Schweitzer campaigns began expressing concerns about the race's insecure online voting system where members were emailed PINs they used to identify themselves and log in to vote. These concerns grew as the leadership election approached.

In the midst of voting, the two campaigns expressed concern about the ease with which members could get a new voting PIN. They accused Kenney's campaign of distributing VPN software, which would allow supporters to vote multiple times. "Secret use of software to falsify the sender's IP address, expressly designed for the purpose of evading detection, is an obvious badge of suspicious behaviour," said a submission from Schweitzer's campaign, which along with Jean's, called for the vote to be postponed to no avail.[24] Their concerns were well founded.

Calgary-Greenway MLA Prab Gill was forced from the UCP caucus after admitting, and then denying, he stuffed ballots at a local riding executive election, but he claimed he was a patsy. Gill went to the RCMP with allegations the Kenney campaign signed up "thousands" of new members and attached fraudulent email addresses to their membership applications, which campaign officials used to intercept their voter PINs and vote for Kenney.[25] CBC News spoke to a dozen people who had fake email addresses attached to their party registration and never voted, many of whom were newcomers to Canada whose families signed up en masse as a gesture of respect. "They know that most people in our community, like my parents, who have a language barrier, are not going to log into a computer and vote," said one member of the Punjabi community.[26] Online news outlet PressProgress spoke to 17 people who were listed as party members but never signed up, 13 of whom were listed as having voted.[27] Some weren't citizens, and another person said they didn't know who Jason Kenney was. Once again, Kenney appeared to be weaponizing immigrants for political purposes. The Kenney campaign has strenuously denied being aware of any fraudulent activity. As of this writing, the RCMP is still investigating allegations of voter fraud six years later; it interviewed Kenney for its probe in February 2022.

Kenney ultimately secured the UCP leadership with 66 percent of the vote on October 28, trouncing Jean and Schweitzer, who proceeded to forget electoral irregularities ever occurred. Jean temporarily left politics, while Schweitzer set his sights on becoming the UCP MLA for Calgary Centre. The kamikaze and voter fraud scandals might have fuelled the perception of Kenney as a carpetbagger, but few on the right seemed to care as long as Kenney could deliver on his promise to win the election, cut their taxes, and take a belligerent approach toward Ottawa. With his leadership secure, Kenney directed his attention to his next opponent, Rachel Notley, whom he depicted as a "surrogate" for Justin Trudeau, tying her to the alleged federal overreach he promised to protect Albertans from. "We need a watchdog for Alberta not a lapdog for Ottawa," he told the *Calgary Sun*'s Rick Bell on the eve of his leadership win.

The Art of the Fair Deal

During the UCP leadership race, while Kenney was hitting the single note of his grassroots guarantee, with some anti-carbon tax sentiment mixed in for good measure, Brian Jean summoned the spirit of the Firewall Letter, calling for Alberta to push for a "fair deal" from the federal government.[28] After defeating Jean in the leadership race, Kenney picked up on this thread. He called for a referendum on abolishing the equalization program altogether, which he insisted would somehow "force binding negotiations with the federal government."[29] This sentiment was echoed by Fildebrandt, who went on to form his own Freedom Conservative Party, but Fildebrandt brought this anti-equalization fight to its logical conclusion — an explicit threat to separate.

Kenney couldn't risk losing support to Fildebrandt's upstart party, so he continued beating the equalization drum while merely implying what Fildebrandt said out loud. Kenney "doesn't endorse separation. But he's happy to stoke the flames," noted Calgary-based *Toronto Star* columnist Gillian Steward on New Year's Day 2019. Fildebrandt came in third place in Chestermere-Strathmore, losing handily to Leela Aheer. Fildebrandt's presence gave Kenney a moderate aura as he repeated similar arguments about Alberta's role in Canada.

The big gripe with equalization, which Kenney characterized as a "slap in the face" to Alberta, was that Quebec received billions of dollars from the program, despite frequently running surplus budgets, while an indebted Alberta had to pay into it even when oil prices were low. The problem with this logic was that, as University of Calgary economist Trevor Tombe noted, Alberta was the richest province in Confederation "however you slice it." The province's deficits weren't reflective of poor finances but of making a political choice in favour of low taxes.[30] Another equalization grievance was rooted in Quebec's opposition to pipeline expansion, which was why fair-deal rhetoric couldn't be considered in isolation from Kenney's "fight-back" strategy against environmentalists.

When a federal court temporarily quashed the Trans Mountain Pipeline expansion in September 2018, Kenney told *CTV News* he "would not be surprised if a significant and growing minority of Albertans are entertaining [separatism]." Proclaiming himself a proud federalist, Kenney added, "the frustration is real." A few months later, a poll from Research Co. showed a quarter of Albertans agreed that "Alberta would be better off as its own country."[31] While the poll's headline dismissed this figure as "negligible public support for separation," one in four people represented a significant constituency. Kenney needed their support to be able to pursue his broader agenda, so he strategically embraced their cause, but wasn't full-throated enough to turn off those who weren't captured by separatist fantasies.

Once in power, Kenney convened a Fair Deal Panel to travel the province in late 2019 and early 2020 based on the predetermined premise that Alberta was being marginalized by the Feds, with a mandate to determine how Alberta could flex its provincial muscles. Delivered in June 2020, it made 25 recommendations, many of which echoed the contents of the Firewall Letter, although it notably cautioned against Alberta going its own way on tax collection. Kenney promised to study the panel's calls to establish an Alberta pension plan and police force, despite the majority of people surveyed for the panel rejecting both ideas. Finally, he followed through on his promise to hold an equalization referendum, another recommendation, which occurred during Alberta's 2021 municipal elections, with 62 percent of voters opting to remove it from the Constitution. The referendum allowed equalization opponents to blow off steam without changing the fact that a single province couldn't rewrite the Constitution, something the former federal Cabinet minister certainly understood. This gesture was always part of Kenney's populist facade.

During the 2019 election campaign, the NDP attempted to use Kenney's regressive social views and electoral fraud allegations against him while Kenney ensured the campaign's focus was on economic issues, which he tied into questions of autonomy. "We're here to talk about jobs, the economy, pipelines, and a fair deal for Alberta," Kenney said at his March 19 campaign kickoff at a quiet oil field services yard in the Edmonton suburb of Leduc, dedicating his campaign to "the people who have been damaged by the ideological, job-killing policies of the NDP government and their alliance with Justin Trudeau." He hit all the right notes of Alberta's political code.

It didn't matter that Kenney's campaign attracted some highly unsavoury figures — Justice Centre for Constitutional Freedoms leader John Carpay, an old friend of Kenney's, who compared the LGBTQ+ Pride flag to a swastika; Adam Strashok, who ran the call centre for Kenney's UCP leadership campaign while running a white supremacist memorabilia store; three Edmonton–West Henday nomination candidates who posed for photos with the far-right outfit Soldiers of Odin; and numerous candidates who expressed anti-LGBTQ+, Islamophobic, and racist views.[32] This pattern, and the unavoidable question of why such forces were attracted to the UCP campaign to begin with, was overlooked as much as allegations of voter fraud in the leadership race. People simply didn't care. Most UCP voters just wanted to see their taxes cut, while a vocal and electorally significant minority wanted to fight the Feds.

The focus was firmly on returning Alberta to its prosperous glory days. With that approach, the UCP project appeared headed for smashing success, receiving 55 percent of the votes with a remarkable 70 percent turnout on Election Day. Clearly, Kenney's approach was working, but that sense of triumph would be relatively short-lived. As quickly as he had united the right in Alberta, his coalition would come crashing down. Before that could happen, however, he began his term in office doing something all members of his coalition could agree on — cutting taxes, gutting regulations, and suppressing organized labour.

6

WAGING WAR ON THE PUBLIC SECTOR

ONCE THE DUST SETTLED FROM JASON Kenney's resounding electoral victory and the Alberta Legislative Assembly reconvened, the premier
announced the impending "summer of repeal." He moved hard and fast
to undo most of his NDP predecessor's legacy in time for the Calgary
Stampede in July. "Speed creates its own momentum. It also makes it harder for the opponents of reform to obstruct it," he explained in an April 2019
interview with the *Edmonton Journal*. He was single-minded in his approach
to reducing burdens on big business; this was central to his economic ideology. But Kenney ultimately went farther than reversing NDP policies to
what they were prior to 2015, shifting the goalposts even more rightward.
He combined a charitable approach to the ruling class with an aggressive
posture toward anyone who stood in the way of this goal. He fattened the
private sector with one hand while starving the public sector with the other.
Kenney reduced taxes and then claimed there weren't sufficient revenues
to justify a public sector of Alberta's size. However, it wasn't simply about
cutting taxes and regulations for business as an excuse to cut public expenditures; Kenney set out to use his bully pulpit to crush organized labour,
which he viewed as a hindrance to economic growth. Through a series of
draconian pieces of legislation in his first year in office, the UCP handi-
capped unions from fighting back against his broader privatization agenda.

Beyond the ideological component, there was a petty, personal, and partisan reason for the incoming government's anti-labour animus — he saw organized labour as an extension of the NDP. While the point is often brought up in bad faith by Kenney, the UCP, and its online troll brigade, it is nonetheless true that the NDP, in both its federal and Alberta incarnations, has deep-seated ties to the labour movement. Lou Arab, a spokesperson for CUPE Alberta, is NDP leader Rachel Notley's husband; Alberta Federation of Labour (AFL) president Gil McGowan ran for the federal NDP in Edmonton Centre in 2015; Shannon Phillips, the NDP's environment and parks minister during its sole term in government, used to work as a researcher for the AFL; and the NDP's constitution requires two AFL members to sit on its provincial council. Kenney regarded organized labour not only as an ideological enemy to be crushed on the path to prosperity but also as a proxy for his political opponents.

In reality, Kenney was facing enemies both in opposition and inside his own party, a product of the PC/Wildrose divide he attempted to mend. His initial austerity agenda was something the entire caucus could get behind, patching over differences within the caucus while presenting a united front in the government's earliest days. Doug Schweitzer, for example, who was regarded as the standard bearer of the party's more moderate PC wing when he ran against Kenney and Brian Jean for the UCP leadership, promised on the leadership trail to implement "the biggest tax relief in Alberta history immediately" by imposing a flat budget for four years. When it came to pursuing a pro-corporate agenda, former rivals Kenney and Schweitzer were in total alignment, and Schweitzer proceeded to become one of Kenney's most bullish partisans as justice minister. Members wouldn't express any discomfort with Kenney's agenda until the Covid pandemic, which tossed a wrench into Kenney's economic plans and brought about his demise.

Setting the Agenda

The first four pieces of legislation the UCP passed in May 2019 outlined Kenney's economic program and set the tone for what was to come, presenting a dichotomous view of labour and the public sector, on one hand, and unconstrained free enterprise on the other. This perspective permeated Kenney's approach to the environmentalist movement, public education, the drug-poisoning crisis, and public health care, in which the interests of private entities were placed at the forefront of public policy decisions.

Kenney's first order of legislative business, announced on May 22, 2019, was the elimination of the NDP's carbon tax by the end of the month. Announcing the introduction of the Act to Repeal the Carbon Tax in the Legislative Assembly, Kenney declared: "Promise made, promise kept," which would soon become his catchphrase. However, he could only eliminate the *provincial* carbon tax, which cost consumers $30 per tonne at its 2018 height, up from $20 when it was introduced. Without its own carbon tax in place, a federal tax would be imposed on the recalcitrant province, which suited Kenney just fine, fulfilling his prophecy that the Feds were trying to pin Alberta down. Kenney teamed up with Ontario premier Doug Ford and Saskatchewan premier Scott Moe for a costly court battle with the Feds, which they lost in March 2021. Getting rid of the provincial carbon tax cost the province $1.3 billion in foregone revenue.[1] Cutting taxes allowed Kenney to reward the private sector while creating a pretext to deepen his attacks on the public sector; for him, it was a win-win. But the carbon tax cut was small potatoes compared to what was to come.

The following week, Kenney introduced a suite of employer-friendly labour reforms for his second piece of legislation, dubbed the Open for Business Act, the centrepiece of which was partially reversing the $15 per hour wage the NDP gradually phased in from 2016 to 2018 in the face of united opposition from business lobbyists, who were quite content with the $10.20 per hour pre-NDP minimum wage. While lowering adult wages could cost Kenney at the ballot box, he would have no such problem with youth, so Kenney created a two-tiered minimum wage of $13 for youth who worked fewer than 28 hours per week. "Thirteen dollars an hour is a heck of a lot more than $0 an hour, and that's the option here. We're talking about part-time, teenagers who are typically in high school, working typically 20 hours a week or less," he said, as if that made their labour less valuable than those of their adult colleagues who did the same work.

Kenney used this legislation to fire his first salvo against the labour movement by eliminating card check, which made union certification automatic if organizers could collect the signatures of 65 percent of a workplace's employees. The NDP introduced this policy in 2017, leading to more than a doubling of union certifications in that year alone.[2] Kenney returned to the pre-2017 status quo of mandatory ballots, which tilted the process in the favour of employers by giving them time to mobilize against the union drive. Kenney would, naturally, tout this reversion as a victory for "fairness and democracy in the workplace," which would protect workers from "intimidation and bully tactics" — just not from their bosses. The legislation, additionally, eliminated time-and-a-half overtime pay. While that would significantly reduce wages for people who worked overtime, Kenney said it would provide "flexibility" for their bosses.

The most consequential piece of legislation the UCP introduced in its first month was Bill 3, the Job Creation Tax Cut Act, which slashed Alberta's corporate tax rate from 12 percent to 8 percent over four years, rolling it back further than it was before the NDP came to power, with the goal of Alberta having by far the lowest corporate taxes in the country. This legislation blew a massive hole in Alberta's budget, giving the government a pretext for austerity by using the oldest trick in the book — the cupboards were bare! The news release announcing the bill included an estimate from "leading economist" Jack Mintz that the tax cut would create "at least" 55,000 new jobs, failing to disclose the pertinent fact that Mintz sat on the board of Imperial Oil. Mintz, a fellow at the neoliberal Fraser Institute, could always be depended on to advocate tax cuts as a solution to any problem, which just so happened to benefit companies like the one whose board he was on.

The NDP Opposition repeatedly referenced the cost of Kenney's tax cut as $4.5 billion over four years, contrasting the UCP's generosity toward corporations with the government's cuts to public services. This $4.5 billion figure, however, severely underestimated the tax cut's impact. Alberta's five biggest oil companies *alone* projected a combined $4.277 billion in savings in their quarterly reports after the cut was announced, *PressProgress* reported in November 2019. Leading the pack was Canadian Natural Resources, which estimated a $1.618 billion windfall, followed by Suncor with $1.116

billion, Imperial with $662 million, Cenvous at $658 million, and Husky, which would be purchased by Cenovus in 2021, at $233 million. These earnings, it turned out, allowed the companies to *eliminate* jobs by investing in automation while increasing compensation for shareholders and executives,[3] like Mintz.

While the NDP's minimum wage increase to $15 per hour over three years was regarded by Kenney as too fast a change, lifting corporations' tax burden couldn't come soon enough. In fact, the government dropped the corporate tax rate to 8 percent 18 months ahead of schedule under the guise of its July 2020 Covid recovery plan. Independent Lethbridge-based journalist Kim Siever found that the number of jobs created in the three years after the corporate tax cut didn't keep up with population growth. While Alberta added 83,600 more jobs from June 2019 to September 2022 — a 3.65 percent increase — the working-age population grew by 5.43 percent. And of these 83,600 jobs, just 40,000 were full-time. The connection between the tax cut and increased employment, in any event, is tenuous, since corporations have a fiduciary to increase shareholders' earnings, not to create jobs. "No one is going to hire more workers just because they have more money on hand, unless demand was already increasing for their products and services, and they needed more workers to keep up with that demand," Siever noted.

After the corporate tax cut was announced, Kenney introduced the Red Tape Reduction Act, which a May 29, 2019, government news release said would "reduce the regulatory burden on businesses and speed up approvals to grow businesses." Rural southern Alberta MLA Grant Hunter was appointed the new associate minister of red tape reduction. Kenney promised to cut red tape for businesses by one-third and stop it from "creeping back," which he said would make Alberta the "freest economy in Canada," although it was unclear how one measured red tape, let alone freedom. Red tape reduction applied *strictly* to businesses; the government would increase red tape whenever that suited its agenda. While this suite of pro-business, anti-labour legislation was rolled out in the UCP's first month, a panel was preparing a report that would retroactively justify Kenney's predetermined policy agenda of dismantling the administrative state.

Fresh off his April 2019 election victory, Kenney boasts to the business-friendly audience at the Canadian Club in Toronto of his plans to cut corporate tax rates by four percentage points.

One Panel to Rule Them All

Prior to passing a single piece of legislation, Finance Minister Travis Toews, a corporate cattle farmer and former accountant from Grande Prairie, announced the formation of a Blue Ribbon Panel on Alberta's Finances, which was specifically instructed to find a way to balance Alberta's budget by 2022–23 "without raising taxes," gaming its conclusions to the government's liking. During former NDP finance minister Joe Ceci's last fiscal update, the province had a deficit of $6.9 billion, significantly decreased from the projected $8.8 billion in his 2018–19 budget, although the province's debt was projected to rise to $96 billion by 2024, which Kenney highlighted to demonstrate the province was in a "critical fiscal situation." But addressing this fiscal imbalance by downsizing the public sector, which would reduce the debt, while cutting taxes, which would exacerbate it, was a deliberate ideological choice.

The Blue Ribbon Panel was the first of many panels and task forces Kenney convened with a composition and mandate that could only result in recommending the policies he had already planned on pursuing, and its results had wide-ranging implications for many ministries. "[The] Kenney government may as well have announced a task force on nutrition, populated it with children and ice cream manufacturers, and limited their mandate to determining what we should eat for dinner," quipped *Maclean's* columnist Jason Markusoff in September 2019 after the government unveiled a panel on the minimum wage stacked with small-business owners.

Janice MacKinnon, who served as Saskatchewan's finance minister during Roy Romanow's NDP government in the 1990s, was tapped to lead the panel, which was announced on May 7, 2019. Kenney would point to her former party affiliation as a symbol of its non-partisan, common-sense nature. Columnist Graham Thomson, writing in *iPolitics* the next day, observed this was a conscious effort "to inoculate himself against criticism that he is a right-wing ideologue out to slash government spending by gutting government services after only listening to conservative voices."

MacKinnon was Kenney's kind of New Democrat. *Regina Leader-Post* columnist and long-time Saskatchewan politics observer Murray Mandryk called her politics "very chameleon-like."[4] And the austerity-crazed 1990s were the age of political chameleons. Governments from across the political spectrum, from Jean Chrétien's federal Liberals (1993–2003) to NDP governments led by Bob Rae in Ontario (1990–95), Romanow in Saskatchewan (1991–2001), and Mike Harcourt in British Columbia (1991–96), as well as PC governments led by Ralph Klein in Alberta (1992–2006), Gary Filmon in Manitoba (1988–99), and Mike Harris in Ontario (1995–2002), embraced, to varying degrees, the neoliberal consensus of the day, focusing obsessively on deficit and debt concerns.

Romanow's 1993 budget, which MacKinnon delivered as finance minister, closed 52 rural hospitals, ended the province's children's dental plan and universal prescription drug program, and slashed funding to schools, hospitals, universities, and local governments by anywhere from 5 to 13 percent. But it also raised the provincial sales tax, which Alberta doesn't have, and the gas tax, while cutting taxes for the manufacturing and processing sectors.

In an interview with the *Edmonton Journal*, MacKinnon insisted Alberta would be able to avoid such deep cuts, which reporter Emma Graney presented with skepticism, pointing to MacKinnon's 2013 report for the right-wing Macdonald-Laurier Institute advocating health-care privatization and a 2017 report co-authored with Jack Mintz, Kenney's favourite economist, calling for cuts to public sector wages.

On May 10, 2019, the *Calgary Herald* published an op-ed with MacKinnon's byline, arguing that making significant cuts now, or "measured choices" in her parlance, would avoid even worse cuts in the future. She repeated the classic neoliberal trope comparing government debt to household debt, ignoring the fact that governments, unlike households, can raise taxes. But for Kenney's UCP, new taxes were out of the question, an omission from the panel's mandate the op-ed attributed to the need to rush the report out in time for October's budget, promising taxes "will be reviewed at a later date." As of this writing four years later, that date hasn't arrived.

It turned out the government practically wrote this op-ed for MacKinnon, as well as her talking points for the press conference announcing the panel, according to emails obtained by the AFL through a freedom-of-information request, shattering any illusions of MacKinnon's impartiality. "Premier's office would also like an op-ed to go out from you as Chair. Can you take a look at the following draft, which is based on your speaking notes?" UCP staffer Cheryl Tkalcic wrote to MacKinnon in a May 6, 2019, email. "The op-ed is great. Well done. I have no changes," MacKinnon replied a couple of hours later. Tkalcic offered earlier to provide MacKinnon with "speaking notes" for the press conference announcing the panel the next day, which MacKinnon accepted. Minister Toews, asked for comment from *CTV News*, called the notion that the government even influenced MacKinnon's op-ed "deeply insulting" to MacKinnon.

On September 3, the MacKinnon report was released to the public. It called for deep cuts and privatization, as its namesake was instructed to do. "Cuts around the edges won't get Alberta back to a sustainable balanced budget," the document read, calling for "a difficult but necessary course correction immediately to return the province to fiscal health over the medium- to long-term."[5] To that effect, MacKinnon's panel proposed

26 recommendations for the government to balance the budget, including outsourcing certain health-care procedures to the private sector, which it urged "should be applied to other areas beyond health"; cutting funding to post-secondary institutions and lifting the tuition freeze instituted by the PCs in 2013; legislating wages for public-sector workers, which "in the event of a strike … would form the basis for back-to-work legislation"; and forcing "municipalities to share more in the costs of major projects." In order to implement these changes and more, the report called for a $600 million cut to the budget across the board.

In the report, MacKinnon repeatedly compared Alberta's public-sector costs per capita to those in Ontario, Quebec, and British Columbia, which on average were lower than Alberta's, without inquiring why that might be the case. When that wasn't the case, such as Quebec's spending on post-secondary education, Alberta's government was urged to simply ignore the discrepancy. The report, somewhat defensively, rejected the premise of Alberta consistently having the highest cost of living in the country among provinces and territories, arguing "that might have been true at different times in Alberta but is not the case today."

The Consumer Price Index (CPI), which tracks changes in the price of consumer goods over time, suggested otherwise. In May 2019, the month the panel was announced, the CPI in Alberta was 144, compared to 136.6 nationwide, and 138.1 in Ontario, 132.4 in Quebec, and 131.8 in British Columbia. By the time the panel's findings were released, the CPI in Alberta was 142.9, 136.2 nationally, 137.5 in Ontario, 132.1 in Quebec, and 132 in British Columbia. As of December 2022, it was 160.8 in Alberta, 153.1 nationally, 154.8 in Ontario, 149 in Quebec, and 147.1 in British Columbia. One would hope the cost of the public sector would be higher in Alberta to maintain a similar standard of living as those elsewhere in Canada. But the report claimed Alberta actually had a lower cost of living "measured by a comparison of provincial taxes and utilities in key cities in each of the provinces,"[6] which is simply not how cost of living is measured. It was also an odd argument for a report whose authors otherwise refused to examine taxation.

The report's exclusive focus on public-sector compensation overlooked how private-sector employees in Alberta were compensated more than those elsewhere in the country by an even greater margin, according to a study from the Parkland Institute released on the eve of the inaugural UCP budget. Private-sector workers in Alberta made 17 to 18 percent more than their counterparts in the rest of the country, while public-sector workers made 9 to 10 percent more. The MacKinnon report disingenuously depicted Alberta as having a uniquely bloated public sector without accounting for the fact that the percentage of people employed by the government in Alberta was identical in 2018 to the percentage nationally at 10.23 percent. It simply came down to higher wages to account for a higher cost of living. But when you're a hammer looking to attack the public sector, everything is a nail of excessive government spending.

The glaring methodological flaws of the report were seldom recognized in news coverage of its findings and recommendations, most of which accepted MacKinnon's framing uncritically. In a September *Calgary Herald* column, Don Braid, concluding the report was a "radical document," nonetheless wrote that it was "blunt and accurate in its assessment of how successive governments — mostly conservative — have bungled Alberta's finances." He added that it found "Alberta's cost of living is often lower when tax rates are included," which was incorrect — it claimed Alberta's cost of living was lower than other provinces based *solely* on tax rates and utility costs.

Not even the few commentators who questioned the report's findings and methodology mentioned the cost-of-living question. *National Post* columnist Colby Cosh, while sympathetic to the report's aims, noted a general "cherry-picking" of data.[7] Scott Schmidt at the *Medicine Hat News* noted high public-sector wages were a result of historically high comparator wages in a private sector flush with oil cash,[8] as did Jason Markusoff in *Maclean's*. At the CBC, Graham Thomson wrote that a "combination of moderately reduced spending and moderately increased taxation" could easily balance the books. "But that's not what Kenney wants."[9]

On October 24, three days after that year's federal election, the UCP released its inaugural budget, which aimed for a 7.7 percent reduction in the public sector by 2023. Minister Toews proudly described implementing "surgical cuts" to the budget. It froze health-care funding, despite a growing population, and purported to do the same for K–12 education.

It cut funding for municipal capital projects by $236 million over three years, or 9 percent, downloading these costs onto property owners, who would in turn pass them on to tenants. It eliminated the tuition freeze for post-secondary students, capping increases as high as 21 percent over three years. Most cruelly, it cut Assured Income for the Severely Handicapped (AISH) payments by de-indexing them from inflation. Richard Truscott of the Canadian Federation of Independent Business called the budget "tough medicine, but ... certainly needed medicine." Canadian Press reporter Dean Bennett correctly noted the budget's "austerity will hit some of Alberta's neediest."

While the budget she inspired might have sacrificed Alberta's most disadvantaged on the balanced budget altar, MacKinnon would do just fine. In March 2020, she was appointed to the board of governors at the University of Alberta, which had been given a 11 percent cut in provincial funding in line with her report's recommendation to cut post-secondary funding by forcing students to pay more out of pocket for tuition. This appointment also came a month before the government, again upon McKinnon's recommendation, announced its intention to begin basing a portion of post-secondary funding on arbitrary, inconsistent performance metrics designed to turn post-secondary institutions into job-making factories.

Handcuffing the Labour Movement

In 2017, the NDP government got the province's public-sector unions — Alberta Union of Provincial Employees (AUPE), the Health Sciences Association of Alberta, United Nurses of Alberta (UNA), and the Alberta Teacher's Association — to accept a two-year wage freeze followed by negotiations, and if necessary, arbitration with a hard deadline of June 30, 2019. Athabasca University labour studies professor Bob Barnetson noted in *Alberta Views* magazine that this was widely regarded as an effort "to deny the UCP the opportunity to use public-sector increases as a weapon against the New Democrats in the 2019 election." The benefit of arbitration was assuring unions that even if the NDP lost that election, there would still be "a fair process to decide on wage increases," Barnetson wrote in the magazine's January 2020 edition.

The UCP had other plans. On June 13, 2019, the government announced it would delay arbitration until the end of October, which Toews admitted was intended to buy the government time for the MacKinnon report to come out. He didn't need to wait for the MacKinnon recommendations to cut corporate taxes, but that was because the report's outcome to downsize the public sector was predetermined; the question, if any, was by how much. "In the history of our union, it is the biggest betrayal by government we have ever seen in terms of reaching in and using the power of legislation to alter the terms and conditions of our contract," said UNA president Heather Smith,[10] who was around during Klein's austerity-driven tenure in the 1990s. During the raucous debate on the legislation, whose passage was a foregone conclusion with a majority government, Kenney walked around the aisle of the UCP benches handing out earplugs to his caucus. While the Opposition painted this gesture as a horrible breach of decorum, its symbolism was indicative of Kenney's approach to the labour movement — he was simply not listening.

As negotiations were set to begin in late October, the government revealed that it was looking to impose wage rollbacks of anywhere from 2 percent to 5 percent on the public-sector unions. Meanwhile, the government passed the omnibus Ensuring Fiscal Sustainability Act, which in addition to codifying AISH cuts into legislation, allowed the government to hire scabs and prevented unionized workers from filing employment standards complaints, forcing them to go through the formal grievance process. On January 31, 2020, an arbitrator awarded a 1 percent pay increase to most AUPE workers and freezes to auxiliary nurses. Toews complained this would cost the government $35 million and threatened job cuts, or what he euphemistically called "adjustment to work force levels." The government only had the power to eliminate unionized public-sector jobs. A suite of legislation it soon brought forward served to impact the labour movement as a whole.

The first piece of the UCP's second legislative session was the Critical Infrastructure Defence Act, which occurred under the backdrop of two key developments — rail blockades conducted in February 2020 in solidarity with Indigenous land defenders opposing the Coastal Gas Link pipeline in British Columbia, and closer to home, the cancellation of the Teck Frontier tar sands mine. Ostensibly, it aimed to prohibit environmentalists from blockading pipelines, and other oil and gas infrastructure, to maintain investor confidence. However, it was much more far-reaching, with significant implications for the labour movement. The legislation, passed in May, imposed a fine of up to $25,000 or six months in jail for anyone deemed to have entered, damaged, or obstructed "essential infrastructure," as the government defined it. Given that the entire purpose of strike action, or any other protest, is to disrupt business as usual, the bill allowed the state to conscribe where these actions could take place. Another bill introduced and passed in 2020 formalized these constraints on organized labour.

The centrepiece of the UCP's anti-labour onslaught was the Restoring Balance in Alberta Workplaces Act, or Bill 32, which was introduced in July 2020. Based on the faulty premise that the NDP's mild labour reforms gave workers excessive power, the act placed onerous restrictions on union activity. Chief among them were where unions could picket, prohibiting workers from demonstrating outside secondary sites — workplaces that weren't their own but were connected to theirs, whether it was other worksites operated by their employers or businesses that indirectly depended on their labour — without explicit permission from the labour relations board. If their employers hired scabs, the unions would be forbidden from blocking, or even delaying, the scabs to their worksites.

Another key part of this bill would force union members to explicitly opt in to what the government deemed "political activities," artificially dividing union activity into core activities, such as bargaining and grievance settlement, and the rest. Never mind that its non-core activities would have already been voted on by union membership; unions would be forced to file detailed paperwork on where their dues were going. This component of the legislation was intended to starve unions of funding that would go toward fighting against the UCP agenda on multiple fronts.

The dues portion of Bill 32 represented a brazen attack on the Rand formula, named after Supreme Court of Canada justice Ivan Rand, who in 1946 ruled that all union members must pay dues, regardless of their level of involvement in the union, since whether they liked it or not, they benefited from the union's obligation to provide fair representation in the event of a grievance and any gains made through collective bargaining. Kenney put this formula in his crosshairs by framing the matter as one of individual choice.

A week after the bill was introduced, Kenney revealed what sort of initiatives he didn't want union dues to go toward, arguing rank-and-file members might not want their dues to go toward "union boss political activities," such as opposing efforts to overthrow the government of Venezuela or inviting environmentalists to speak at conferences. Upon the bill's introduction, AUPE secretary treasurer Jason Heistad noted Kenney's invocation of individual preferences provided a smokescreen for "dismantling our collective power." Labour Minister Jason Copping admitted the legislation would create "red tape" for unions, but that it was important to recall that the government's red tape reduction efforts were aimed squarely at businesses. For Kenney, it was prosperity first, and unions were seen as a major roadblock toward prosperity by agitating for wages and working conditions beyond those determined by the market.

Addressing inadequacies in the market through collective bargaining — organized labour's raison d'être — is inherently political. Any division between bargaining activities and other political agitation was entirely fictitious, noted labour lawyer Joshua Mandryk. "What unions are able to achieve and defend for their members is impacted by larger social and political issues and it's not restricted to the bargaining table," he told *Rank & File Radio — Prairie Edition* in a July 2020 episode. He cited the examples of beloved universal programs such as Medicare, the Canada Pension Plan, and unemployment insurance as the products of labour agitation. These were, not coincidentally, all programs Kenney's separatist base wanted to opt out of.

Bill 32 had far-reaching implications beyond weakening unions' ability to support a political agenda that benefited their members. As a result of the legislation, which wasn't implemented until August 2022, unions cut their charitable donations by $2.5 million, or 38 percent of the $6.5 million they spent on charity before the legislation went into effect. Jason Foster, an Athabasca University labour studies professor, co-authored a Parkland Institute report a month after the legislation's implementation examining its impact on unions' charitable contributions. He told me the UCP's anti-labour animus blinded it to the range of union activity outside bargaining and wages. "In their rush to try and stick it to the unions, they didn't pause long enough to realize that this has negative consequences for groups other than unions," Foster said. With their perception of unions "as these big bad entities that get in the way of prosperity," the UCP government overlooked the active role unions play in their communities.

Unlike bosses, labour leaders were subject to the democratic mandate of employees. If workers didn't like their union's policies, nothing was stopping them from getting involved and attempting to convince enough of their fellow workers to change them. Kenney put his thumbs on the scale through legislation to constrain unions' democratic mandates. If there was collateral damage to that, then so be it. If individual workers wanted to give money to charity, they were welcome to do so, but having workers collectively pool their resources to fulfill a collective vision was out of the question.

A resolution at the UCP's October 2020 convention calling for Alberta to adopt U.S.-style "right-to-work" laws, in which employees could opt out of being part of a union altogether, passed with 81 percent support, revealing the party's preferred endgame. Kenney never adopted right-to-work legislation, partially because his political career was cut short and partially because it might not have been electorally viable, but his suite of labour legislation clearly set Alberta on that path.

Kenney's anti-labour animus was a clear expression of his view that the hierarchies created by capitalism were a natural order that ought not to be disrupted. Within this framework, the only permissible collective institutions were those that could be used to uphold, rather than subvert, these social relations, whether it was the Chamber of Commerce, the church, or right-wing political parties. Organized labour was correctly identified as posing a barrier to full marketization.

Kenney's disdain for the labour movement was only exceeded by his hatred for environmentalists. The labour and climate justice movements were intimately connected as different means to the same end — slowing down the pursuit of profit for the collective good — despite efforts by the UCP and NDP to conflate opposition to fossil fuels with opposition to fossil-fuel workers, livelihoods. In his zeal to combat the environmentalist movement and promote the oil and gas industry, Kenney would abandon any preferences toward the free market or fiscal conservatism that he espoused elsewhere.

7

BURNING DOWN THE HOUSE

FOLLOWING A YEAR-LONG STINT AS A tobacco lobbyist,[1] Ezra Levant published *Ethical Oil*, a book-length love letter to Alberta's oil sands in 2010. An old chum of Jason Kenney from their Reform Party days, Levant argued that, contrary to environmentalists' claims that endlessly extracting bitumen from the oil sands[2] was an unsustainable burden on the environment, public health, and Indigenous rights, continued extraction was a moral imperative. "Oil is an international commodity," he wrote. "Even if the oil sands were to completely shut down, the world wouldn't use one barrel less. It would just buy that oil from the oil sands' competitors: places like Saudi Arabia, Iran, Sudan, and Nigeria."[3] Levant accused environmentalists of "driving consumers into the hands of oil producers who are worse by every ethical measure," including the environment. But there was a gaping hole in his environmental criteria. Levant claimed that "human-caused global warming is a theory that isn't uniformly accepted in either the scientific or lay community," dismissing climate concerns as a "last-gasp attack on the oil sands."[4]

Explicit climate denial aside, Levant presented an exceptionally shoddy strawman argument. Few environmentalists would argue that Canada should purchase Saudi or Nigerian oil rather than Albertan oil; this false dichotomy distracts from the primary issue. Instead, environmentalists insist that we need to phase out the oil sector altogether on an international scale and that Canada has a *moral* obligation to lead the transition toward renewable energy, which Levant dismissed as "some perfect fantasy fuel," due to a combination of Canada's immense wealth and the uniquely deleterious effects of tar sands oil on the planet and Indigenous treaty rights.

Levant's book was a hit, winning the *Globe and Mail*–sponsored 2011 National Business Book Award. The nominally left-leaning *Toronto Star* sent reporter John Goddard in September 2010 to sit down for an interview with the author. Goddard referred to the book as a "sweeping study," arguing that Levant was making a "left, liberal case" for the tar sands. "Levant argues not that the oilsands are good because they keep the wheels of capitalism spinning," he wrote, "but because they produce a morally superior product to all other oil sources when economic justice, minority rights, freedom from oppression and, yes, even environmentalism are taken into account." What Goddard described as fresh "left, liberal" arguments were, in fact, boilerplate neocon moralism.

Upon its release, Kenney urged his Twitter (now "X" but referred to hereafter as "Twitter") followers to check out his buddy's "fact-packed polemic," whose argument he said was difficult to dispute: you could buy either *our* ethical product or *their* unethical product. This essentially became the official position of the Stephen Harper Conservatives. On January 7, 2011, the day after Environment Minister Peter Kent bemoaned the "bad rap" tar sands crude had gotten, insisting the product "is absolutely ethical … in every sense of the word," Harper announced that his government would work to "explain to the world" how great Canadian oil was.[5] A week later, the *Globe* hailed Levant as "Harper's oil sands muse."[6] Levant, who later founded the far-right media enterprise *Rebel Media*, now known as *Rebel News*, was cast out of polite company in 2017, in part due to the outlet's sympathetic coverage of the deadly Unite the Right rally in Charlottesville, Virginia. Kenney, UCP leadership rival Brian Jean, and federal Conservative leader Andrew Scheer distanced themselves from Levant's media outlet, but that didn't prevent Kenney from echoing his slippery talking points at every turn.

In 2012, an obscure North Vancouver–based blogger named Vivian Krause expanded upon Levant's narrative, arguing that well-funded U.S. interests were intent on sabotaging the ill-fated Northern Gateway Pipeline by funding domestic environmentalists through a supposedly shadowy out-fit called the Tides Foundation. Krause, who has admitted that 90 percent of her funding from 2012 to 2014 came from the oil and gas industry,[7] became a key figure in Kenney's anti-environmentalist campaign in Alberta.

Upon returning to Alberta in 2016 in pursuit of making the NDP a one-term government, Kenney ramped up his attacks on the environment-alist movement, spending an inordinate amount of time personally vilifying prominent environmentalists Tzeporah Berman and Ed Whittingham, who were both appointed to roles by the NDP in a futile effort to bridge the gap between environmentalists and industry. Kenney promised to adopt a "fight-back" strategy against perceived enemies of the oil sands once in power, explicitly centred around "intrepid researcher" Krause's claims.

There was an entire section in the UCP's 2019 platform entitled "Standing Up to Foreign Influences." The core of this strategy was two-pronged: a $30 million "energy war room," which would "respond in real time to lies and myths told about Alberta's energy industry," and a $2.5 mil-lion inquiry into Krause's theories of a foreign plot targeting the tar sands. The war room quickly became a laughingstock, in which I played a minor role, and the inquiry, after repeated deadline extensions, essentially found nothing. It is tempting to write off either of these initiatives as a "fiasco," "dud," or "nothingburger," and these descriptors are all technically correct. But this dismissive language obscures the role Kenney's efforts to cast a shadow of suspicion over the entirely legitimate aspirations of environment-alists played in establishing an authoritarian populist consensus.

In every year following the publication of *Ethical Oil*, save for 2020, oil and gas production increased in the tar sands.[8] At 56 tCO2 per person in 2017, Alberta alone emitted almost four times more carbon per capita than Saudi Arabia's 15.2 tCO2 and nearly double that of Qatar, the worst polluting nation, at 31.2 tCO2. This will only increase as Alberta expands oil and gas production. From 2005 to 2016, Canada's greenhouse gas emis-sions dropped a pitiful 3.8 percent, while Alberta's *increased* by 14 percent.[9] Simply put, Alberta is weighing Canada down on its climate commitments. Business as usual in Alberta's oil and gas industry poses a unique threat to the planet's existence. This is precisely why Levant's puerile arguments were

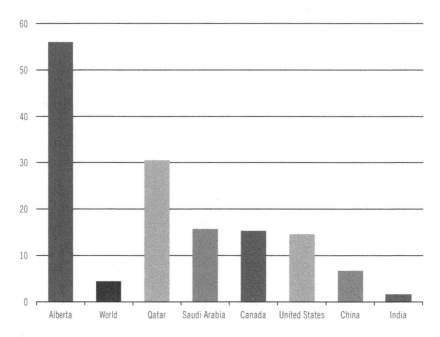

In 2017, Alberta alone emitted more than triple the carbon per capita of Saudi Arabia, nearly double that of Qatar — the planet's worst per capita polluter — and almost 13 times the global average. Source: Barry Saxifrage/VisualCarbon.org and International Energy Agency.

so useful to Kenney. They shifted the focus from the tar sands' deleterious impact on the planet toward irrelevant metaphysical criteria. If our oil was uniquely moral, that would make its opponents immoral, so Kenney set his sites on vilifying those who stood in the way of untrammelled tar sands expansion.

The NDP's Climate Half Measures

Kenney began his smear campaign by relentlessly targeting one environment-alist in particular — Tzeporah Berman — appointed in 2016 to co-chair the NDP's Oil Sands Advisory Working Group, tasked with developing a climate plan acceptable to both activists and industry, upon the request of industry lobbyists. Berman, who participated in blockades against old-growth logging in British Columbia in the 1990s and sought to halt oil sands' expansion as the executive director of the Tar Sands Network, had developed an unlikely alliance with the then Canadian Association of Petroleum Producers (CAPP) president Dave Collyer, working, over several years, to facilitate dialogue between oil and gas executives, scientists, and environmentalists to overcome a paralysis in climate policy. Berman lived a somewhat double life at this time, attempting to find pragmatic, mediated policy-oriented solutions with her opponents in industry while working with environmentalist nongovernmental organizations (NGOs) to create ad and protest campaigns to shift the political conversation in environmentalists' favour. But, by Berman's own admission, her work in Alberta ultimately demonstrated the profound flaws of this approach.

In an interview, Berman described Kenney as a "poisonous and annoying kind of weasel." Kenney exploited her opposition to tar sands expansion and demands to shut the industry down by mid-century, deliberately conflating her views with the NDP government, ignoring that industry boosters wanted someone with Berman's credibility as an environmentalist to be part of the discussion. The NDP took Kenney's bait at every opportunity, protesting that *it* was the party that would, in fact, get pipelines built and expand tar sands production. The party never articulated a vision of an Alberta no longer dependent on the vicissitudes of the oil and gas market.

NDP leader Rachel Notley was more critical of the oil and gas industry during the 2015 provincial election, which she shocked the nation by not only winning but also by consigning the 44-year PC dynasty to history. Notley did so in part by painting the ruling PC party's fealty to the oil and gas industry as detrimental to Albertans, criticizing Premier Jim Prentice for having "focused only on more export pipelines for unprocessed bitumen — sending our jobs to Texas,"[10] while promising to "reduce our province's over-dependence on raw bitumen exports." There was nothing radical about this platform, but it did suggest a mild break with the past when the provincial government let the oil and gas industry do essentially whatever it wanted. Once Notley came to power, though, it became increasingly clear that very little would change. Big Oil continued to rule the day.

In August 2015, three months after the election, Notley fulfilled a promise to appoint a panel to review royalty rates, similar to what PC premier Ed Stelmach did in 2007, earning him unhinged backlash. Industry was elated when Notley's panel returned in February 2016 with the conclusion that royalty rates should remain the same. This recommendation was largely expected, given the downturn in oil prices, with the West Texas Intermediate benchmark falling to its lowest in 16 years at $26.68 per barrel in January 2016, but the panel didn't chart a path to increase rates once the price of oil went back up, nor did the government even politely suggest doing so. The panel appointment was the last time the NDP expressed any desire to challenge the oil and gas industry's stranglehold over the province.

The NDP turned to its Climate Leadership Plan, announcing a proposed cap on tar sands emissions, which permitted emissions to grow substantially from 70 megatonnes per year to 100. To implement this cap, the government established the Oil Sands Advisory Group, appointing Berman to co-chair it alongside CAPP's Collyer and Melody Lepine of Mikisew Cree First Nation. Berman's presence immediately drew ferocious backlash from all the usual suspects, including Kenney, who a week earlier had announced his intention to seek the PC leadership.

On July 13, 2016, Kenney posted a Berman quote about the need to *"shut down* the tar sands [emphasis in original]" on Facebook over an NDP orange background. "Disagree? Help us Unite Alberta," he wrote in the comments linking to his website. On July 14, Kenney posted another Berman quote — "Oil is corroding our democracy" — again using her remarks to solicit support for his campaign. Kenney's attacks were buttressed by a "Fire Berman" petition and ad campaign from Levant's *Rebel Media*, which launched on July 15. If there was any evidence to support Berman's point about oil's corrosive impact on politics, it was the ease with which Kenney was able to worm his way back to Alberta and tap into the anger, frustration, and most importantly, fear of the thousands of Albertans who had lost their jobs in the oil sands since prices crashed in late 2014.

Berman pointed out that prior to Kenney's attacks the most outspoken critics of her involvement with the advisory group were other environmentalists, who saw her as selling out their cause by collaborating with the very people who caused the climate crisis. These criticisms of Berman weren't new. In April 2009, she was harshly rebuked for endorsing then B.C. Liberal premier Gordon Campbell's carbon tax — the first in Canada — and criticizing the B.C. NDP for what she regarded as its counterproductive opposition to it. Berman didn't endorse the Liberals, who in British Columbia were essentially conservatives, wholesale. But she told the *Georgia Straight* that she believed the Liberals' "climate strategy and their commitment to conservation efficiency and an economy-wide price on carbon and their commitment to expand the renewable-energy sector is leadership," despite misgivings about its expansion of the province's oil and gas sector and building more highways at the expense of public transit. In response, marine researcher and fish-farm opponent Alexandra Morton wrote an open letter in the *Tyee*, accusing Berman of chasing headlines, pre-emptively blaming her for "all that follows" if Campbell was re-elected. Such criticisms from the environmentalist movement paled in comparison to the coordinated harassment campaign from Kenney and his supporters.

As the attacks intensified, including Wildrose Opposition leader Brian Jean's November 2016 accusation that Berman was "declaring war" on the oil sands, Berman began receiving torrents of anti-Semitic and misogynistic abuse online. The vilification campaign came to a head in May 2017 when Berman was assaulted by a man at the Edmonton airport. "They grabbed my shoulders and spat right in my face and were shaking me. I tried to wrench myself away and then I fell down and then I ran into the bathroom. It all happened fairly quickly, and I got away fairly quickly, but it was pretty traumatic," she recalled. Kenney never denounced, or even acknowledged, this physical assault on her. Berman felt particularly betrayed by the oil and gas industry people, with whom she shared cordial discussions about the threat of the climate crisis, who refused to come to her defence. She ultimately reached a "mutual decision" with the NDP government to leave the advisory group the following month. Interestingly, Kenney's attacks on her intensified *after* she left. Each time Berman attended a rally against pipelines, or criticized the tar sands, Kenney reminded his online followers that Notley appointed her to the Oil Sands Advisory Working Group, conveniently ignoring who requested her involvement.

Berman told me the "funny part" of Kenney's quixotic crusade against allegedly foreign-funded environmentalists was that she was fully willing to comply with it; he just never asked. "I would have happily provided the government with all of the information and all of the budgets and all of the data, because it was not illegal and it was a drop in the bucket compared to what industry was spending. I know because I saw the industry plans and ad plans, et cetera, because I was working with the industry," she said.

Through her experience, Berman learned that the pledges of oil and gas executives were essentially meaningless. "Even if we're able to reach agreements with people within industry on specific policies," she told me, "what I later discovered is those same people won't stand up to their CEOs, or to the oil and gas industry associations, when those associations attack the same policies that they agreed to." Just 20 months after the CEOs of four of Alberta's five biggest oil companies — Suncor, Cenovus, Canadian Natural Resources Ltd., and Shell — stood onstage with Notley and Environment and Climate Change Minister Shannon Phillips to announce the Climate Leadership Plan, which including the emissions cap, a $20 per tonne carbon tax, and phaseout of coal, all but Steve Williams of Suncor had left their positions.[11] Berman said the carbon tax, one of the first policies Kenney nixed once in power, ultimately served as cover for further pipeline expansion.

The Alberta NDP internalized the view that indefinite fossil-fuel expansion is beneficial for society. This was exemplified in February 2018 when Notley banned the import of B.C. wines in retaliation for B.C. premier John Horgan's opposition to Kinder Morgan's Trans Mountain Pipeline expansion (TMX). For this stance, Mark Scholz, head of the Canadian Association of Oilwell Drilling Contractors, praised Notley's "incredible leadership." CAPP spokesperson Jeff Gaulin offered similar praise, thanking Notley for "standing up for Alberta, standing up for jobs and standing up for fairness in Canada."[12]

The likelihood that any of these people voted for Notley in 2019, rather than Kenney's "Jobs, Economy, Pipelines" platform, is net zero. "Rachel Notley," Berman explained, "is never going to be more pro-pipeline than Jason Kenney. He's always going to be the pipeline prince because those are his politics." But that didn't stop Notley from trying. She went further than even Prime Minister Justin Trudeau, who, in May 2018, purchased TMX for $4.5 billion because Kinder Morgan was no longer interested in building it, in her fealty to the oil and gas industry. In August 2018, when a federal court ruling temporarily quashed the pipeline expansion, she refused to participate in the federal government's climate plan, which included nationwide scheduled carbon tax increases, until the "federal government gets its act together."

TMX, which, as of May 2023, is at least $23 billion over-budget, will almost triple the existing Trans Mountain Pipeline's capacity for transmitting Alberta bitumen starting in 2024. Notley continued boasting of her pipeline-building prowess as the 2023 election approached. "Let's come together to solve our greatest challenges and ensure everyone succeeds," she tweeted in December 2022. "That's how we got TMX built. United, we can do great things." Berman confessed that at the end of the day her critics in the environmentalist movement were correct when they said there was no sense working with the oil and gas industry, because those in power would never accept any limitations on their bottom lines. "In a lot of ways, it felt like a waste of four years of my life," she said. "We are living in a climate emergency. I don't have time for that."

Foreign-Funding Fantasies

In January 2018, Vivian Krause posted an executive summary of a new "report" on her blog, Fair Questions, titled "The Tar Sands Campaign Against the Overseas Export of Canadian Oil: Activism or Economic Sabotage?" This document expanded upon her earlier 2012 polemic, arguing that the U.S.-based Tides Foundation, under the umbrella of "Tar Sands Campaign," was funding environmentalist activism in Canada, including groups such as the Great Bear Rainforest Initiative, Environmental Defence Canada, Greenpeace Canada, the Pembina Institute, and Ecojustice, among many others. "While the information herein is believed to be accurate and reliable," Krause wrote in a disclaimer at the beginning of the post, "it is not guaranteed to be so," urging readers to "exercise due diligence to ensure the accuracy and currency of all information."[13] Clearly, this wasn't a serious scholarly exercise.

She wrote that while the "strategy of the [Tar Sands Campaign's] U.S. funders was not entirely clear" when she began researching the topic in 2010, "now it is." Krause insisted that the Tides Foundation and its well-endowed U.S. backers were pulling the strings behind the various actors in Canadian environmentalist groups via the Tar Sands Campaign. She accused them of "demarketing" Alberta oil "by instilling fear, uncertainty and doubt, not only in the minds of consumers, the broader public, policy makers and investors but also most insidiously, within the mind of industry itself."[14] Some of the nefarious strategies to hamstring fossil-fuel development she included were participating in fossil-fuel projects' regulatory review, generating negative press attention, and supporting legal actions initiated by First Nations. Krause threw around large dollar amounts in the millions and hundreds of thousands, and the names of wealthy backers, like the Rockefellers and the Hewletts, conveniently leaving out what percentage of these organizations' budgets were foreign-funded, while failing to express even the slightest curiosity about foreign funding of industry lobbying efforts. She concluded by calling the tar sands the "whipping boy, the punching bag" of environmentalists,[15] a line Kenney explicitly echoed in December 2019.

For some reason, the CBC's *Calgary Eyeopener* conducted a softball interview with Krause in November 2018, reminiscent of Ezra Levant's gushing media coverage in 2010, in which she was able to articulate her theories with little pushback. The program described Krause as a "researcher" "investigating" the foreign funding sources of the anti-oil sands movement. Krause claimed to care about the environment as much as anyone, but that anti-tar sands activists weren't helping the cause. Echoing Levant nearly verbatim, she said shifting away from fossil fuels "just means the oil gets produced by other countries instead of Canada." Almost three weeks after the segment ran, a revealing clarification note was affixed to the online transcript: "A previous version of this story did not make clear how Vivian Krause earns her income and that her views are controversial to some."[16] Indeed, her views might be "controversial to some," but a more pertinent question was whether they painted an accurate picture. And the answer to that question was a resounding no.

Energy journalist Markham Hislop explained in a May 2019 deep dive how Krause's narrative tapped into a sense of aggrievance among junior and intermediate oil producers who were most hard hit by the 2014 downturn in the patch. "Albertans are mad as hell," he wrote. "They understand that oil and gas busts are unavoidable, but they firmly believe that booms are a birthright and that they have been cheated out of the latest one." He pointed out that American donations to the Tar Sands Campaign were by no means its main drivers. With 10 to 20 percent of Canadian environmental NGOs' budgets receiving American funding, depending on their size, this funding was relatively minimal. Most of the funding for these groups is Canadian. Krause's narrative, Hislop added, ignored that these campaigns were led by Canadians and First Nations "who are almost absent from her narrative" and that, in any event, the Tar Sands Campaign had been largely dormant since the NDP Climate Leadership Plan.

Later that year, at *Canada's National Observer*, journalist Sandy Garossino wrote what was likely the most well-known takedown of Krause's theories, although she attributed these views to Kenney.[17] Likening the foreign-funding theory to a "house of sand, where every pillar crumbles to the touch," Garossino argued that the purpose of these claims was to "discredit, silence and intimidate environmental dissent, and ultimately to choke off resources to activist groups."[18] After consulting charitable grant data, publicly accessible tax returns, and financial statements from 2009 to 2019, Garossino found that "every core tenet of Kenney's conspiracy theory is flatly and demonstrably false."

In the decade examined, U.S.-based foundations provided $4.9 billion to climate charities worldwide — of those funds, $2.9 billion went to American causes, $2 billion went to groups in the European Union, India, and China, and just $51 million went to Canadian groups, of which $40 million were involved in the Tar Sands Campaign, compared with $1.97 billion in charitable grants Canadian groups received across all sectors. Given the scale of Canada's oil production, most of which comes from the massive reserves in the tar sands, "it's actually quite remarkable how little international climate funding we attract," Garossino observed. While the Tar Sands Campaign received $40 million in foreign funding, 43 percent of the Canadian oil and gas industry was foreign-owned, which in 2017 totalled $180 billion, in addition to billions more in dividends paid to foreign owners and investors. Simply by looking at the data Krause cited, as well as the data omitted, Garossino thoroughly debunked Krause's theory without even naming her.

Despite its sloppiness, Kenney continued to use Krause's work to vilify environmentalists in the runup to the 2019 election, but he wasn't alone. Days before Albertans headed to the polls, NDP leader Rachel Notley told *Edmonton Journal* columnist David Staples that she, too, believed there was a foreign conspiracy against the tar sands. "Vivian Krause and people like her have done a good job of really laying bare the details of this and really showing us the degree to which this had been going on and building over time."[19] The lies embedded deeper into the political discourse and informed attacks on Kenney's next personal target.

Fire Ed Whittingham

One person early to debunk Kenney's "ethical oil" talking points was Ed Whittingham. "It's a rhetorical device; it's [a] bait and switch," the then director of the Pembina Institute said when Ezra Levant's ideas gained currency with the Harper government. "It's designed to make us forget about the negative environmental impacts we have in Canada because you are comparing to a completely lower standard in other countries."[20] Like Berman, the NDP government brought Ed Whittingham on board to find common ground with industry. The attacks on his ultimately brief appointment to the board of the Alberta Energy Regulator (AER) began almost immediately in February 2019 with a video from Levant's *Rebel Media*, entitled "NDP Appoint One Last Anti-Oil Activist to Alberta Energy Regulator." From *Rebel*, this framing made its way into Krause's blog, and from there it entered the mainstream. "The NDP learned nothing from the Tzeporah Berman appointment in 2016," Jason Nixon, one of Kenney's most loyal acolytes, who became the UCP's inaugural environment minister, tweeted on March 5, linking to a video of himself complaining about Whittingham's opposition to the ill-fated Keystone XL and Energy East pipelines.

That same day, *Calgary Herald* columnist and UCP member Licia Corbella published a piece headlined "NDP Government Appoints Anti-oil Activist to the Alberta Energy Regulator," writing "Whittingham's appointment is Tzeporah Berman 2.0 — only worse." She didn't explain how Whittingham's appointment, whose approach to the oil and gas industry was far more conciliatory than Berman's, was worse. Corbella complained that when Notley announced the Climate Leadership Plan, "Whittingham was standing by her side at the podium," failing to acknowledge the oil and gas executives who stood alongside Notley and Whittingham, since that didn't fit her narrative. The smears spread like wildfire. *Red Deer News Now*, owned by billionaire Jim Pattison, affixed a bizarre headline to a May 6 Canadian Press article that referred to Whittingham as an "anti-oil activist" (without the quotation marks).

Released a month later, the 2019 UCP platform included, alongside promises to establish a war room and foreign-funding inquiry, another extraordinary pledge: "Fire Ed Whittingham from his position at the Alberta Energy Regulator." Whittingham, whom I interviewed from his home in the mountain town of Canmore, less than an hour's drive west of Calgary, said he found it peculiar to see himself named in a political platform, "and moreover, not just named, but told his public execution would be imminent if the party won."

Whittingham is a very middle-of-the-road kind of guy. In a May 2019 interview with the *Narwhal*, Michael Crothers, the president and national chair of Shell Canada, who worked with Whittingham from 2016 to 2018, praised his "balanced voice" and spirit of "dialogue and collaboration." The two co-authored a November 2016 *Globe and Mail* op-ed, in which they expressed support for carbon pricing, using its revenues to subsidize investments in clean technology, and capping oil sands emissions "as an expression of confidence in the energy industry's continued ability to innovate to reduce CO_2 emissions." Still, Whittingham acknowledged that his AER appointment was "manna from heaven" for Kenney, as it gave the UCP leader a convenient target for his anti-environmentalist campaign so close to the election in April, "not [for] my actual record, but the person that they made me out to be."

Whittingham likened his response to the attacks to a scene in D.A. Pennebaker's 1967 Bob Dylan documentary *Don't Look Back* where Dylan reads a newspaper article about himself. After taking a big puff on his cigarette, Dylan says, "Thank God, I'm not me." Unlike Berman, whom he says he respects greatly, Whittingham had no reservations about working with industry. While the demonization campaign against him was irritating, he didn't receive the same amount of abuse as Berman, or then environment minister Shannon Phillips, who was inappropriately surveilled by several Lethbridge police officers in 2017 and 2018, some of whom objected to her government's phaseout of off-highway vehicle (OHV) use on specific trails in Castle Provincial Park outside Lethbridge. Whittingham correctly attributed the disparity in treatment to misogyny.

On April 29, the day before Kenney was sworn in as premier, Whittingham announced his resignation from the AER post, citing the coordinated "smear campaign" against him. Kenney responded with a tweet: "It was gracious of Ed Whittingham to resign a day before we could fire him." I asked Whittingham why he quit, rather than force Kenney to fire him. "I'm not going to allow myself to be publicly frog-marched to the gallows and then let them fire me, like out of principle," he replied. "I don't want to work for your government. I have major concerns. You've treated me this way, so yeah, I'm going to exit on my own terms."

Kenney Goes to War

Offering a sharp contrast to the misguided efforts of consensus-building on display when the NDP announced its Climate Leadership Plan in 2016, when Kenney announced his energy war room in June 2019, he was onstage with, among others, Vivian Krause and the founder of the pro-industry Oil Sands Strong advertising outfit, Robbie Picard, who carried a photo of Tzeporah Berman with her face crossed out. Kenney simply couldn't let Berman go, resulting in another deluge of death threats sent her way. *CBC News* didn't mention this disturbing visual in its story on the announcement, merely indicating that Kenney "reiterated criticism" of her and referred to "foreign-funded radicals." Kenney indicated that the war room's $30 million annual budget would be partially funded by a tax on large emitters, meaning this tax would be partially returned to the industry in the form of free advertising, but otherwise that conference was scant on details.

Energy Minister Sonya Savage, previously employed by Enbridge and the Canadian Energy Pipeline Association, previewed what was to come when she wrote letters to *Politico* and *National Geographic* to complain about unfair coverage. For the *National Geographic* piece, headlined "This Is the World's Most Destructive Oil Operation — And It's Growing," Savage noted a few relatively minor factual errors, which had already been corrected, calling the article "unacceptable." The letter to *Politico* lectured the editors about how the United States would need Canadian oil for years to come. "It was more [of a sales] pitch than anything resembling a correction," noted *CBC News* reporter Drew Anderson in a June 2019 story. The purpose of her complaints to media outlets was to put journalists on notice that if they wrote something the Kenney government disliked, the government would use its power to publicly shame them.

Kenney set a similar tone in September after Amnesty International expressed concern about the potential impact of his public vilification campaign on environmentalists' freedom of expression. In an open letter to the human-rights organization, faithfully published in full in the *National Post*, Kenney, oozing equal parts sarcasm and smarm, wrote: "I understand it must be hard for you. When you look around the world and see the rise of authoritarian governments, civil war, human trafficking, genocide, and other gross violations of human rights, it must be a tall order to find *something, anything* to denounce here in our gelid but placid Dominion [emphasis in original]." Kenney listed various Amnesty reports into human-rights abuses in other oil-producing nations. The message appeared to be that while other countries jailed dissidents, we merely targeted them for publicly funded vilification and harassment while applauding our commitment to human rights. As a historical artifact, Kenney's letter revealed the author's Manichean world view that you either supported *our* oil and gas or *theirs*.

The same day he penned his letter to Amnesty, Kenney told a room of oil and gas executives in Fort McMurray that Russia jailed Greenpeace activists who protested an offshore oil rig, sending them to Siberia for six months "and funnily enough they've never been back." He further said: "I'm not recommending that for Canada, but it's instructive." The latter point of his story was, in fact, false; Russia did jail activists in St. Petersburg for three months, but the activists successfully sued the government afterward for illegally boarding their ship.[21] But the exaggeration, and the description of it as "instructive," demonstrated Kenney's deep-seated authoritarian impulses.

In December, Kenney officially launched the war room, innocuously named the Canadian Energy Centre (CEC). At the announcement, Kenney vowed the war room would operate with "respect, civility and professionalism" before calling environmentalists liars in his next breath. He couldn't help himself. Tapped to lead the CEC was Tom Olsen, frontman of alt-country band Tom Olsen and the Wreckage, a former *Calgary Herald* editor, and failed UCP candidate in the 2019 election. Its staff included former *Herald* city hall reporter Grady Semmens; former *Herald* reporter Shawn Logan; former *Financial Post* columnist Claudia Cattaneo; and Fraser Institute alum Mark Milke, author of *The Victim Cult: How the Grievance Culture Hurts Everyone and Wrecks Civilization* and an occasional *National Post* contributor.

So deep were the CEC's ties to Postmedia, owner of the *Calgary Herald*, the *Financial Post*, and the *National Post*, that the company hired former Kenney staffer Nick Koolsbergen to ask how it could get "involved" with the war room.[22] In October 2019, prior to its launch, the CBC reported that the centre was incorporated as a private entity, so despite being largely government-funded, it would be exempt from freedom-of-information inquiries. Savage said the government wanted to run the CEC like a corporation because it would give it "more freedom to be efficient," and though the CEC's board was composed of three Cabinet ministers — Savage, Nixon, and Justice Minister Doug Schweitzer — its designation as a private entity has repeatedly been upheld by the province's privacy commissioner.

As a reporter at the *Medicine Hat News* also tasked with writing columns, the war room was too absurd not to write about. "At best," I concluded in a piece published Saturday, December 14, 2019, "the war room is an expensive joke. At worst, it's a grave threat to our right to dissent." On Monday, my boss and I received an email from Grady Semmens. "Good morning," it began, "I just wanted to reach out to let you know that we will provide a response to clarify many of the comments and inaccuracies in Mr. Appel's column.... I will have you something on Monday afternoon and would appreciate if you could run it as an OpEd [*sic*] as quickly as possible." I was officially the first journalist in Alberta targeted by the war room.

At the spur of the moment, I decided to tweet a screengrab of the email with the caption: "Bring it on, war room." Almost immediately, members of the media raised concerns: Was the government demanding a rebuttal to my piece or kindly expressing disagreement? Some compared it to Premier William Aberhart's 1937 Accurate News and Information Act, which required newspapers to run government rebuttals to content officials disliked. *Calgary Herald* columnist Don Braid, normally sympathetic to the CEC's aims, called me a "tough young reporter-columnist in the Hat." My employer, much to my chagrin, decided to run an incredibly boring response from Olsen, which made no reference to any inaccuracies in my piece. As a journalist, you never want to become the story. Fortunately for me, my run-in with the war room was quickly overshadowed by other ineptitudes from the CEC.

James Keller at the *Globe and Mail* revealed that the war room's public-relations team was impersonating journalists when reaching out to sources for propaganda purposes. Some businesses featured on the CEC website appreciated free advertising from the Alberta government, but Vancouver-based chef Donald Gyurkovits, declaring his opposition to pipelines, was infuriated that he was being used by a government propaganda service promoting the oil and gas industry. Canadian Association of Journalism president Karyn Pugliese said the CEC was "welcome to spin, but when they masquerade that as journalism, it's completely dishonest."[23] Compounding the series of embarrassments, Olsen was forced to apologize in February 2020 for a bizarre 20-tweet tirade, in which the CEC account accused the

New York Times of anti-Semitism, bias, and not being the "most dependable source" for a completely innocuous article on international investors' lack of confidence in the tar sands.

Easily the most absurd campaign occurred in March 2021 when the CEC chose to go to war with Netflix over a children's film about Bigfoot. The CEC accused Netflix of "brainwashing our kids with anti-oil and gas propaganda,"[24] urging supporters to send a form letter to the streaming service, because *Bigfoot Family* portrayed an oil and gas company kidnapping Bigfoot when he catches wind of their plot to blow up an Alaska nature reserve to access oil. Olsen called the campaign, which generated 1,200 emails, 60 percent from outside Canada, an example of the "important work" the CEC was engaged in. Kenney agreed, making international headlines by calling the children's film "vicious" and defamatory.[25] This incident was peak war room, which, given its partial funding from a tax on large emitters, was itself foreign-funded.

One positive outcome of the war room, beyond complete embarrassment, was a major funding boost for the local activist outfit Climate Justice Edmonton (CJE), which immediately after Kenney's election began fundraising for "A War Room to Beat Kenney's War Room" and raised $20,000 from an initial goal of $3,000, which would be used to fund a province-wide canvassing campaign about the connections between social and environmental justice.[26]

CJE co-founder Emma Jackson noted the apparent contradiction between the government spending millions of dollars on a glorified social media campaign and the fiscal conservatism Kenney otherwise espoused.[27] Jettisoning free-market principles when they risked disrupting the established order is textbook Kenneyism. Nowhere was this more apparent than in his approach to the oil and gas industry, especially his decision to blow $1.3 billion in public funds on the Keystone XL Pipeline, which never got built. His publicly funded demonization campaign against anyone who stood in the way of perpetual tar sands extraction added yet another layer to this approach, of which the war room was just one component.

The Grand Inquisitor

While the war room provided many laughs, the inquiry into environmental activism, for all its fumbles, revealed the overall campaign against environmentalists was serious business. Forensic accountant Steve Allan was hired as inquiry commissioner in July 2019. Kenney said Allan's goal was to investigate the "shadowy funding" of Canadian environmentalist groups who were engaged in a "premeditated, internationally planned and financed operation to put Alberta energy out of business," which he speculated could be a Russian plot.[28] Schweitzer said the inquiry would determine if any of these actors engaged in "illegal activity" and had the power to compel testimony from witnesses. A final report was supposed to be submitted by July 2, 2020.

The official terms of the inquiry shifted repeatedly. On June 25, the government adjusted expectations by tweaking its mandate slightly from looking "into the role of foreign funding in anti-Alberta energy campaigns" to looking "into the role of foreign funding, *if any* [emphasis mine]." While the definition of "anti-Albertan" in the government's original terms of inquiry referred definitively to the "dissemination of misleading or false information," the government tweaked this verbiage in August to say it "*may include* the dissemination of false or misleading information."[29] The following month, Allan said fact-checking environmentalists' claims was too much of a "colossal undertaking" for him to complete, so that would remain beyond the scope of the report.[30]

On November 14, CBC investigative reporters Charles Rusnell and Jennie Russell revealed that Allan had handed a $905,000 single-source contract to Dentons — the law firm where Schweitzer served as a partner before getting elected to the Legislative Assembly and Allan's son, Toby, was a partner — to provide legal advice to the inquiry. The next day, Rusnell and Russell reported that Allan had donated $1,000 to Schweitzer's failed 2017 UCP leadership campaign, in addition to $750 to the UCP in 2018, and that Allan would be paid a handsome $290,000 for his work on the inquiry. Schweitzer called it "frankly ridiculous to suggest that donating one-fourth of the maximum annual allowable amount over two years ago somehow secures an appointment."

The reporting duo revealed on November 19 that not only had Allan given Schweitzer's campaign money, but he also actively campaigned on his behalf, co-hosting a Schweitzer fundraiser in June 2018. Allan also wrote an email to colleagues in April 2019, urging them to vote for Schweitzer, because "if the UCP wins, there is an excellent chance Doug will be in Cabinet." Despite these revelations, Ethics Commissioner Marguerite Trussler ruled in July 2020 that there was no conflict of interest in Schweitzer awarding Allan the role because the two men "were not friends and their relationship was not close."

Allan's July 2020 deadline also proved incredibly flexible, extended to October 30 and provided a $1 million top-up from the war room's budget a week before the original due date. Two days before the second deadline, the government announced the inquiry would receive another extension until January 31, 2021, with no new funds. This was then pushed back to May 31 and again to July 30. "People [who] dig into these issues often need more time," Kenney said after the announcement of a fourth extension. "That's fine. We've said that the important thing is that they come up with a useful report that can help to govern our future actions by Alberta's government in defending the women and men who work in our energy industry."[31]

Meanwhile, commission participants were encouraged to brush up on their knowledge of climate change with denialist tracts such as *False Alarm: How Climate Change Costs Us Trillions, Hurts the Poor, and Fails to Fix the Climate* and *Apocalypse Never: Why Environmental Alarmism Hurts Us All.* The inquiry also commissioned its own reports, including $28,000 to British author Tammy Nemeth for a bizarre, conspiratorial tract alleging that an international Marxist conspiracy had infiltrated the media, banks, NGOs, governments, the United Nations, and large corporations with the aim of bringing about the destruction of Western civilization, starting with the tar sands.

The 657-page inquiry report was finally submitted for its July 2021 deadline. "No individual or organization in my view," Allan noted in the report, officially released in October, "has done anything illegal. Indeed, they have exercised their rights of free speech."[32] Nor did he argue that participating "in an anti-Alberta energy campaign is in any way improper or constitutes conduct that should be in any way impugned," acknowledging that environmentalists were "driven by an honest concern about the threats of climate change." The report also found that the CEC did more harm than good to the cause of boosting the oil and gas industry, arguing that the "reputation of this entity has been damaged beyond repair."[33]

Vivian Krause was apoplectic, accusing Allan in an October 30 *Calgary Herald* column of "giving environmentalists exactly what they wanted," echoing the Dude in *The Big Lebowski* ("That's just like your opinion, man") by complaining that the report was Allan's "personal opinion, not a professional legal analysis." She expressed disappointment that the UCP failed to use the full weight of the law against environmentalist groups. But, in the two years of the Allan inquiry, the damage was already done to environmentalists' reputations. "Falsehood flies, and the truth comes limping after it," Anglo-Irish author Jonathan Swift wrote in 1710, "so that when men come to be undeceived, it is too late, the jest is over, and the tale has had its effect."[34]

Sandy Garossino, who so thoroughly debunked the inquiry's premise before it even blew past its first due date, wrote after reading a leak of the entire draft report:

> In the years to come, history will forget Steve Allan and Jason Kenney.
>
> Tomorrow's heroes will be those who never stopped sounding the alarm, no matter the cost. The ones who lie awake at night, staring at the ceiling and wondering how bad this could get, if they are in danger and if they should be putting their kids through this ugliness.
>
> And who then get up in the morning, put the coffee on and somewhere find the courage to keep going.
>
> Clear their names, Jason Kenney.
>
> Take it all back.

Suffice to say, Kenney didn't do that.

For this reason, five environmentalist NGOs targeted by the inquiry — Environmental Defence, West Coast Environmental Law, STAND.earth,

Dogwood, and the Wilderness Committee — filed papers to sue Kenney and the Alberta government for defamation in February 2022, with their statement of claim calling his allegations "malicious, high-handed, arrogant, and reckless." The litigants asked for $15,000 each in actual damages and $500,000 in punitive damages from Kenney "to dissuade him and other Canadian public officials from using the power of their office to bully their critics."[35] As of this writing, that litigation is ongoing.

Removing Climate from the Agenda

While Kenney dedicated so much time and effort into attacking environmentalists, the climate crisis continued unabated. A report commissioned by former NDP environment minister Shannon Phillips into the impact of climate change on Alberta was shelved by the Kenney government for six months before quietly being uploaded onto the government's website in February 2020. Co-authored by Canadian climate scientist Katharine Hayhoe and Texas Tech University postdoctoral research fellow Anne Stoner, it found a warming climate "will profoundly impact Alberta's natural environment, and have the potential to affect the province's agriculture, infrastructure, and natural resources, as well as the health and welfare of its inhabitants." If climate action is delayed, Hayhoe told *Global News*, underscoring the report's urgency, "it's going to be too late to make the choice. Just like if we are being loaded onto the ambulance, being taken to the hospital for a heart attack, it's too late to say, 'oh, I'll join a gym and I'll eat healthy.' We have to make those decisions earlier in the same way."[36]

Alberta is a petrostate, with oil and gas embedded deeply into the province's fabric, and it didn't become that way by letting the free market do its work. It got that way by putting the thumb of the state on the scale in favour of the oil and gas industry, conflating the collective interests of Albertans with companies that seek to suck the earth dry and rob the population blind until nothing remains. Kenney was by no means the first politician to help facilitate this tragic scenario, but his anti-environmentalist crusade added a unique moral zeal and nastiness to the cause, tarring the industry's opponents at the very time when mining and drilling operations needed to be wound down. It wasn't enough to simply dismiss environmentalists as alarmists; they needed to have a sinister ulterior motive attributed to them. Kenney's obsession with defending the industry at all costs had everything to do with an ideology that venerates tradition as much as it does untrammelled capitalism. Oil and gas have historically been at the forefront of Alberta's economy, enriching some Albertans in the process. Any change to this established order is naturally frightening, particularly for those whose livelihoods depend on the industry's success. Kenney exploited this sense of insecurity, channelling collective anxieties toward not the oil and gas companies themselves but anyone who stood in the way of increased oil and gas production, whom he regarded as an enemy to be vanquished.

This anti-environmentalist crusade ultimately couldn't be confined just to the environmentalist movement. In February 2018, famed environmentalist and former CBC broadcaster David Suzuki was scheduled to speak at the Alberta Teachers' Association convention; in April, he was invited to receive an honorary degree from his University of Alberta alma mater; in September, Tzeporah Berman was invited to address teachers. Kenney found a trifecta of his favourite targets — environmentalists, unions, and public education. "No wonder people are concerned about the curriculum review when the teacher union's social studies wing regards Tzeporah Berman as an objective source," he told sympathetic *Calgary Sun* columnist Rick Bell. Promising to "ensure balance and objectivity in our education system, instead of ideology and dogma," Kenney would do precisely the opposite.

8

EDUCATION FOR THE FEW

ON MAY 7, 2018, ABOUT A year from the provincial election, Jason Kenney spoke at the inaugural UCP convention about the NDP's "secret curriculum changes," which his team promptly uploaded as a Facebook video — his favoured means of communicating with voters in the leadup to the election. This notion that the NDP was allegedly hiding something nefarious from parents and updating the province's badly outdated K–12 curriculum, parts of which hadn't been updated since the 1980s, to turn children into socialist foot soldiers was a ubiquitous refrain from Kenney as the 2019 election approached.

In his speech, Kenney said he feared the "deepest damage" the NDP would do if re-elected wasn't their economic policy, which he expressed confidence he could roll back, but their changes to the province's education system. Kenney pivoted immediately to attacking Education Minister David Eggen, a former teacher, for his alleged support of boycotting Israel to protest its treatment of the Palestinians — one of Kenney's favourite lines of attack from his time in Ottawa. More importantly, for our purpose, he called Eggen a "long-time opponent of Alberta's successful tradition of school choice."

"School choice" refers to Alberta's policy of removing funds from the public school system to place them in the coffers of unaccountable private actors in the form of so-called charter schools, which are intended to provide special programming not offered in the perpetually underfunded public system. Alberta also funds up to 70 percent of tuition for full-blown private schools. Charter schools, unlike public, separate (Catholic), and francophone schools, don't have publicly elected boards and are able to reject students. For the purposes of this chapter, I'll refer to public, separate, and francophone schools as "public" to distinguish them from private and charter schools. Although separate schools are a form of religious educational choice that receives public funds and has been normalized in several provinces, including Ontario and Alberta, a critique of that system is beyond the scope of my analysis.

Alberta is the only province with charter schools, a status quo that Eggen and the NDP largely maintained. While Eggen rejected the applications for two Calgary charter schools in February 2016, public education advocates have long asked the government to phase out private and charter school subsidies altogether and dedicate those funds toward strengthening the public education system. The NDP could have gradually whittled away at the percentage of private school tuition publicly funded, but it didn't.

However, Kenney, who has never attended a public school, isn't one to let a good strawman go to waste. Calling Eggen a "true believer" in the public school system, as if that were an insult, he accused the NDP of pushing "social engineering and more failed teaching fads" into the school system. "Let me be clear," Kenney said, "if the NDP decides to smuggle more of their politics into the classroom through their curriculum, we will put that curriculum through the shredder and go right back to the drawing board … and we will do this in an open and transparent way."

Kenney made good on his promise to shred the NDP's curriculum, but there was just one problem — it wasn't the NDP's curriculum. The process of rewriting Alberta's curriculum began under the watch of the PCs, the very party Kenney led before merging it with the Wildrose to create the UCP. It began in 2008, with Premier Ed Stelmach instructing Education Minister Dave Hancock to establish a long-term and long-needed update to the provincial curriculum. Hancock's office issued a 2010 report, dubbed *Inspiring Education*, which outlined a vision of education for the year 2030. The NDP merely attempted to bring the work that began under Stelmach to fruition, which was slated to be in classrooms by 2022. It was accompanied by online surveys and in-person information sessions to incorporate parental feedback. That work was ultimately for nothing. The UCP's replacement curriculum did precisely what Kenney accused the NDP of doing — smuggling politics into the curriculum through an opaque process. This chapter will focus specifically on the social studies component of the curriculum, since this was where the curriculum's alleged politicization under the NDP, and actual politicization under the UCP, occurred.

Kenney appointed Adriana LaGrange, a former Red Deer Catholic Regional Schools trustee and board chair who was previously the president of Red Deer Pro-Life, as education minister. Toward the end of LaGrange's tenure as a trustee, which lasted from 2007 to 2018, Red Deer Pro-Life showed students at École Secondaire Notre Dame a video comparing abortion to the Holocaust. In 2018 and 2019, multiple schools from that very board bussed students to the anti-choice March for Life in Edmonton. "I do encourage young people to get involved in political debates and activities," Kenney said when asked about the bussing at a May 2019 news conference.

While Kenney and LaGrange fiddled with the curriculum to make it more amenable to their world view, they expanded the reach of charter schools and cut funding to the public system. They blurred the distinction between private and public education systems, which was already murky in Alberta, taking steps toward fully marketized education, in which parents were regarded as consumers and children's education was the product. The curriculum chaos they instituted served to sow confusion in the public system, ultimately leaving individual teachers on their own to figure out how to teach each subject. With the expansion of private education, the government would have to worry less about dealing with the pesky Alberta Teachers' Association (ATA), which doubles as a professional association and teachers' union.

This approach to K–12 education is fully consistent with what we know about Kenney's ideology. He used the power of the state to gradually transfer resources from public to private actors, and did so at the service of a world view that regarded a strong public education system as an inhibition toward promoting traditional values. He manufactured a common sense that Alberta's values were under attack by public educators. Under the umbrella of school choice, it would be increasingly easy for those who wanted their children to escape the chaos of the public system to send them to a private school, segregating their children from the unwashed masses, whether for religious, ideological, or socioeconomic reasons.

Manufactured Curriculum Dissent

In the summer of 2018, a parent who bought into Kenney's pitch that the new curriculum was riddled with left-wing ideology took incomplete, decontextualized draft curriculum documents from an engagement session and leaked them to *Edmonton Journal* columnist and Kenney loyalist David Staples. The ministry scrambled and released the full draft version of the K–4 curriculum, which focused on six subject areas — arts, mathematics, social studies, science, French, wellness — months ahead of schedule to allay concerns they were being developed in secret. In his July 18 column, headlined "In New Social Studies Curriculum, There's No Such Things as Albertans," Staples complained that the draft curriculum, as leaked to him, contained no references to Alberta or Canada. His *Journal* reporter colleague, Janet French, whose work on education issues in Alberta was indispensable, subtly pointed out in a story the next day, after the documents were released publicly, that Staples's claim was patently false. As one example, the draft asked Grade 4 students to identify "how the actions of individuals and groups prior to 1905 in what is now Alberta shaped their communities."

Staples wrote that while the social studies curriculum contained six references to "settlers," it included more than 30 references to First Nations, Inuit, and Métis peoples, and a dozen references to francophones. Acknowledging a need to "delve deeply into the often appalling treatment of Indigenous people," Staples claimed "this new and polarizing curriculum goes far beyond, essentially creating two categories of Albertans: settlers and their victims." He was also offended by the presence of "buzzwords of the social justice movement," such as "equity, fairness, giving, sharing, inclusion and diversity." Staples complained: "Self-reliance and fortitude aren't mentioned, let alone the virtues of free speech or healthy competition." He argued the curriculum would create "intolerant zealots weaponized by social justice ideals."

Kenney pounced on this column from his media toady, releasing a Facebook video the same day praising Staples for getting a "bootleg copy of the draft NDP K–12 curriculum" when, in fact, it was only part of the draft K–4 curriculum. Kenney, repeating all the ubiquitous right-wing buzzwords, contended the documents were a smoking gun and that the NDP had smuggled "intersectionality" and "critical race theory" into the curriculum, which Kenney defined as "an obsessive focus with people's racial or ethnic origins and ... historical injustices, as opposed to an actual objective and balanced historical narrative about how our society came to be." He bemoaned the fact that the leaked portion of the K–4 curriculum didn't include anything about Canada's "Westminster parliamentary institutions" and their "European roots," financial literacy, or military history. Kenney ended the video by reiterating his call to scrap the curriculum and write one that was more "balanced."

University of Alberta education professor Carla Peck, one of the country's foremost experts in curriculum, worked with Alberta Education under the NDP to shape the curriculum update first initiated by the PCs. She's worked as a consultant on curricula in New Brunswick, Manitoba, and the Northwest Territories, in addition to Alberta. While Peck's academic duties precluded her from helping write the curriculum update, she did sign up as a reviewer for the social studies portion of the curriculum, which is her specific field of expertise.

The PC/NDP curriculum was imperfect, Peck noted, but it was at least drafted in a way that could be improved. The curriculum was slated to be done in three stages: K–4, scheduled to be finished by the end of 2018; 5–8, planned for completion in late 2019; and then high school, to be developed in phases from 2020 to 2022. Peck said she was "not happy at all" with the social studies curriculum, specifically its plan for a "common architecture" across subjects within each phase, which was helpful for elementary school teachers tasked with teaching all subjects to classes but contributed to a "generic approach" to social studies, failing to go into sufficient detail within each specific social studies subject. "They just treated concepts as if they lived outside of history or lived outside of geography, and they didn't honour the disciplines within social studies," Peck recalled.

For all its faults, the PC/NDP curriculum did "focus on big ideas, it did focus on connecting concepts, and there was a logical progression from one grade to the next," she said. "It was still a million times better than what was produced under the UCP. The UCP's was literally a list of facts with no connecting concepts, no big ideas. It was as if somebody just went to an *Encyclopaedia Britannica* from the 1950s and just copied it and put it into another document."

With the UCP in power, Minister LaGrange began the process of dismantling the curriculum progress made under previous governments. And it wasn't just the curriculum that would be put through the shredder. On August 17, 2019, LaGrange announced the province was scrapping a memorandum of understanding that the 50,000-member ATA signed with the NDP government in 2016, which promised teachers equal partnership in curriculum development. The government informed the ATA of the news late Friday afternoon — the day before LaGrange announced it publicly on Twitter.

LaGrange tweeted the agreement was "not one I would have signed, it is too restrictive," arguing the union was merely "one of many partners" who needed to be consulted, as if the input of the people tasked with teaching the curriculum were as good as anyone's. Perhaps Cypress–Medicine Hat MLA Drew Barnes revealed more than intended about the government's motivations when he told me for an August 22, 2019, *Medicine Hat News* story that "parents and families need to be sure that as the main *customer* of education, their voice is heard [emphasis mine]." He added: "Let's grow the pie. Let's make it so more interested and informed voices with education are heard." The tearing up of their agreement, for which the teachers were given a month's notice, would set the tone for relations between the UCP government and the ATA, which was fully consistent with Kenney's anti-labour animus.

Less than a week after scrapping the memorandum of understanding with the ATA, on August 22 the minister announced a 12-person curriculum advisory panel, which included zero active K–12 teachers but did include CEOs, administrators of colleges and technical institutes, and three university professors, only one of whom had expertise in curriculum. It was chaired by Angus McBeath, a former Edmonton Public School Board (EPSB) superintendent. McBeath's son, William, is a Conservative stalwart. He worked for the federal Conservatives from 2004 to 2010, then the Wildrose until 2014, before landing a gig with the Manning Centre think tank, named after Reform Party founder Preston Manning (now known as the Canada Strong and Free Network). Since 2018, he's been the chief operating officer of the far-right news site True North. Angus McBeath is, of course, not his son, but William's career path is indicative of his father's partisan political connections.

The panel delivered its recommendations to the government in December. They included the use of standardized testing to evaluate students' progress from Grades 1 to 5 and "to bring the needs of Alberta's employers into the curriculum-development process," including an emphasis on "resource development." There were also constructive, albeit vague, recommendations to continue incorporating Indigenous perspectives into the curriculum, ensure the final product "reflects the diversity of Alberta's students," and that "knowledge outcomes in curriculum are clear in order to foster student reasoning in each discipline," as well as for classrooms to "have access to a broad range of learning resources, representing a range of mediums."

At a January 29, 2020, press conference announcing the panel's findings, LaGrange said that while "the teacher has control over his or her classroom, and they bring in the resource or speakers or information that they would like to share," they must teach issues in an "unbiased" fashion. "Do we believe there's climate change? Absolutely. Climate change is real. But we do want that presented to our children in a balanced way," she said. When *National Post* reporter Tyler Dawson asked her what she meant by a "balanced" approach to climate change, LaGrange said there were instances brought to her "by parents and others of extremist views that have been brought into the classroom," citing a "particular document" telling students "that they are the final generation to deal with climate change."

While individual teachers were free to teach as they saw fit, they had to do so in a manner that was consistent with the government's ideology that climate change wasn't of particular urgency. The UCP's crusade against the climate movement played a role in its assault on public education, with state power used to marginalize perspectives that called into question the logic of endless economic growth. To pull this off, you had to start when kids were young and beginning to question the world around them, making K–12 education an ideal target.

Jason Schilling, a teacher from the Palliser School Division surrounding Lethbridge, was elected president of the ATA in July 2019, right around the time the UCP government announced it would halt the field-testing of the PC/NDP curriculum. He said the government scrapping its memorandum with the ATA and then appointing an ideologically driven panel to guide the curriculum writing process was an example of the UCP engaging in the very secretive curriculum rewrite it accused the NDP of doing. "We saw it sort of become kind of a closed-door development of curriculum with this panel, none of whom were active teachers in the field at the time," Schilling told me. "And it created the mess of a curriculum that we have now."

Based on the panel's recommendations, LaGrange drafted a new ministerial order, which said the purpose of K–12 education was to "promote the *acquisition* of skills and the pursuit of knowledge with wisdom, while valuing equality of opportunity, parental responsibility, personal responsibility and excellence, and respect for difference and the inherent dignity of each individual." Students would "*inherit* a rich, interconnected knowledge base and be practiced in free, lively, and respectful dialogue with varied viewpoints [emphases mine]." The use of the words *acquisition* and *inherit* was noteworthy because they implied a transactional, top-down approach in which students had knowledge drilled into their heads by their teacher, who was regarded as the ultimate disseminator, or gatekeeper, of knowledge. This wasn't an approach conducive toward critical thought, laying the groundwork for the disastrous social studies curriculum that followed.

The day the new order was signed, a rambling, incoherent press conference revealed the calibre of advice LaGrange received from her advisory panel's chair. McBeath said there were "two portals in education that if either falter, kids' education will falter and their *work potential* may falter [emphasis mine]" — literacy and numeracy. Once again, note the emphasis on the student as a future worker, rather than an informed citizen, but McBeath's remarks got weirder and more revealing. Recalling the first conversation he had with LaGrange, McBeath said in a tangent that needs to be read in full to believe:

> You can have a really bright young person graduate from high school and they get a job. And they're fast and they're quick, and they know how to field orders and they wait on customers. But if they steal you blind, are you sure you got a good one? So we want to teach students a certain reverence for honesty, integrity, perseverance, stick-to-it-ness, resilience, respectfulness and other virtues we think it's important to possess.... I don't mean to put down any industry in this country, but some people are nervous when they go to buy a used car. It's possible that they may think they won't hear the whole truth and nothing but the truth about that car and its history. Well, we want every Albertan that we produce through our schools, along with their families ... to be the kind of person you'd want to be selling you a used car, because you can trust them.

The discomfort on LaGrange's face was palpable. "I have never seen anything so embarrassing in terms of curriculum development [or] education policy-making as that one press conference," Carla Peck recalled.

McBeath's bizarre remarks served not only as an apt metaphor for the incoherent K–6 draft social studies curriculum to come but also for Kenney's broader approach to education, in which the masses of children in the public education system were trained to be honest used-car salespeople while the powerful and privileged sent their children to specialized private schools to be moulded in their parents' image. In both cases, the goal was to keep the wheels of the established order churning with increased alacrity.

Chris Champion Returns

The week after the August 6 presser, the ministry announced an eight-person all-male panel of advisers to oversee the curriculum writing process. Noteworthy in his inclusion on that panel was one of Kenney's old hands from Ottawa — Chris Champion, who played an extraordinarily hands-on role in Kenney's review of the citizenship guide at the Department of Citizenship and Immigration. If Kenney was genuinely committed to keeping politics out of the curriculum, he couldn't have picked a worse emissary.

Even more troubling were the views Champion published and espoused in the *Dorchester Review*, a right-wing history journal he founded in 2011. That year, he published an unbylined piece calling an Australian history curriculum "light on facts and heavy with guilt about aboriginals and immigrants." The writer compared the Australian curriculum to the Canadian "preoccupation with victimhood mostly centred on Japanese Canadians and residential school 'survivors.'" Note the scare quotes around "survivors." In response to a request for comment from the CBC, Alberta Education spokesperson Colin Aitchison said the piece wasn't authored by Champion and that the publication offered a wide array of perspectives. He added that while Champion worked for the Conservatives as recently as 2015, he went on to become an "established academic" and Canadian Armed Forces member. From 2013 to 2014, Champion worked as a history lecturer at the University of Ottawa before returning to work for Kenney in 2015 at the Department of Defence.

On August 14, the day after Champion's appointment as a curriculum adviser, University of British Columbia education professor Lindsay Gibson tweeted two photos of an article from the print copy of the *Dorchester Review* from Spring/Summer 2019, written by C.P. Champion, entitled "Alberta's Little History War," in which he applauded Kenney's "finely-calibrated counterattacks" against the PC/NDP curriculum. The article went on to call adding more First Nations perspectives into the curriculum a "fad" and the Kairos blanket exercise, which was intended to teach children about the damaging impacts of colonization on Indigenous peoples, "deplorable agit-prop … which brainwashes children into thinking of themselves as 'settlers' stealing the land." This anti-Indigenous vitriol was written about a year prior to Champion's appointment. He would continue making anti-Indigenous remarks after he was done working for the government, accusing Indigenous people of feeling "entitled to some unique aristocratic victim status" after hundreds of suspected unmarked graves were discovered on the grounds of the former Kamloops residential school in the summer of 2021.[1]

The *Progress Report* later revealed Champion's intimate role in drafting the curriculum, with a bureaucrat referring to fulfilling his "vision" in an email exchange with Champion. "I am sharing with you the most recent working drafts of Culture, Philosophy and Religion K–6. The social studies team built this from your vision and previous feedback. They are looking forward to the additional feedback that you are working on to continue to strengthen these drafts," reads an October 2 email from a bureaucrat to Champion obtained through a freedom-of-information request. Moreover, the drafts themselves were redacted from the request because they were sent to Kenney and his Cabinet for approval, a practice Carla Peck described as "unheard of."[2] For his troubles, Champion was compensated $15,400 for 38 days of work.

In October 2020, a draft of the K–4 fine arts and social studies curriculum proposals was leaked to the CBC.[3] The document's content, which placed a disproportionate emphasis on memorization, clearly had Champion's paws all over it. It said learning about the horrors of residential schools should be delayed until students were "more mature and are less emotionally vulnerable to traumatic material," advising it to be taught as an example of "harsh schooling" in Grade 9.

In Grade 1, students would learn about the "three great" monotheistic religions, which the document said, with a distinctly Christian tinge, "are built on the idea that God revealed himself to humans ('revelation') who have the capacity to discover the truth about Him." At the same time, a section recommending teaching students about sustainability and different ways of using land was crossed out, with someone — likely Champion — writing "sounds like mysticism." They wrote: "One could equally say 'water sustains everything,' or 'the fire of the Sun,' or 'Oxygen,' or 'the Holy Ghost.' All would be true in their way." By Grade 3, students would learn that Indigenous cultures "are often themselves influenced by Christian social teaching." In the same section, the mysterious editor said they removed references to "equity" because it was "probably a politically partisan and charged buzzword." Grade 4 students would learn that most non-white Albertans, identified as being primarily from Japan, South Korea, the Philippines, and China, were Christian.

Professor Keith Barton, a specialist in social studies curriculum and instruction at Indiana University in Bloomington, told the CBC that adopting the proposals would turn Alberta into a "laughingstock," calling its recommendations "utter nonsense." Barton added, "It just showed no familiarity with how children think and learn. And it certainly showed no familiarity with the past 30 or 40 years of research theorizing about what history and social studies education should look like." Dwayne Donald, an education professor at the University of Alberta specializing in Indigenous teaching and curriculum, and a member of the Papaschase Cree Nation, said the document "makes me feel sick," describing it as racist and demeaning.

The official draft, which was for all subjects across K–6, was released in March 2021. According to Peck, its social studies component wasn't much of an improvement. "It had been trimmed down a bit, but the overall tone and orientation of the document was the same — here's lists of facts to be memorized, [with] content that was wildly inappropriate for kids in elementary school, just in terms of the complexity and interest, and what we know about how kids learn," she told me. "That first document in October very heavily influenced the one we saw in March." A good social studies curriculum, Peck said, needs to be oriented around "big questions" that can be examined from multiple angles for the purpose of "developing citizens … who are knowledgeable, who are able to think critically and deeply about the societal questions that we're all swimming in every single day." It was more than just facts anybody could look up on Google.

As a result of the broader curriculum's shortcomings, 56 of 61 school boards in Alberta, representing 95 percent of students, outright refused to pilot any of it throughout 2021,[4] leading the government to concede defeat in December, agreeing to scrap the social studies component and start from scratch while delaying implementation of fine arts, French, and science. The ATA called on the government to ditch the entire curriculum until "an independent, open and full review and rewrite can occur,"[5] unsurprisingly to no avail. The government was further humiliated when the Northwest Territories, which had used Alberta's curriculum for decades, announced it would instead use British Columbia's, which was more recently updated and included emphasis on Indigenous knowledge.

None of the five Alberta school boards that did pilot the curriculum wanted to touch the social studies section. However, seven private schools agreed to pilot the social studies curriculum at various grades from March 29 to September 30, 2021, according to documents obtained by the CBC, demonstrating the relative malleability of private schools compared to schools operating under the oversight of publicly accountable school boards. While the social studies curriculum imbroglio sowed confusion in the K–12 education system, the Kenney government proceeded apace with privatizing education.

A Brief History of Alberta Charter Schools

Alberta's experiment with charter schools dates back to 1994, with then premier Ralph Klein introducing them as part of his broader neoliberal shift in the early 1990s toward market-based solutions toward everything. Klein decided to apply this logic to the education system, as advocated by the American guru of neoliberal economics, University of Chicago economist Milton Friedman, who argued the state ought not to have a "monopoly" on education, questioning the "special treatment of education even in countries that are predominantly free enterprise in organization and philosophy." Friedman concluded that while schools should remain publicly funded, they should be privately operated to encourage competition.[6]

Klein's introduction of charter schools, which was announced amid massive education cuts in January 1994, was somewhat obscured by Klein's move to remove school boards' taxation powers, giving the province full education funding responsibility. Interestingly, these efforts at centralization earned a rebuke from a young Jason Kenney, then at the Canadian Taxpayers Federation, who expressed fear of an "aggrandized provincial bureaucracy in education." Kenney further said: "If anything, I think we need to radically decentralize." However, in characteristic fashion, he applauded Klein's efforts to get off the "debt-servicing treadmill" through deep cuts to public services.[7]

An unsigned editorial in the *Calgary Herald* expressed skepticism of charter schools later that month, warning they could serve as a "Trojan Horse permitting the extensive privatization of the public system." Indeed, that was precisely the point. Echoing Friedman's terminology in an interview with a Medicine Hat radio station, Jim Dinning, Klein's provincial treasurer, said the government's goal was to end the "monopoly" of public schools on education.[8] These schools were depicted explicitly as a way for parents and teachers to seize control of education from school boards and teacher unions.

In its February 1994 budget, the Klein government expressed a desire to establish between 50 and 100 charter schools in the next two years.[9] By November, the government backtracked, with Education Minister Halvar Johnson instituting a cap of 15, among other charter school regulations, such as an inability to turn away students for being members of a protected class, although this restriction proved flexible. Red Deer–based Dr. Joe Freeman, a prominent charter school booster, said it was unrealistic to expect charter schools to accommodate kids with complex needs. "The school has an obligation to take all children, but not into a classroom where they won't *profit* from the instruction [emphasis mine]," he told the *Calgary Herald*.[10] In 1995–96, the first year school year charters were introduced, they represented 0.04 percent of student enrollment in Alberta. By 2019–20, before the UCP introduced reforms making it a whole lot easier to open one, charter school enrollment was 1.34 percent, representing a 335 percent increase.[11] Enrollment percentages alone, however, don't do justice to the disparity between public and private education in Alberta.

Backpack Full of Cash

Barbara Silva, a former high school Spanish and math teacher in the Calgary area, co-founded public education advocacy group Support Our Students (SOS) in 2015 due to the "slow creep to privatization that had been happening in Alberta." Silva, who now lives on Vancouver Island and is no longer formally involved with SOS, said she was motivated by the contrast between conditions in charter and public schools. While charter and public schools

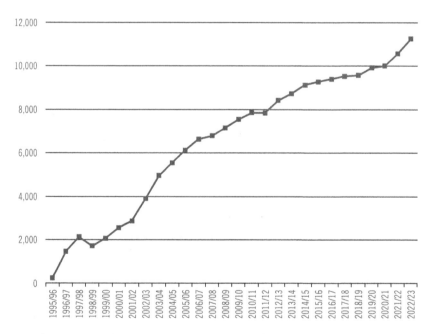

Since their inception for the 1995–96 school year, the number of students enrolled in publicly funded, privately operated charter schools has consistently increased, reaching 10,000 students for the first time in the 2020–21 school year, when the United Conservative Party loosened restrictions on how many could operate.

Source: Alberta School Authority Population/Government of Alberta.

receive equal funding per student, and neither are permitted to charge tuition, charter schools charge parents exorbitant fees for uniforms, transportation, textbooks, elective classes, physical education, and other activities. "All of this was happening while the general public's kids were having to make makeshift classrooms on stages in the music room, music classes were being cancelled, kids were having lunch in the hallways, we were losing education assistants, we were having to fundraise for books, for replacing tiles in the schools," Silva told me. Public schools also charge fees, but they're much more limited, and low-income students can have those fees waived, since public schools are unable to turn anyone away. Charter schools may waive fees, but they're under no obligation to do so.

SOS takes the broader view on charter schools that it's unacceptable for, in Silva's words, "certain sectors of students to get a type of education that other students don't have access to. If one child needs a special program, the likelihood is that other children in society do as well. And it should be offered across the board, free, at point of access, with no barriers. So if someone has identified a need within the system, then we fix the system. We don't just fix the individual need. And that's what charters do."

Jason Schilling of the ATA shares this critique but also points to a lack of transparency over where charter school funds are allocated. "Public schools have publicly elected trustees who are the stewards of that school division or that school authority and that includes the fiduciary responsibility of their budget. Charter schools don't have that. They don't have a public oversight of the money," he told me. The ATA has no problem with charter school teachers or programming, but objects to the way they're structured. Charter school teachers are also not ATA members, unless they've been temporarily seconded from a public board, which might further elucidate Kenney's fondness for them.

The word *charter* refers to the permission these schools are supposed to get from their local school board to operate special programming that's absent from the public system — a requirement the UCP removed after a year in power. For example, the Almadina Language Charter Academy, which has three campuses in Calgary, is specifically oriented toward students whose second or third language spoken at home is English. The mandate of others, such as the Centre for Academic and Personal Excellence in Medicine Hat, is vaguer, offering students a "personalized integrated program," which is facilitated through "community partnerships, partnerships with parents, collaboration with external services, and a counselling approach to discipline." The only thing stopping the public system from offering these sorts of programs is a lack of funding to do so.

Another key term in the charter school discussion is *voucher*, referring to the system in the United States where parents are given a stipend to spend on the school of their choice. Alberta technically doesn't have a voucher system, but Silva says in practice that's precisely what school choice is. Public money follows a student to the school of their parents' choice, whether it's public or a charter school, like a backpack full of cash. *Backpack Full of Cash* happens to be the name of a 2017 documentary about the voucher system in the United States, narrated by actor Matt Damon, which SOS has hosted screenings of across the province because it shows the direction in which the province has been heading since Klein's reforms, which Kenney and LaGrange accelerated. "It has been the pillar and the point of pride for many Albertans that Alberta does not have a voucher system, that our charter schools are not like the American charter schools, when in fact they entirely are. They're just Canadian versions of them. But the intention behind them, the way that they operate, the way that they are funded is entirely the same," Silva said.

While charters can be run for profit in the United States, they must be operated by non-profits in Alberta. But Silva said this distinction is entirely superficial, pointing out that the Fédération internationale de football association (FIFA), an organization not exactly known for its altruism, is technically a non-profit. "It's a tax status, it's not a moral code. It's absolutely no indication that you're doing something out of morality or sense of justice or a sense of obligation to the greater good or social benefit."

When the UCP came to power, there were 13 charter school authorities in Alberta — two below the cap reluctantly established in 1994. However, there was a loophole in this cap. Charter authorities were permitted to set up as many campuses as they could, so while there were 13 authorities, they contained within them 23 brick-and-mortar schools. But the UCP eliminated this cap in June 2019, allowing even more authorities to open even more campuses. As of this writing, there are now 21 authorities operating 37 campuses.

Rather than have charter school operators demonstrate the need for their school to their local school board, the May 2020 Choice in Education Act made it so they only had to go to the minister, who would then take their proposal to the local school board on the charter school's behalf, which LaGrange admitted was intended to speed up the approval process. Justifying these changes, Kenney said, "we believe that parents know better than politicians or bureaucrats about what's in the best interests of their kids" and called school choice a "fundamental human right."[12] This policy was neoliberal in applying market logic to schooling, but neoconservative in its framing as a matter of human rights and family values.

Funding Discord

The UCP insisted it would maintain $8.223 billion funding for education from the previous NDP budget, which would have in practice still been a cut due to population growth, since school boards at the time were funded based on projected enrollment. After the inaugural UCP budget, it became increasingly clear that public schools were getting shortchanged.

The province's largest school board, the Calgary Board of Education (CBE), received a $32 million cut, due to the elimination of three grants and insufficient one-time transition funding, despite enrollment having increased by 2,400 students. After the board announced it would lay off more than 300 temporary teachers, LaGrange ordered an audit of its finances, citing the CBE's "history of questionable, irresponsible decision-making when it comes to its finances," a reference to an audit of the board's finances under the NDP, which found a $9.1 million bookkeeping error but concluded it had no impact on the board's finances.[13] The following month, the board announced it would use a $15 million infrastructure and maintenance renewal grant to keep these educators employed, naturally coming at the expense of the board's aging infrastructure.

The audit returned without finding any examples of egregious spending, but made 25 recommendations, consisting of minor tweaks alongside calls to enhance long-term planning. The minister threatened to fire the entire board if it didn't implement the majority of the recommendations, which it did. This threat, with its sheer belligerence toward the province's largest school board, occurred exactly a week before the government introduced the Choice in Education Act.

The ATA had to file a freedom-of-information request to discover the overall budget was, in fact, cut by $136 million. With province-wide enrollment growth of 13,000 students, that amounted to a 4 percent funding reduction overall.[14] These documents came out just as the UCP moved the goalposts on school funding, introducing a new, convoluted formula that based per-student funding on three-year enrollment averages, which the government acknowledged would place rural school boards with declining enrollment at an advantage while punishing boards in big cities with rapidly growing enrollment.[15] The 2020 budget downloaded $121 million in costs onto school boards themselves, which would have to either come from reserves, or if the board's reserves were depleted, by increasing school fees. In the days before the 2019–20 school year began, the UCP removed the NDP's ban on school boards charging fees for bussing in students who lived more than 2.4 kilometres, or farther, away from their school. Downloading additional costs onto school boards left them no choice but to pass them onto parents, further eroding the line between public and private education while revealing the empty sloganeering of *school choice*.

Once Covid struck, the government used the opportunity to rob schools of an additional $128 million under the guise of redirecting these funds toward unspecified pandemic-response measures, leading to thousands of layoffs, which the government vowed would be temporary. Boards able to avoid eliminating jobs, like Medicine Hat's public and separate school divisions, had to cut costs elsewhere, such as maintenance, repairs, and classroom supplies. This made sense as a short-term measure while kids were out of class, but the 2021 budget didn't provide additional resources for a return to classes or curriculum implementation, resulting in the loss of almost 2,000 jobs, which the government proceeded to blame on the boards themselves.[16]

Most of the assistants who were laid off at the outset of Covid did get their jobs back, but these jobs were increasingly precarious, with fewer hours and resources at their disposal. The 2022 budget, which was tabled on February 24 — the same day Russia invaded Ukraine — finally increased education funding, including funds for curriculum implementation, academic and mental health supports, and transportation, but these additional funds were insufficient to keep up with enrollment growth.

Meanwhile, charter and private schools, with their immense revenue sources outside public funding, would be mostly insulated from the whims of the provincial pocketbook. Kenney's assault on public K–12 education, whether through sabotaging curriculum, fiddling with boards' funding, increasing the number of competing charter schools, or his minister's efforts to publicly humiliate the province's largest school board, will have long-term impacts for kids who went through the school system during the tumult of the Kenney years. Kenney's policies exacerbated the disruptions of the pandemic.

Marketizing Post-Secondary Education

The austere approach to K–12 education was matched by vicious cuts to the post-secondary sector, which left university and college students paying more, while beginning the process of tethering remaining funding to the job market. This was a key recommendation of the MacKinnon panel, which repeatedly insisted Alberta get its spending in line with that of Ontario, Quebec, and British Columbia, except when it came to post-secondary funding. That was because Quebec, at 62 percent, offered more generous post-secondary grants than Alberta's 54 percent,[17] which didn't suit the panel's predetermined narrative that spending in Alberta was out of control.

In its inaugural budget, the UCP cut provincial grants by 7.9 percent and lifted a tuition freeze first imposed by PC premier Alison Redford in 2013, in addition to increasing interest on student loans, which students from disadvantaged backgrounds would have to depend on to pay higher tuition, and removing tax credits of up to $1,000 per year for students who took out loans. It did increase funding for the trades, which Finance Minister Travis Toews said would "strengthen the connection between students and jobs effectively."[18] Tuition hikes were capped at 7 percent, but the province allowed programs to apply for an even greater increase.

Just as it had with K–12 education, the government didn't stop at cuts — it also restructured the funding formula to suit its desired outcomes. In January 2020, the government announced it would tie increasing amounts of post-secondary funding to "performance-based" criteria, starting at 15 percent. After its implementation was delayed due to the pandemic, the government announced in March 2021 it would begin at 5 percent, which would be solely based on the ability of post-secondary programs to get students work experience relevant to their programs.

In a January 26, 2020, analysis piece for *CBC News*, journalist Drew Anderson cautioned against measuring schools' performance based on metrics rather than the quality of education. He wrote that "there are unintended consequences whenever a government decides post-secondary performance is something that can be distilled on a spreadsheet, or that the value of a university education is in its contribution to the workforce, to the future earnings of its grads." When we look at this policy in the context of Kenney's world view, it becomes quite clear these consequences were very much intended.

Tying funding to employment would turn post-secondary education into a job-making enterprise, punishing those fields in the arts and humanities designed to make students think critically but might not land them jobs immediately. "What they've done is they've taken a ceramic, smashed it on the ground, and now they're daring to claim that only they have the tape and glue to fix the vase," Carolyn Sale, an English and film studies professor at the University of Alberta and past president of the university's Association of Academic Staff, told me for a January 2020 *Medicine Hat News* story as the government announced its intention to introduce the new funding formula. "This is about taking a system that their cuts are already going to so drastically undermine and then use the chaos that they have created to start redirecting funding to the technical institutes [and] more job-oriented programs."

The 2020 budget cut post-secondary grants an additional 6.3 percent, shrinking post-secondary funding to $5.1 billion from $5.4 billion in the previous budget just four months earlier. Toews said these cuts would allow schools "to be more entrepreneurial and to raise additional own-source revenue," meaning invest more in employment-oriented programming while charging students more for tuition.[19] In 2021, the post-secondary budget was cut a further 1.4 percent, bringing it down to slightly more than $5 billion and leading to 750 job losses.

While grants were slashed a total of 7.7 percent in the 2020 and 2021 budgets, it wasn't spread evenly among schools. The University of Alberta was hit the hardest, with its funding cut a wildly disproportionate 20 percent. The University of Calgary and University of Lethbridge each lost 12 percent of their funding, but five small private universities, as well as MacEwan University and Lakeland College, managed to walk away relatively unscathed with just a 2 percent funding reduction each. "You can't help but at least contemplate that there are political reasons for some of the cuts," University of Alberta microbiologist and Confederation of Alberta Faculty Associations president Kevin Kane told the CBC.[20] The University of Alberta was ultimately forced to make up for this funding loss by cutting 800 non-academic positions between 2019 and 2021, in addition to hundreds of academic staff let go through attrition. This had a disproportionate impact on arts faculty teaching subjects such as history, politics, and environmental and social policy. "This knowledge is being lost to students, as well as to journalists and citizens trying to make sense of politics and policy issues in Alberta," wrote University of Alberta political scientist Laurie Adkin in the September 2021 issue of *Alberta Views* magazine.

This trend continued, even with a $500 million surplus, as the government slightly increased the post-secondary budget in 2022, including $171 million over three years to expand enrollment for specific fields such as energy, health care, aviation, finance, and finance technology, as well as high technology, which included computer science, information technology, and data modelling. With this targeted increase, the arts-and-humanities-focused University of Alberta suffered another $52 million cut.[21]

It's worth recalling that Kenney never finished his university degree in philosophy. His particularly brutal assault on post-secondary education, which was even harsher than his approach to K–12 education, could be read in part as the product of a deeply held grudge against academia for rejecting him. But his approach was also profoundly ideological. Kenney saw students, whether in the K–12 system, university, or college, as units of economic measurement, judged by the ability to get a job, consume, start a traditional family, and not ask too many questions. To fulfill this vision, he offloaded expenses from public to private actors while using state power to make it harder for the public side to function. This formula replicated itself with an even greater dose of neoconservative moralism, and more deadly impacts, in Kenney's approach to the drug-poisoning crisis.

9

REJECTING HARM REDUCTION

AT A MARCH 2018 CAMPAIGN STOP in Lethbridge — a small city of
about 100,000 in southwestern Alberta that became the location of North
America's most frequented supervised consumption site (SCS)[1] — Jason
Kenney came out in blanket opposition to the philosophy of harm reduction for people who used drugs. "Helping addicts inject poison into their
bodies is not a solution to the problem of addiction," he told the *Lethbridge
Herald*. Kenney insisted the drug-poisoning epidemic, which was driven
largely by overdoses from a street opioid supply cut with powerful substances
like fentanyl, was best dealt with as a strictly criminal matter, rather than
a question of public health. Throwing fuel onto the Alberta separatist fire,
he demanded an increase in Canada Border Service Agency funding "to
interdict the import of deadly drugs from China and elsewhere" and promised to boost police funding so they could "chase down every source in the
criminal world to find out who is dealing poison on the streets of Lethbridge
right now."

This tough-on-crime talk was reminiscent of former prime minister
Stephen Harper's harsh criminal justice policies, which increased the number of incarcerated Canadians by 17.5 percent, despite declining crime rates,
and almost doubled the budget of the federal corrections system from $1.6
billion when Harper came to power in 2006 to just under $3 billion in 2012.[2]

Harper's criminal justice agenda included mandatory minimum sentences for crimes involving guns, drugs, and sexual assaults; less credit for time served for criminals who weren't granted bail and tougher restrictions around parole; and making it easier to deport non-citizens who committed crimes. The former prime minister opposed Insite in Vancouver's Downtown Eastside, which at the time was the sole SCS in Canada, but his effort to have it shut down was kiboshed by a unanimous Supreme Court decision in 2011, which argued people who used drugs had a Charter of Rights and Freedoms entitlement to access supervised consumption services.

That didn't stop Harper from placing onerous restrictions on opening new SCSs, including a letter of approval from the head of the local police force; statistics and other information on crime, public nuisance, and inappropriately discarded drug paraphernalia in the vicinity of the site; and a report on consultations with a vague array of "community groups."

Kenney used the spirit of this legislation, which Prime Minister Justin Trudeau declined to repeal when he was elected,[3] to justify his all-out assault on harm reduction as Alberta premier. The premier's hamfistedness regarding harm-reduction measures was matched with an unprecedented generosity to private abstinence-only recovery clinics, which suited his ideology with their religious-infused approach to putting people who used drugs on the path to righteousness.

A few days after his comments in Lethbridge, Kenney slightly dialled back the rhetoric on a visit to Vancouver, acknowledging the Supreme Court's 2011 decision, but with the caveat that he wanted "properly to consult with local communities about the placement of facilities." He said he supported "reasonable harm-reduction efforts" but didn't specify what those were, calling the "notion that this is a panacea for the consumption of some of these really toxic opioids ... a bit naive."[4] This entirely misrepresented the perspectives of harm-reduction advocates who saw the SCS as an important tool, but not the sole one to address the drug-poisoning crisis. It didn't matter, because to Kenney these were "NDP drug sites,"[5] which had to be removed as a vestige of his predecessor's rule.

Since 2018, when there were 815 opioid-poisoning deaths, the crisis had only grown worse, according to the government's own substance-use surveillance system, which it unveiled in December 2020. While the total of opioid-poisoning deaths decreased to 626 in 2019, it skyrocketed during the pandemic, coinciding with a major downturn in the use of supervised consumption services. In 2020, the total was 1,186, increasing to 1,628 in 2021, before a slight decrease to 1,510 in 2022 left the figure higher than it was in 2020. Each one of these deaths was preventable through enhancing access to harm-reduction measures, including the expansion of SCSs and opioid agonist treatment and the provision of a pharmaceutical-grade, safer supply.

Kenney's government, however, was possessed by a moralistic view that drug use was sinful, downloading responsibility for ending the drug-poisoning crisis onto individual drug users. Jason Luan, Kenney's inaugural associate minister of mental health and addictions, made this perspective clear in a May 2020 *Edmonton Journal* op-ed where he wrote "addiction does not exist in drugs; it exists in people," meaning "the solution exists in people and not in tinkering with the drug supply." In other words, the problem is *you*, not the increasingly toxic drug supply. Individual drug users were shamed into treatment, while the few options for them to use substances safely dwindled.

When Kenney came to power, there were seven SCSs in the province — one in Lethbridge, one in Calgary, four in Edmonton, and one in Grande Prairie. Since then, the Lethbridge site and Edmonton's Boyle Street location have been shut down, and as of this writing, the Calgary site is in the process of closing down. Those that remain were subject to onerous identification requirements that only deterred people from using them. Meanwhile, private recovery clinics were lavishly subsidized with public funds without having to demonstrate any measurement of efficacy. It might have made a good sound bite to say you're giving people who are down and out the opportunity to get their lives on track, but it was cold comfort for those who had already lost loved ones to an increasingly toxic illicit drug supply.

Stopping the Harm

Petra Schulz lost her youngest son, Danny, to an accidental opioid overdose on April 30, 2014, when he was 25, and the drug-poisoning crisis that has spiralled out of control today was in its infancy. He had been in and out of rehab, and during one of his relapses took a fatal dose of pure fentanyl that had been sold to him as heroin. Danny, who was a trained chef by trade, was gay, which wasn't an issue in his family, who accepted him fully, but did lead to him getting bullied in school. He also had social anxiety, which Schulz said pushed him toward drug use as a coping mechanism.

"I can't capture him in just a few words, and as you can tell, we miss him so much still," Schulz told me in an interview. "It's eight years and it comes and goes. Sometimes it's worse and sometimes it gets a little better. Like, you get used to the pain, of course. It never goes away, but you get used to living with the pain." Shortly after Danny's death, Schulz, who resides in Edmonton, began hearing reports of opioid deaths on the Blood Tribe reserve, the largest First Nations reserve in the country, and was upset by the focus on statistics, rather than the lives of people. The Truth and Reconciliation Commission hearing in Edmonton occurred the month before Danny died, and after his passing, Schulz says she couldn't stop thinking about the harrowing stories of Indigenous peoples' immense pain and trauma due to Canada's genocidal policies, and the courage they showed in its face. This brought her to the realization she should connect with others who have suffered loss due to the drug-poisoning epidemic and advocate for evidence-based interventions.

She was spurred into action. With two of her friends, Schulz established the organization Moms Stop the Harm, which has been at the forefront of the fight against the UCP government's war on evidence-based drug policy. *Moms* is a bit of a misnomer in retrospect, Schulz says, since the organization includes siblings, romantic partners, and other relations with people who have died from overdoses. When Moms Stop the Harm was formed, the province's long-governing PCs were in power, and the government was somewhat receptive to the group's call for supervised consumption sites in Edmonton, despite its conservative leanings. "They didn't slam the doors in our faces like the current Alberta government does," Schulz recalls. "They listened."

For all its flaws, the Alberta NDP government that came to power in 2015 was strongly in support of harm-reduction policies, with Health Minister Sarah Hoffman establishing a Minister's Opioid Emergency Response Commission, which was co-chaired by Dr. Elaine Hyshka, a staunch harm-reduction advocate and public health professor at the University of Alberta, and Dr. Deena Hinshaw, Alberta's chief medical officer of health, and included Schulz as a member. Hoffman accepted "each and every recommendation" the panel made, including funding for supervised consumption sites and opioid agonist therapy, but the NDP government "moved them forward too slowly," Schulz says. Then, in 2019, Kenney and the UCP came to power, setting out to "destroy what we built." She said the group's efforts to have Kenney and the UCP even listen to them were unfruitful. "I once ran into Kenney in a café in Calgary and gave him my business card. I even shook the man's hand. I would not do that anymore. These days, I think his hand is contaminated," Schulz says. "There's too much blood on it."

Supervised Consumption and Its Discontents

In Lethbridge, the Arches SCS, which was named after the social agency that operated it, opened in March 2018, and by August 2019 averaged 663 visits per day, making it the busiest site in North America. For its unhoused clients, the SCS serves as a "sanctuary — one of the few places they can simply be without feeling unwanted or being accused of loitering," wrote reporter Nadia Yousif in an in-depth piece for *StarMetro Edmonton*, for which she spent 12 hours at the Arches site. Many of the site's clientele were Indigenous people from the nearby Piikani and Kainai First Nations, who used drugs to numb the pain of decades of intergenerational trauma from experiences of colonization, residential schools, and the Sixties Scoop, in which Indigenous children were taken from their parents to live with settler families. The site was open 24 hours a day, with 13 injection booths, each with a mirror and needle disposal box, as well as two inhalation rooms for people who smoked drugs — one for meth, the other for heroin. It was the only site in Canada to offer inhalation services, with each room able to accommodate four people at a time. People could use the site as many times as they wanted, with the only restrictions being that buying and selling drugs on the premises was prohibited, and a 45-minute time limit in the booths.

Yousif spoke to a worker at the site, Sam Mackey, who once used meth and heroin and was the site's first overdose. When plans were underway for the site, Mackey was asked to participate in consultations on what people who used drugs would like to see there. She told *StarMetro* that before the site opened, she was "probably at the worst of my worst" — homeless, kicked out of her partner's home, and overdosing regularly. When she was offered a job at Arches after the consultation, she felt a sense of redemption. "I have a purpose, I have meaning," Mackey said. According to Arches, the site reversed 2,500 overdoses in its first 17 months, but most notably made 9,000 referrals to detox, recovery, and mental health services. These numbers showed that the binary between harm reduction and recovery that Kenney's government perpetuated was false. Through creating a close bond with clients who often had nobody else, Arches staff were able to guide people to recovery when they were ready to do so. Local backlash to the site, however, was ferocious.

Dan Hamilton, owner of the neighbouring Hamilton Carpet and Flooring, began posting photos on social media of left-behind drug debris and people loitering on social media, and then started a 24/7 YouTube stream of the site's west entrance, which was adjacent to his store. "I should not be prevented from making known, and visible, that which is killing my business and threatening the viability of our downtown," Hamilton said in a statement to *StarMetro*. He feigned sympathy for the people who used the site but maintained that his business interests outweighed the lives of people who used drugs. Lethbridge-based journalist Kim Siever told me that Hamilton put up a FOR SALE sign on his business, which he immediately took down once Arches was closed.

This pattern of vicious rhetoric repeated itself elsewhere in the province, often, though not always, uncritically repeated in local media. In Calgary, there is just one SCS for a city of 1.3 million — Safeworks at the Sheldon

Chumir Centre Hospital. A condo board member told *Global News* in July 2019 that residents were "just afraid to walk out of the building." Stuart Allen, the owner of Buzzards Restaurant & Bar in downtown Calgary, called the presence of people who used drugs a "cold sore" on the neighbourhood.[6] In a story that was a bit too on the nose to be believed, in January 2019, a local funeral home owner told the *Medicine Hat News* that a proposed SCS would harm his business interests.

Concerns surrounding public safety near the sites weren't without merit, but the rhetoric with which they were expressed reflected a total lack of compassion for the people who used the sites. Kenney and his local allies seized on this anger from small-business owners to justify an all-out assault on harm-reduction services during his three years as Alberta's premier. Calgary city councillor Sean Chu, who was later accused of pulling a gun on an underage girl before sexually assaulting her when he was a cop in the 1990s, called the city's sole SCS a "shooting gallery."[7] Former Calgary city councillor and failed mayoral candidate Jeromy Farkas likened the site near Chumir to a war zone. "You can't drop a bomb in a neighbourhood and wish for the best. You break it, you fix it," he told the *Calgary Sun* in March 2020. "We've reached a breaking point in our communities," he said elsewhere.[8]

Back in Lethbridge, Blaine Hyggen, a right-wing city councillor who is now the city's mayor, put forward a motion in August 2019, which asked the province to cut funding for the site until a proposed provincial review of SCSs' impact on surrounding communities was completed. Citing "hundreds and hundreds and hundreds of emails" he received from concerned citizens, Hyggen blamed the site for rising crime and disorder in the area where it's located. He said Arches' clientele were caught in a "vicious circle of injecting, coming out, creating crime, getting money to feed that habit, going back in and doing the same thing." Mayor Chris Spearman opposed the motion, arguing the problem in Lethbridge was a lack of funding for intox, detox, and homeless shelter services, not the consumption site, which he called the "one positive" development in response to the drug-poisoning epidemic. "If that went away, we would lose contact with the drug users and the drug issue would go from the supervised consumption site to every area in the city."[9]

The motion was defeated 6–3 after a tense debate, with supporters and opponents rallying outside city hall separated by a steel fence. During the debate, Hyggen bemoaned that the site was "pumping with music and fun." He further complained: "Drug users come around and are warmly greeted by their fellow users — it's like a big party. At times, they are even supplied with chocolate bars, pizza, chips, take-out food, etc."[10] Luckily for Hyggen and likeminded municipal politicians, a government that shared their perspective was already in power and would soon use a politically motivated audit to override municipal governments and crack down on SCSs.

The Crackdown

The month after the tense debate in Lethbridge, Kenney announced a freeze on new funding for SCSs, pending a review he promised into the socio-economic impacts of the sites on surrounding communities. The merits of harm reduction as a policy were not to be considered. In a familiar pattern, Kenney formed an ideologically driven committee to provide him with the pretext to do what he had already decided to do. The eight-person committee convened a travelling road show of town halls across the province's major cities — Calgary, Edmonton, Lethbridge, Red Deer, Grande Prairie, and Medicine Hat — for just over two weeks in September. In one example of the many grievances the panel heard, Teresa Swerhan of Grande Prairie complained that her neighbourhood had become a den of "hookers, thieves, dealers, and junkies." She said: "You go for a walk and you don't see a normal person anymore."[11]

The panel's report was handed to the government in March 2020. Unsurprisingly, given its narrow mandate, it concluded the sites were a magnet for social disorder and crime, citing the presence of needle debris in the surrounding vicinities, as well as the "aggressive and erratic behaviour of substance users leaving the sites." The report also brought up rumours of "inadequate oversight and the lack of accountability mechanisms at the sites," and bemoaned a perceived "lack of focus on referrals to detoxification and treatment resources."

While Jason Luan called the report a "wake-up call" that revealed a "system of chaos" in the sites' vicinities,[12] experts panned the panel's methodology. University of Alberta public health expert Cameron Wild called the report a "political document and not an objective or scientifically credible evaluation." University of Calgary sociologist Jenny Godley said it "wouldn't pass my undergrad stats class." Saint Mary's University criminologist Jamie Livingston said the "blatantly biased" report worked backward from an assumption that crime was out of control near the sites and cherry-picked data of calls to police, rather than criminal charges, to justify its predetermined conclusion,[13] for which there was no evidence.[14] Livingston and Godley joined 40 academics in an open letter to the government calling on the report to be retracted entirely.

The day before the committee's report was released to the public, the government set its sights on Arches' funding, announcing an audit of alleged financial irregularities at the site. The audit from accounting firm Deloitte was released in July 2020. It found $1.6 million in unaccounted public funds, as well as thousands of dollars in inappropriate expenses, including gift cards, unauthorized overtime pay, a television, and travel expenses to Portugal. The province could have imposed new management on the facility to ensure continuity for its clients but instead discovered a pretext to cut the site's funding. With three-quarters of its funding coming from provincial government grants, the site's operators were left with no option but to close by the end of August. The matter was referred to a criminal investigation by the Lethbridge Police Service, who in December 2020 announced that it had found the funds, declining to press criminal charges, but by then the damage was done. "The threshold for what we spend tax dollars on is a lot different than the threshold of a potential successful criminal conviction," Kenney said, citing the misspent funds and concerns from nearby residents about needle debris and general disorder.[15]

On August 31, mere weeks after Deloitte's audit revealed misspending among Arches staff, the *Calgary Herald* reported that members of the supervised consumption site review panel exceeded their budget by more than $10,000 while they were on tour, spending lavishly on "excessive" meals, including prime rib dinners, avocado toast, and booze, despite repeated warnings from the ministry to keep their spending within budget.

After the government closed Arches, it allowed Alberta Health Services to operate a mobile overdose prevention site out of a white cube-shaped van, which was criticized as woefully inadequate. The van had three booths, down from 13 at Arches, and operated 20 hours per day, down from 24 at Arches. While Arches included a booth for smoking substances, the van was strictly for injections. According to an open letter to Luan signed by four local physicians, patients were required to wait up to five or six hours to use the mobile site, but many of them needed to use every two or three hours to avoid severe withdrawal symptoms. Users also had to start from scratch in establishing trusting relationships with the staff at the mobile site. Unsurprisingly, the closure of Arches resulted in increased overdoses and needle debris, which spread across the city, as well as to nearby First Nations reserves, such as Blood Tribe, rather than being confined to downtown Lethbridge, in the two weeks after the site stopped operations.[16] But Kenney wasn't done whittling away at the province's harm-reduction infrastructure.

In April 2021, the government announced it would permanently close the Boyle Street SCS, one of three in central Edmonton, with the government arguing there were simply too many SCSs in the same location. The services offered at Boyle Street are slated to be moved to a barer-boned overdose prevention site in the Old Strathcona neighbourhood, which provoked a predictable backlash from local residents. In May, the Cabinet decided to close Calgary's Safeworks and move it to two undetermined locations. These decisions made no sense, according to Dr. Elaine Hyshka, the Canada Research Chair in Health Systems Innovation at the University of Alberta. "If anything, we need to be keeping all the SCSs we have and making new ones to support other parts of our cities and the province that could benefit from having these life-saving interventions," she told the *Calgary Herald* in a May 21 story. The government revealed in March 2022 that neither of these two sites would be SCSs but overdose prevention sites. As of April 2023, the location of the Calgary overdose prevention sites hasn't been determined, let alone opened.

The government then imposed new barriers to the use of the remaining SCSs. As of September 30, 2021, the sites had to sign a "good neighbour agreement"[17] with the surrounding communities, including a dispute-resolution process and an outline of responsibilities for each side, further pitting SCSs against their neighbours. Far more onerously, SCSs were required to ask clients for their health card information. Mike Ellis, a former Calgary cop who replaced Jason Luan as associate minister of mental health and addictions in July 2021, admitted in an *Edmonton Journal* op-ed that these "quality standards" were designed to set people who used drugs onto a path of the government's choosing. The sites would be forced to partner with treatment and recovery programs of the government's preference, "ensuring they get the care they need to improve their lives sooner rather than later." The government was closing the walls around harm-reduction services to facilitate its recovery-centric approach to the drug-poisoning crisis. To help with this policy, which would provide a windfall for non-profits willing to play ball, Kenney brought in a big gun from neighbouring British Columbia.

The Mysterious Mr. Smith

While Kenney advocated a tough-on-crime approach to the drug-poisoning epidemic when he was on the campaign trail, once elected, he opted to provide a more compassionate veneer to the same failed drug war policies. To this end, he imported a man named Marshall Smith to serve as chief of staff to Jason Luan and then Mike Ellis. Smith served as a key architect in the government's shift away from harm reduction to a recovery-centric approach. He was an up-and-comer in the Gordon Campbell–era B.C. Liberals, a party that had more in common with Alberta's UCP than its federal namesake, working in the attorney general's office and then serving as chief of staff to the minister responsible for Vancouver's 2010 Olympic bid until he was arrested twice in 2004 for selling cocaine and crystal meth.

After a few years of living on the streets, Smith got sober and soon became an evangelist for the sort of rigid, abstinence-only approach to recovery championed by Kenney. In 2008, he began work at the Baldy Hughes

Therapeutic Community Farm, an unlicensed and unaccredited recovery facility in Prince George. Online news outlet the *Tyee* unearthed a damning 2011 B.C. government-commissioned review of the facility, which found "numerous examples of non-conformance with licensing standards ... in all cornerstones of the facility and program." Clients, who paid upward of $3,000 per month, were offered little more than a 12-step abstinence program from staff who lacked "core competencies." There were few wrap-around supports and frequent medication errors. Clients who had medical issues were forced to visit a nearby walk-in clinic, because there were no physicians on staff. The program had a 45 percent success rate, measured by at least three months of abstinence following completion.[18]

According to investigative reporting from Glacier Media reporter Jeremy Hainsworth, Smith allegedly coerced patients into phone banking for B.C. Liberal leadership candidate Kevin Falcon in 2011, calling party members to solicit support. Confidential sources told Hainsworth they had no choice, because many of them were court-ordered to attend Baldy Hughes, and Smith pressured those who were reluctant to pick up a phone, a claim Smith strenuously denied, insisting that the phone banking was volunteer work. According to one source, Smith was given the boot from Baldy Hughes as soon as Falcon was defeated.[19]

Whether the allegations of forced politicking are true or not, it's evident Smith is an intensely political figure. In a revealing October 2015 interview with *Talk Recovery Radio*, he summarized his cold approach toward people suffering from addiction. "When we talk about reducing the shame and stigma, we're talking about the shame and stigma of recovery," he said. "I think a certain shroud of stigma needs to remain around addiction." Smith was so adamant in his opposition to harm-reduction measures that he resigned from his position at the B.C. Centre on Substance Use when the organization began advocating for compassion clubs — members-only co-operatives where health-care professionals provided people who used heroin with their drugs of choice. This mentality would make him fit right in with a government dead set on stigmatizing people who used drugs while placing recovery on a pedestal as an individualized solution to the collective problem of drug-poisoning deaths.

The Recovery Racket

With Marshall Smith on board, the government formed a 23-person panel on addictions and mental health in November 2019, which set out to develop the so-called Alberta model of funnelling money to private recovery clinics. The panel was co-chaired by Mustard Seed Ministry founder Pat Nixon — the father of UCP MLAs Jeremy and Jason — and Canadian Mental Health Association Calgary executive director Laureen MacNeil. Of particular note were three appointees from the upper ranks of the abstinence-only private recovery industry: Simon House founding director and former Kenney CTF colleague Andrew Crooks, Fresh Start Recovery Centre executive director Stacey Petersen, and Poundmaker's Lodge Treatment Centres executive director Brad Cardinal. By the time it delivered its advisory report to the government in March 2022, which predictably recommended the government invest in recovery, Crooks had been quietly dropped from the council.

In the meantime, Petersen's and Cardinal's clinics were recipients of government largesse. In December 2019, Kenney announced a $1.4 million grant for Poundmaker's Iskwew Healing Lodge, built just north of Edmonton on the site of a former residential school, to fund 28 new beds and seven existing beds. A news release announcing the funding included a statement from Cardinal applauding the government, which didn't identify him as a member of the government's advisory panel. A few months later, the government announced as much as $1.56 million per year over three years for Fresh Start to fund 294 additional treatment spaces in Calgary. Petersen called the funding "unprecedented" and a "game changer" in a news release, which again, didn't identify him as a member of the advisory committee. In the same announcement, Lloydminster's Thorpe Recovery Centre received $2.21 million per year to fund an additional 1,722 treatment spaces and Sunrise Healing Lodge got $518,300 to fund 156 beds, both over three years.

Rebecca Haines-Saah, a University of Calgary health sociologist, criticized the government's superficial fixation on numbers of beds as a "political talking point" with no rhyme or reason, noting the government's

dogmatic approach to recovery at the expense of a wide spectrum of interventions for the drug-poisoning crisis. "They've pitted harm reduction
against treatment, as if to say that funds for harm reduction somehow
take away from treatment, that the two are in competition, or that people
who support or advocate or benefit from harm reduction are opposed to
treatment."[20]

Later in 2020, the government announced it would subsidize all fees
for licensed private recovery clinics at an estimated cost of $8.2 million per
year, presaging a significant transfer from the public to non-profit sector. The
government was markedly less generous with publicly run recovery facilities,
shutting down the AHS-operated McCullough Centre for homeless men in
Gunn, Alberta, in February 2021 to save provincial coffers just $3 million.
In March 2022, the government announced it would eventually be reopened
as a publicly owned but privately operated "recovery community." Plans were
also underway for similar facilities on the Blood Tribe Reserve as well as in
Lethbridge and Red Deer. The site in Lethbridge was being conveniently
built on government-owned land adjacent to Fresh Start's Lethbridge facility. According to documents obtained by the *Calgary Herald*, the government planned to "re-evaluate [the] need" for an overdose-prevention site in
Red Deer once its recovery facility opened.

To its credit, Kenney's government expanded the use of drug-treatment
courts, doubling capacity in Edmonton and Calgary, where they already
existed, and adding new ones in Lethbridge, Red Deer, Grande Prairie, and
Medicine Hat, which provided an alternative to criminalizing people convicted of non-violent offences. Even then, the policy was explicitly framed
around funnelling people into strictly abstinent recovery where they would
be subject to "frequent and random drug testing, and the use of sanctions
and rewards," according to Matthew Reid, whom Kenney put in charge of
the file.[21] The government announced a fundamentally coercive policy of
allowing police to offer people they had just arrested the option of entering
the "recovery-oriented system of care" once they were in jail.

In December 2021, at the tail end of the deadliest year for drug-poisoning
deaths on record, Kenney and Ellis boasted the government had exceeded its
goal of funding 4,000 treatment spaces by double while announcing plans

for a new app to assist people who used drugs in developing a "recovery plan," with Ellis admitting, "right now we are completely focused on recovery." Eroding the province's minimal harm-reduction infrastructure while integrating a particularly rigid form of recovery into the criminal justice system was a form of neocon social engineering. Rather than address the root causes of the drug-poisoning epidemic, Kenney used the weight of the state to force society's most vulnerable people into his traditionalist conception of moral behaviour.

Where's the Data?

There's a growing body of academic literature suggesting that harm-reduction policies are more effective than the rigid regimen of abstinence Kenney poured public funds into. This reality is reflected in Alberta Health Service's (AHS's) explicit endorsement of harm reduction, which "acknowledges that abstinence is not always a realistic goal for some people" and recognizes the necessity of "meeting people where they are." These policies "recognize the inherent value of human beings and the importance of an inclusive community that can support people who use substances with compassion," AHS's harm-reduction explainer on its website reads, noting that people need to feel supported as part of a broader community in order to seek assistance when they're ready.[22]

According to an August 2019 study from the Alberta Community Council on HIV, which was submitted to the government to no avail, SCSs had zero fatalities after responding to 4,300 overdoses. A March 2017 peer-reviewed literature review in *Canadian Family Physician* compares the efficacy of abstinence-only recovery and opioid agonist treatment based on 66 studies, finding an overwhelming consensus in favour of harm reduction. "Individual patient characteristics and preferences should be taken into consideration when choosing a first-line opioid agonist treatment," the review reads. "However, the most important factor to consider is that opioid agonist treatment is far more effective than abstinence-based treatment."

Sara Fox, development coordinator at Thorpe, one of the private recovery clinics benefiting from UCP largesse, said its 42-day abstinence-only program has a 79 percent completion rate, but beyond that it was difficult to determine how successful the program was. "For, what is success? One day of abstinence? One month? One year? It is misleading to claim that someone will be 'cured' after programming," Fox said. Through a freedom-of-information request, journalist Duncan Kinney received heavily redacted documents revealing that between 2016 and 2021 at least three people died at recovery facilities in Alberta, including Thorpe patient Joshua Corbiere. There has been no independent analysis of success rates at the various publicly funded private recovery centres across the province, nor was there information on how many publicly funded beds there were province-wide, how often they were used, and how many people were on wait-lists.

Dr. Hyshka identified this lack of transparency as a major problem. "These basic metrics could be easily incorporated into the substance-use surveillance dashboard the province already publishes, but for some reason there's just no appetite to share any information about these operators and the funding that goes to these services," Hyshka said. "The province is investing hundreds of millions of dollars in these services, but there's just no accountability in terms of their performance and whether they're achieving their stated objectives."[23] Edmonton-based investigative journalist Charles Rusnell noted in a July 2022 story for the *Tyee* that it was "now impossible to track whether the government's abstinence-based recovery policy is working because it doesn't track how many people enter treatment or how many successfully complete it."

There's also an absence of data on the harm-reduction side of the equation, with no localized data on overdoses across the province publicly available since mid-2020, despite the government continuing to collect that data based on emergency medical service (EMS) calls for overdoses in Edmonton and Calgary. Rusnell obtained heat maps showing EMS responses to overdoses in the inner-city Edmonton neighbourhoods of Eastwood, Woodcroft East, and Woodcraft West increased by 171 percent over a year, from 1,164 in 2020 to 3,155 in 2021. These figures exclude instances in which a person is revived using naloxone and thus no ambulance is called. Harm-reduction advocate Rylan Kafara told Rusnell he has no doubt this increase is related to the closure of the Boyle Street SCS, underscoring the urgency of reopening the site, opening more sites elsewhere, and ending the disciplinary approach to drug use.

The government's surveillance dashboard solely focuses on aggregate data for Edmonton, Calgary, Fort McMurray, Grande Prairie, Red Deer, Lethbridge, and Medicine Hat regions at the expense of rural areas, making it difficult for front-line workers to respond adequately. Prior to the release of the surveillance dashboard, the government provided geospatial data in its quarterly reports on drug-poisoning deaths. Through a freedom-of-information request, the *Edmonton Journal* and Edmonton Zone Medical Staff Association (EZMSA) obtained data on how the drug-poisoning crisis is impacting specific geographical zones across Alberta, including rural areas. For 2021, the provincial opioid death rate was 33.72 people per 100,000. Some rural areas had death rates significantly higher than the provincial average, such as Canmore with 103.13 and Cardston-Kainai, which includes the Blood Tribe reserve, with 107.81. Edmonton-Eastwood had the highest death rate in the province at a staggering 291.85. Calgary Centre, where Safeworks is located, had a rate of 195.58.

Associate Ministry of Mental Health and Addiction spokesperson Eric Engler admitted to the *Edmonton Journal* that the government made a "deliberate choice to not publicly share neighbourhood-level data," a decision he attributed to privacy concerns and not wanting to stigmatize racialized communities.[24] According to EZMSA, this conscious decision "leaves communities in the dark and grappling with deadly situations on their own, without key information which could be used to advocate for additional resources. This further perpetuates a cycle of trauma, shame, and loss." This secretive approach might be bad for the purposes of sound public policy, but it enabled the Kenney government to justify its evidence-free, recovery-centric response to the drug-poisoning crisis. Recovery should be freely accessible for those who want it, but it shouldn't be done on the backs of those who continue to use drugs.

Toward a Future Conservative Drug Policy

When Danielle Smith officially replaced Kenney as Alberta's premier on October 11, 2022, Marshall Smith (no relation) received a major promotion, becoming Premier Smith's chief of staff. Ellis was shifted to the Ministry of Public Safety, and Calgary-Currie MLA Nick Milliken was put in charge of a full-fledged Ministry of Mental Health and Addiction. Smith made it clear she would go even further than Kenney in her recovery-first approach to the drug-poisoning crisis. In February 2023, *Globe and Mail* reporter Alanna Smith (no relation) revealed the UCP drafted legislation to force people with severe addictions into recovery against their will — the first law of its kind in Canada.

On the federal level, Conservative Party Leader Pierre Poilievre, who served alongside Kenney in the Harper Cabinet from 2013 to 2015, made explicit his desire to emulate Alberta's approach. In a video entitled *Everything Feels Broken*, Poilievre sits outside a homeless encampment in Vancouver, shamelessly using it as a prop to depict many of its residents as "hopelessly addicted to drugs, putting poison in their bodies" — a clear echoing of Kenney's campaign-trail rhetoric. Poilievre proceeds to argue that the struggles of these people "are the result of a failed experiment" that is a "deliberate policy of woke NDP and Liberal governments to provide taxpayer-funded drugs [and] flood our streets with easy access to these poisons."

To justify his argument, Poilievre cherry-picks data from November 2021 to July 2022 to argue Alberta has "managed to cut overdoses in half," while using data from 2016 to 2021 to contrast these statistics with a tripling of overdoses in British Columbia since Justin Trudeau became prime minister, as journalist Paul Wells noted.[25] But if we look at Alberta's statistics since Kenney became premier, opioid overdoses went from 65 in May 2019 to 100 in July 2022. Not as stark an increase as in British Columbia, but a far cry from the 50 percent reduction Poilievre claims. However, if we put partisanship aside and look at the numbers in Alberta from 2016 to 2021, as Poilievre does for British Columbia, overdoses in Alberta more than quadrupled from 40 in January 2016 to 175 in December 2021.

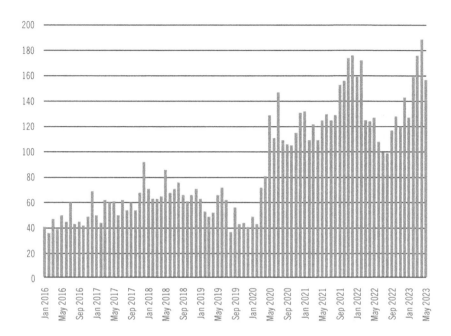

While drug-poisoning deaths decreased over certain months in 2022, they remained higher than they were at any point prior to the pandemic.
Source: Alberta Substance Use Surveillance System/Government of Alberta.

Poilievre's main contention that safe supply is responsible for increasing overdoses in British Columbia is pure hokum, as the academic literature clearly shows. The notion that there's this massive supply of government-funded drugs is similarly false. British Columbia's safe supply program has been highly limited since its inception. While the B.C. government claims 12,000 people have accessed its safe supply program, the actual number is closer to 500. The B.C. NDP government deceptively includes in that figure people who have received prescriptions for substances that were already legal, such as oxycodone and hydromorphone. By contrast, there are at least 83,000 British Columbians with opioid-use disorder, according to a March 2022 report in the *Tyee*. It's not the existence of a safe supply then; it's insufficient implementation that's killing people.

Kenney created a template for future conservative drug policy by demonstrating that old-school, tough-on-crime conservatism can only go so far. A compassionate face needs to be put on these policies, and his "recovery-oriented system of care" does just that. Kenney deserves credit, however slight, for removing financial barriers to accessing recovery, which no doubt helped many disadvantaged people who wanted to access recovery do so. The way in which he did so, however, served as a bait-and-switch to distract from his broader agenda of hollowing out the state's functions to a bare minimum while enriching unaccountable private actors. Like charter schools, these privately operated recovery clinics will enjoy lavish public subsidies without any element of public accountability. By fully subsidizing private recovery and empowering law enforcement to compel people into treatment without addressing any of the material causes for why so many are dying of drug poisoning, he ensured an endless supply of clients for his allies.

Not everybody is ready to enter recovery, and an unwillingness to do so shouldn't be a death sentence. This hyperfocus on recovery is rooted in Kenney's strict moralism. Either you're a sinner who's using drugs, or you're setting yourself on the path to righteousness by entering treatment; either you abstain, or you're a failure. There's no neutral ground in this view. Kenney's shifting of resources from evidence-based interventions to an approach more suitable to his ideological leanings is a microcosm of his attitude toward health care. Once the pandemic hit, Kenney's public health positions were torn between ideology and political calculus.

10

THE PLAGUE

A SERIES OF DECISIONS PRECEDED THE disastrous handling of the Covid-19 pandemic across Canada, which as of September 2023 has killed 53,644 people across the country and decimated its long-term-care homes. The country was set up for failure, thanks to the hollowing out of the public health-care system as a result of cuts during the administrations of prime ministers Brian Mulroney and Jean Chrétien, when the size of government came under increased scrutiny. Under Chrétien, Kenney cheered on his cuts as the head of the Canadian Taxpayers Federation while pushing him to go further. In 1984, when Mulroney became prime minister, there were 6.8 hospital beds per 1,000 Canadians; by 2018, there were 2.5.[1] "Some of those beds would've come in handy during the pandemic," noted Paris Marx in the online news outlet the *Breach*.[2]

Of all the calamitous government responses to Covid, none produced as strong a backlash against a government as Alberta's. Canadians living in other provinces could look at their governments, for all their failures, and conclude at least they weren't living in Alberta, whose premier was driven by, on the one hand, an ideological inclination toward strengthening capitalist relations, and on the other hand, practical considerations regarding his own political fortunes. Lorian Hardcastle, a University of Calgary professor of health law, told me that of all the Canadian provinces, Alberta should have had the least difficulty during the pandemic. "We aren't the poorest province, we aren't the province with the fewest doctors per capita, we aren't the province with the fewest ICU beds per capita, we aren't the oldest province," she said. "On any metric, we really were set up for success, but we just didn't have a government that was willing to impose restrictions."

University of Calgary political scientist Lisa Young references the political "comorbidities" Kenney faced going into the pandemic, which were largely reflective of the tensions within his fragile UCP coalition that were brought to the fore.[3] It's difficult to disentangle Kenney's Covid response from his sagging political fortunes and vice versa. His response to the pandemic was an incoherent mess, which attempted to please both those who sought a more activist government role in combatting the pandemic and those who wanted to do nothing, which was roughly divided along urban and rural, or PC and Wildrose, lines.

The most fatal flaw in Kenney's response was his ideological inclination to put the needs of a smoothly functioning economy over those of protecting lives. When he repeatedly jettisoned this approach temporarily, he appeared weak to his base, exacerbating the political tensions within the party he created. While Alberta's initial pandemic response has largely evaded scrutiny, his "prosperity-first" mentality, as University of Alberta political scientist Jared Wesley called it,[4] was present well before the pandemic and manifested itself early with Kenney's efforts to push through health-care privatization while keeping as many businesses open as possible. The Covid crisis laid bare the folly of this approach.

Kenney reluctantly implemented the most basic pandemic restrictions, with various ebbs and flows throughout based on political calculations, but he repeatedly did so when it was too late to have a significant impact. In Covid's first year, Kenney's ideological preferences were on full display, with his cuts to the public health-care system, which continued throughout the plague, and his minimization of the ultimately fatal outbreak at the Cargill meat-packing facility; in 2021, as the political tensions within his caucus came to the forefront, his response oscillated more wildly; and in 2022, it all came crashing down.

Amid the talk of the pandemic's impact on Kenney's political fortunes, it's crucial not to lose sight of the coronavirus's human toll. As of August 2023, at least 5,818 Albertans have officially died of Covid. Deaths from the pandemic, the drug-poisoning crisis, and the general strain on the public health-care system led to 10,232 excess deaths — that is, more deaths than one could expect based on normal mortality rates — in Alberta from January 2020 to November 2022, according to a study from University of Toronto researcher Tara Moriarty, who argues Covid deaths were under-reported, particularly during the late 2021 Omicron surge.

Early Privatization Efforts

In February 2019, Kenney unveiled his public health-care guarantee, which assured voters a UCP government would maintain or increase health-care funding and preserve a publicly accessible publicly funded system. This rested uneasily beside his 2017 promise to defer all policy decisions to the UCP membership. At the 2019 UCP convention, delegates voted against a motion to ensure any health-care reforms conformed to the 1984 Canada Health Act, which prohibits financial barriers toward accessing health care, previewing the tensions between Kenney and the party grassroots that would characterize his erratic pandemic response.

With the UCP in power, Health Minister Tyler Shandro announced a $2 million contract to the Ernst & Young consulting firm to review Alberta Health Services, intended in part "to drive greater efficiencies" — a common euphemism for the early stages of privatization. Shandro promised the government wasn't "blowing anything up," which is never a good sign. After the UCP's inaugural budget slightly increased health-care funding, Shandro, who owns shares in his wife's private insurance brokerage company,[5] appeared outside a private Calgary optometry clinic to announce the government's goal of contracting out 80,000 surgeries to the private sector over four years, including hip and knee replacements and cataract surgeries, to reduce pressure on the public system. The Ernst & Young report hadn't yet been released, but the MacKinnon panel had already recommended the province offload certain procedures to private actors to save money.

Privatization, however, doesn't save money, nor does it reduce pressure on the public system, Hardcastle explains. Private clinics are reluctant to conduct more complex surgeries because they're less profitable, leaving them to an increasingly underfunded public system. The basic procedures private clinics do provide end up costing the public more for the same reason. Privatization, Hardcastle adds, led the public system to respond to deficiencies in the private system, rather than the reverse, citing the short-lived Health Resources Centre in Calgary, which offered private orthopedic surgeries before it went bankrupt. Its 900 patients were transferred to the public system, which also had to pick up the tab for the clinic's insolvency. So while health-care privatization doesn't serve its stated practical aim, it does afford a valuable investment opportunity for a select few, allowing them to diversify their portfolios at public expense. Kenney later boasted of his government "massively" expanding the reach of private health care while expressing regret that the pandemic prevented the government from going "further and deeper into health-care reform."[6] It wasn't for lack of trying.

On February 3, a week after the first Covid case was detected in Canada, but six weeks before the coronavirus was declared a pandemic and a state of emergency announced on March 17, Shandro unveiled the results of the Ernst & Young review. It provided 72 opportunities to save a total of $1.9 billion in health spending. Some of its recommendations, such as closing underused hospitals and trauma centres, were deemed too radical for the UCP, no doubt reflecting electoral concerns. Others, which Shandro attempted to implement — namely, its calls to reduce physician compensation and outsource non-medical hospital services to the private sector — contributed to the demoralization of health workers at the worst possible time.

Most physicians were compensated by charging the government fees per visit. These were worked out in negotiations with the government, which allowed doctors to bill a $41 base fee per visit, with an additional charge, known as a "complex modifier," for visits that lasted more than 15 minutes. Shandro used an impasse in contract negotiations with the Alberta Medical

Association (AMA) to impose on it a new contract that fitted the Ernst & Young report and MacKinnon panel recommendations. The new contract, which AMA president Dr. Christine Molnar learned about through media reports, unilaterally cut the fee complex modifier by 50 percent — from $18 per visit to $9 — beginning April 1, with the goal of eliminating it entirely in 2021. It also stopped funding overhead costs for hospital services. Molnar said the imposition of a contract on physicians was unprecedented since the introduction of public health care. The two sides ultimately reached an agreement 30 months into the pandemic, with less than half of physicians turning out to vote.[7] In the interim, hundreds of physicians left the profession due to pandemic pressures, which the government's belligerent approach to doctors exacerbated.

Kate Bisby, a Calgary-based doctor who works with vulnerable communities, including the unhoused and people who use drugs, said in an interview that the government's dismantling of the province's harm-reduction infrastructure was just one manifestation of a broader attack on public health care in Alberta; the shredding of the AMA agreement was another. Due to the specific population she serves, Bisby was paid under an alternative relationship plan with the government, which provided doctors with a set income, but she saw the effect of the unilateral fee changes on her colleagues working in hospital settings early in the pandemic.

She recalled doing patient consultations at the Peter Lougheed Centre in northeast Calgary when a fellow physician asked if Bisby's practice had extra funds to cover the first week of their patient's inhaler prescription. Normally, hospitals could absorb the cost of a patient's medication when they were immediately discharged to bridge any gap in insurance coverage. Owing to the government's cuts to hospital overhead costs, her hospital colleage couldn't afford it. "There was a real push at that time to just get people out of the hospital with Covid bearing down, and there was just no money. It was just an absurd situation," Bisby said.

Another early issue Bisby identified was the move to providing virtual care, which naturally caused chaos at the pandemic's outset. For the first week of Covid, physicians were only allowed to charge $20 per virtual visit — less than half of what they were able to charge for an in-person visit, and even less if it took longer than 15 minutes. When the government updated the billing code to compensate physicians the same as they would for in-person appointments retroactive to the beginning of the pandemic, it was conditional upon patients initiating the appointment. This proved troublesome, since many patients, particularly the most vulnerable, were unaware of these changes, yet if the doctor called them to inform them of the changes, they sacrificed full compensation.

While doctors were preoccupied with figuring out how their virtual compensation would work, the government announced that patients would be able to virtually visit doctors through the Telus Babylon Health app, which Kenney hailed as a "new innovative way" to access health care. Doctors opting to use the app were connected with patients on a first-come, first-served basis, severing them from patients with whom they had developed a relationship. Hardcastle told me the government's promotion of a health app owned by a publicly traded company exemplified a disturbing trend toward the "corporatization" of health care, raising concerns about the commercialization of patient data.

A lack of security for this data became a major point of criticism. After investigating the app, Jill Clayton, the province's privacy commissioner, concluded it violated Alberta's privacy standards, expressing particular concern about its use of facial-recognition software, collection of patients' government-issued ID, and recording of appointments. Despite these concerns, as of this writing, the app is still available. The government's promotion of Babylon's profoundly flawed health-care delivery is emblematic of the government placing corporate interests at the forefront of its pandemic response. This pattern would repeat itself to fatal effect in the workplace.

Lives and Livelihoods

On April 7, a few weeks into the pandemic, Kenney delivered a 15-minute special address to Albertans outlining the dire situation the province faced if action wasn't taken, pre-empting Chief Medical Officer of Health Dr. Deena Hinshaw's delivery of the same Covid modelling statistics the following day.

The speech was entitled "Protecting Lives and Livelihoods," which would be the government's mantra throughout the pandemic, placing people's health on the same level as business interests. In the address, Kenney argued that "the two are intertwined." In practice, however, keeping the economic engine running would be placed at the forefront of the pandemic response, with modifications rooted in political expediency.

Despite Kenney's rhetoric of urgency, Alberta's restrictions were looser than those in other provinces. The government outlined dozens of "essential workplaces" where work was expected to continue as normal, including the energy sector, construction, agriculture, and food processing. The Canadian Association of Petroleum Producers, bruised by low demand, drafted a list at the immediate outset of the pandemic of 132 regulations it had long advocated the government cut, meeting in secret with Energy Minister Sonya Savage, who publicly boasted how pandemic restrictions on social gatherings made it a "great time to be building pipelines,"[8] to discuss their requests. Half of them were ultimately granted, including reduced environmental monitoring and Indigenous consultation.[9]

The consequences of Kenney's approach to Covid during the first wave of the pandemic were most immediately apparent in the meat-packing industry, with the Cargill facility in High River — about a half-hour drive south of Calgary — becoming the location of the single largest outbreak in North America. The Cargill plant is the largest meat-packing facility in Canada, responsible for 4,500 heads of cattle per day, amounting to 40 percent of Canadian beef processing. The Minnesota-based company made $2.56 billion in profit the year leading up to the pandemic. Workers, who were paid a starting wage of $17.95 per hour, were either employed on the kill floor, where the cattle were slaughtered, or the fabrication line, where they stood shoulder to shoulder cutting beef carcasses for packaging for eight hours per day.[10]

The workforce at meat-packing facilities in Alberta were two-thirds immigrants, compared to about a quarter of the general population, and 18 percent refugees, compared to 3 percent of the general population.[11] Many would have likely come to Canada as a result, or in spite of, the policies Kenney pursued as a federal Cabinet minister. Somewhere around 70 percent of Cargill's 2,000-person workforce is Filipino. On April 12, the day before 38 Covid cases were reported at the plant, 250 Filipino residents of High River wrote an open letter to Mayor Craig Snodgrass calling for the plant to be shut down for two weeks to avoid further spread. United Food and Commercial Workers (UFCW) Local 401, the largest private-sector union in Alberta, echoed this demand the following day, demanding the company provide full compensation for workers while they isolated. Instead of ordering a temporary shutdown, Cargill opted to temporarily layoff half the plant's workforce, which reduced production by two-thirds.

For the workers who remained, the company staggered breaks and installed plastic dividers in the cafeteria, but their jobs continued as usual in closely cramped quarters. At the same time, workers reported being encouraged to return to work mere days after testing positive for Covid. A $500 bonus the company offered to workers with perfect attendance effectively incentivized workers to show up even if they were ill.[12] An April 15 Occupational Health and Safety (OHS) inspection consisted of a manager taking video of the workplace and sending it to officials at a remote location via a video-conferencing app. Predictably, OHS concluded that "as far as it is reasonably practicable for the employer to do so," the workplace was made safe.[13]

By the time the government and company held an April 18 virtual town hall with the Cargill workforce, which UFCW wasn't invited to, there were 200 cases at the plant. Two hours before the call, Dr. Hinshaw informed several senior health and agriculture officials, including the deputy agriculture minister, that two food inspectors contracted Covid at the plant after Cargill implemented its protective measures. Hinshaw sat alongside Agriculture Minister Devin Dreeshen and Labour Minister Jason Copping, both of whom were briefed beforehand, while Dreeshen baldly lied to the workers, assuring them that "everything that needs to be done both to keep people safe and the food supply maintained is being done." The government faulted everything *but* working conditions for the Cargill outbreak. Dreeshen, echoing Hinshaw, cited overcrowded housing conditions and widespread carpooling as the major culprits.[14] The racialized workers were blamed for their low socio-economic status.

The day after the town hall, one of the employees who contracted Covid, 67-year-old Vietnamese immigrant Hiep Bui, died, and on April 20, Cargill agreed to close the plant for two weeks. At the same time, there was a major outbreak at the JBS meat-packing plant in Brooks — Canada's second-largest. At an April 22 press conference, when there were 96 cases at JBS and 440 at Cargill, Kenney encouraged Albertans to look on the bright side, citing the fact that just two of Alberta's 200 meat-packing facilities had major Covid outbreaks as a "reflection of our success" in having "acted quickly when there have been outbreaks," despite the deception his own government engaged in to keep Cargill open for a week after its workers called for it to be idled. In that time, another racialized worker, 51-year-old UFCW shop steward Benito Quesada, who emigrated from Mexico in 2007, contracted Covid, which he died from on May 12. Three days after the plant's closure, 71-year-old Armando Sallegue, who was visiting his Cargill worker son from the Philippines, got Covid, which killed him on May 5, the same day it was revealed that 949 Cargill workers — almost half the workforce — had been infected. These deaths were direct casualties of Kenney's zeal to prioritize the livelihoods of employers over the lives of their workers.

The Cargill plant reopened on May 4 against the will of 80 percent of workers surveyed by the UFCW. Not even a week after Quesada's death, which later became the subject of an RCMP investigation marking the first criminal probe into a workplace-related Covid fatality, Kenney began the process of reopening the economy. By late May, he was referring to Covid, which he previously likened to the struggle during the First World War and the Great Depression, as a mere "influenza that does not generally threaten life apart from the elderly and the immunocompromised."[15] As bad as Kenney's response to the first Covid wave was, it only got worse.

Privatization Rears Its Head Again

Throughout the summer of 2020, Covid cases remained relatively low as the government pursued its phased reopening strategy. That began to change in October when daily new cases exceeded 200 for the first time since the initial wave. While cases continued on an upward trajectory, on October 13, the CBC revealed that during the summer, the provincial health authority outlined plans to eliminate 10,700 full-time health-care jobs, impacting 16,700 staff, including front-line workers such as nurses. "There is much to accomplish in a short period of time, and an intensity of impact that must be recognized," the draft plan noted. "The pace and amount of work set out here is not to be understated, with the collection of initiatives truly changing the way health care is delivered in Alberta for years to come."

After CBC reporters Charles Rusnell and Jennie Russell reached out to the Ministry of Health for comment, the government leaked an updated plan to the *Edmonton Journal* that outlined revised plans to cut 11,000 jobs, including 800 front-line positions eliminated through attrition. The changes, which were expected to save provincial coffers $600 million annually, largely consisted of contracting out lab services, housekeeping, and food services to the private sector. In the draft obtained by the CBC, the government acknowledged this posed the risk of provoking labour unrest, which was precisely what occurred about two weeks later after the government put out a request for proposal to outsource laundry services.

On October 26, when the seven-day average of daily new cases reached 450, health-care workers in 35 municipalities — not just large centres such as Calgary, Edmonton, Lethbridge, and Red Deer but also small towns such as Peace River, Whitecourt, Cardston, and Smoky Lake — decided they had nothing to lose and walked off the job in a wildcat strike. The bulk of the people striking were general support staff whose jobs were on the line, but they were joined on the picket line by nurses and health-care aides concerned by the assault on public health care. The government assured workers their jobs would continue under the private umbrella, but this meant a lack of protections offered them by union representation, fundamentally altering the terms of their employment.

Other unions, including the United Nurses of Alberta (UNA), the Health Sciences Association of Alberta, and the Alberta Teachers' Association, expressed support. "We're not going to stand for being ripped apart and discarded, like Kleenex," UNA president Heather Smith said, expressing the sentiments of those who walked off the job. "We are not disposable as a workforce."[16] It certainly didn't help that a week before the job action, the UCP grassroots voted in favour of introducing two-tiered health care. The twin crises of the pandemic and the government's broader attack on a public health-care system that was needed to operate at full strength now more than ever evidently proved too much for workers to bear.

The Alberta Labour Relations Board, upon the urging of Alberta Health Services (AHS), unsurprisingly declared the wildcat strike illegal, demanding workers return to their jobs, which they did on October 27. That same day, AHS revealed it was investigating workers who participated in the strike, with Finance Minister Travis Toews expressing a zero-tolerance approach toward "individual employees" who walked off the job due to the policies his government implemented. The investigations resulted in disciplinary action against 798 participants, consisting primarily of letters of reprimand, with 27 suspensions. The strike didn't prevent large-scale layoffs, which occurred in a piecemeal fashion throughout 2022, with the outsourcing of laundry services, lab services, and in Calgary and Edmonton, hospital food vendors.

Here was a clear example of the Kenney government's efforts to further entrench corporate power during the pandemic, which we also saw with its promotion of the Babylon app and the deadly deception of Cargill workers. On this front, the UCP was united. But as case counts exploded in November, Kenney's decision to belatedly and reluctantly reimpose pandemic restrictions caused him trouble politically, which only grew as the pandemic ground on. He became increasingly torn between the conflicting ideological and electoral impulses that he was able to masterfully balance throughout his career.

None of This Makes Any Sense

As case counts continued to increase in late October, Kenney maintained the future of the pandemic "is in the hands of 4.4 million Albertans in the actions they take as individuals," emphasizing the role of "personal responsibility."[17] This was his default position, which served to offload responsibility for pandemic management onto everyone else — another, more subtle form of health-care privatization. That approach evidently wasn't working, so the day of the wildcat strike, Dr. Hinshaw imposed a 15-person gathering limit, but only in Edmonton and Calgary, in response to growing case counts. These limited restrictions excluded restaurant dining, worship services, wedding ceremonies, conferences, or funeral services, which maintained a 100-person limit. "The warning bell is ringing. I want all of us to hear its call," she said. Suffice to say, they didn't.

In the first half of November, groups of physicians wrote a series of letters to Kenney, Shandro, and Hinshaw calling for the temporary shutdown of all indoor activities and a prohibition on gatherings outside households while keeping schools open to avoid disrupting students' learning. On November 15, two days after daily new cases exceeded 1,000 for the first time, Kenney said he *might* impose new restrictions if Albertans didn't get their acts together, emphasizing the province's "culture of … responsible freedom."[18] Kenney

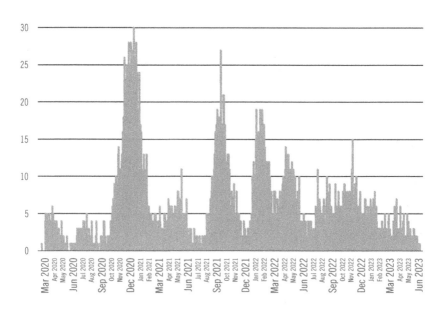

Alberta's deadliest Covid wave occurred in late 2020/early 2021.
Source: COVID-19 Alberta Statistics/Government of Alberta.

then disappeared for 10 days at the outset of what would be Alberta's deadliest Covid wave, with 1,418 deaths from November 1 to January 31.

On November 25, when the seven-day average of new cases was 1,291, Kenney announced a ban on gatherings outside households, unless Albertans wanted to go to a casino, restaurant, bar, or mall, which were permitted to continue operating at 25 percent capacity. Hardcastle, the University of Calgary health law professor, aptly characterized to me the nonsensical nature of this approach, which she described as another example of Kenney prioritizing economic over scientific factors. "There's no way that it's safer to be in the mall with [hundreds] of people with my 10 friends than having two of those people over to my house." Banning private gatherings while keeping the wheels of capitalism churning encapsulated Kenney's harsh approach to the pandemic, in which socialization was only permitted in service of market needs or religious salvation.

The demoralization of health-care workers continued apace. At this point, recruiters from other provinces — namely, British Columbia and Ontario — attempted to draw disenchanted health-care workers from Alberta. One trying to attract doctors to the Vancouver area was quite explicit in its pitch: "Doctors — Escape the Politics."[19] Dr. Bisby went to Vancouver Island to escape the chaos engulfing Alberta, unsure if she was going to continue her medical practice. She knew the Kenney government's management of the pandemic wasn't going to improve from the first wave and would probably get worse. "I didn't feel that there was much if any thought being given to my safety or my patients' safety. I was not comfortable working in that system [so] I decided to take time out." When she returned to Calgary months later, Bisby started working part-time and is unsure if she will ever return to full-time. "It's all been too exhausting."

By December 1, with 100 people in ICUs, the *Toronto Star* reported that Alberta hospitals were double-bunking ICU beds, which AHS euphemistically called "patient cohorting," and rationing oxygen. Dr. Ilan Schwartz, a professor at the University of Alberta's Department of Medicine, told the *Star* he'd never seen anything like it. On December 8, with a seven-day average of 1,766 cases and 128 people in ICUs, Kenney finally shut down restaurants, gyms, casinos, recreation centres, libraries, theatres, and salons, and banned outdoor gatherings, which had hitherto been limited to 10 people, yet churches and retail stores were permitted to remain open at 15 percent capacity. Alberta became the final province to implement a province-wide mask mandate, a responsibility Kenney previously outsourced to municipalities.

At the press conference announcing these restrictions, *Calgary Herald* reporter Sammy Hudes asked Kenney if he felt personal responsibility for his reluctance to impose restrictions as cases skyrocketed. "That sounds a lot more like an NDP speech than a media question. I reject the entire premise of your question," Kenney scolded Hudes before applauding his own "balanced" approach, suggesting the reporter was contributing to "drive-by smears on Alberta." Kenney, who touted the virtues of personal responsibility, refused to take any himself. While this seems hypocritical, it's not when you remember that his political philosophy is rooted in strengthening established power. Personal responsibility is for the plebs.

Kenney, badly bruised from revelations that some Cabinet ministers and his chief of staff travelled internationally while he was tightening restrictions on everyone else, was more cautious in reopening as the vaccine became available in the new year. On January 29, with new cases at a seven-day average of 431, he announced a phased wind-down of restrictions based on hospitalizations, which had exceeded 900 per month earlier. But again, the plan had no rhyme or reason, and enforcement was downloaded onto businesses themselves. If, by February 8, there were fewer than 600 hospitalizations, then restaurants would be permitted to reopen with only six people permitted per table, who had to be from the same household, or designated close contacts of a person living alone; liquor service would have to end by 10:00 p.m. and food service by 11:00 p.m. If, three weeks later, there were fewer than 450 hospitalizations, then restrictions would ease on retail, banquet halls, and conference centres.

The plan never made it past this phase, as case counts and hospitalizations grew in mid-March. On April 1, after physicians called on the premier to implement a two-week "circuit breaker" lockdown, Kenney instead issued a "plea" for Albertans to follow existing, convoluted restrictions with Easter weekend on the horizon. He said he would only introduce tougher restrictions if the province was faced with similar "exponential growth" that had begun in late November,[20] setting the province up for another failure. On April 6, with the week's average daily case count having surpassed 1,000, Kenney announced a reversion to the pre-reopening plan status quo, with libraries closed but malls open at reduced capacity. Notably, he gave restaurants, bars, and cafés three days to shut down indoor dining, allowing the virus more time to spread in those settings.

At this point, opposition to pandemic restrictions became increasingly widespread, particularly within Kenney's own caucus, reflecting an urban and rural divide. The day after he announced new restrictions, 15 UCP MLAs, all from ridings outside Edmonton and Calgary, wrote an open letter decrying a return to restrictions; after the letter's publication, they were joined by two more. The letter called on Kenney to defend Albertans' "livelihoods and freedoms" — an interesting twist on "lives and livelihoods" — by pushing forward with his abandoned reopening plan, adding that they raised these concerns with Kenney, but he didn't take them into consideration. Kenney defended the letter's signatories on free-speech grounds, using it as an opportunity to position himself as a sensible moderate in pursuit of "a common ground that can unite most Albertans."[21] Kenney's pursuit of a non-existent middle ground to mitigate the pandemic indeed unified Albertans — against his leadership.

On May 1 and 2, an illegal "No More Lockdowns" rodeo near Bowden, a town half an hour's drive south of Red Deer, attracted thousands of disgruntled Albertans. Kenney called such a large-scale event in brazen violation of Covid restrictions "a slap in the face to everybody who is observing the rules," and an insult to "Alberta's Western heritage."[22] But days earlier, Kenney legitimized such behaviour when he denied a causal link between restrictions and the spread of Covid. If Kenney truly believed this, then why impose any restrictions at all? The day after the rodeo wrapped up, Alberta became the Covid hotspot of Canada and the United States, with a weekly average of 440.5 daily cases per million people, surpassing Michigan, which averaged 405.9 per million. "When the health system crashes, it'll crash tremendously," warned Calgary-based family physician Dr. Christine Gibson.[23]

On May 4, Kenney enacted further restrictions, including a ban on outdoor dining at restaurants, a 10 percent capacity limit at retail shops, and a 15-person capacity limit at houses of worship. Kenney said he was announcing further restrictions "precisely because, for whatever reason, Albertans are ignoring the rules we currently have in place," again offloading responsibility onto individuals. Jared Wesley, the University of Alberta political scientist, noted that perhaps the issue wasn't so much people violating the rules, but that the rules in place ignored a key source of transmission — the workplace. The government, Wesley said, was acting as if "there's something magical that's happening in Alberta's workplaces that makes them immune to Covid." Kenney, to his credit, in this announcement ordered the shutdown of any workplace that had a Covid outbreak, but that was precisely what he should have done in April 2020, when the meat-packing industry was overwhelmed with infections. That it took him a year to do so was indicative of his ideological inclinations, as well as pressures from the party grassroots encouraging his worst instincts.

The measures announced in early May significantly reduced cases over the next couple of weeks, but they also heightened the caucus tensions highlighted in the letter a month earlier. On May 13, Central Peace–Notley MLA Todd Loewen, one of the letter's signatories, publicly called for Kenney's resignation in a Facebook post that notably didn't mention Covid but referred to the premier's authoritarian leadership style and mixed messaging around various issues. He announced his resignation as the UCP caucus chair but said he was still committed to the premise of the UCP. "We did not unite around blind loyalty to one man. And while [Kenney] promoted unity, it is clear that unity is falling apart."

The same day as Loewen's missive, the UCP caucus met digitally and voted via text message to expel him and another letter signatory, Cypress–Medicine Hat MLA Drew Barnes, who went even further than the others in claiming the restrictions were "just as bad as the Covid crisis."[24] The results of the vote were never disclosed, not even to other caucus members, but Loewen insisted he and Barnes had support within caucus. While Kenney got his way with the removal of Barnes and Loewens, he was politically wounded and thus sought to put the pandemic in the rearview mirror. However, the pandemic had other plans.

Open for Summer

Kenney announced on May 26 his "Open for Summer" plan, which would phase reopening based on a combination of hospitalization numbers and vaccination rates for the first two steps, and just vaccination rates for the third and final phase, signifying the government throwing public health considerations to the wind. If 70 percent of eligible Albertans got their first vaccine dose by June, pandemic restrictions would be almost entirely eliminated, right in time for the Calgary Stampede, which had been cancelled for the first time in a century in 2020. Earlier in the pandemic, this fixation on vaccination was identified as a problem, with 16.4 percent of Albertans expressing no intention to get vaccinated, compared with the national figure of 9.3 percent, in summer 2020. It just so happened that these anti-vaxxers were more likely to be lower-income, politically on the far right, and sympathetic to Alberta separatism[25] — precisely the types of people Kenney cultivated in his campaign to unite the right.

Undoubtedly, 70 percent of eligible people receiving their first vaccine dose was an important landmark, and Kenney behaved responsibly in encouraging Albertans to do so. However, experts questioned whether that would be sufficient to justify the rapid, wholesale reopening of society so Kenney could get a Stampede photo op, particularly as the more deadly Delta variant was beginning to circulate. These skeptical voices were the subject of derision and ridicule from Kenney's online troll brigade, chief among them issues manager Matt Wolf of kamikaze scandal fame, who tweeted in response to a critic on June 2 — "The pandemic is ending. Accept it."

While restrictions remained in place, on the same day of Wolf's flippant tweet, Kenney, Shandro, UCP house leader Jason Nixon, and Finance Minister Toews were revealed to have been enjoying dinner and drinks on the rooftop of the Sky Palace, a penthouse on top of the federal building in Edmonton, whose costly renovation under scandal-plagued Premier

Alison Redford made it a potent symbol of government entitlement. They couldn't have picked a worse location to violate public health orders, which at the time only permitted outdoor gatherings if people were physically distanced two metres apart and forbade them from entering and exiting indoor spaces. The incident laid bare the hollowness of Kenney's personal responsibility rhetoric — something opponents and supporters of restrictions could agree on.

But by then, polling from the Angus Reid Institute suggested Kenney's approval rating was in the gutter, so he gambled on the one thing that might reverse his fortunes — a return to normalcy. On June 18, with 70 percent of eligible Albertans at least partially vaccinated, Kenney and Shandro announced Alberta would be officially open for summer on Canada Day, whereas Ontario and British Columbia more prudently aimed for autumn. Kenney made it clear that his intention was a permanent reopening. "This is open for good, not just for summer." He insisted the deaths of two vaccinated people who contracted Delta in a hospital outbreak shouldn't put a damper on festivities, dismissing them as "very elderly, very frail, immuno-compromised people with multiple comorbidities."[26] Shandro, who was all smiles, agreed, calling the threat of Delta "statistically insignificant." So confident was the UCP of its hands-off approach that it sold BEST SUMMER EVER — ALBERTA 2021 caps on its website, which remained on sale even as cases climbed.

In a surreptitiously recorded video at a July 10 Stampede event, Kenney reiterated his intention never to return to Covid restrictions. "I swear to God," the devout Catholic said, making the sign of the cross with his hands, predicting 80 percent of Albertans would be vaccinated by the fall. When the person recording the video asked him what about the 20 percent who were unvaccinated, Kenney said it was fine because most of them were young. "Covid is not a threat to people under 30, effectively, so the fact that 20 percent of them aren't vaccinated, don't worry about it." For a brief time, it appeared as if this strategy might work. For most of July, case counts remained low, as did hospital admissions.

On July 28, as cases began to increase again but hospitalizations remained stable, Dr. Hinshaw held her first Covid briefing in a month, announcing a "major, major shift" in how the province was going to treat Covid. It would now be treated as "endemic," like any other respiratory infection, rather than the "primary number one risk that all other things are secondary to." Case counts continued to steadily climb after her announcements, as did ICU admissions, which surpassed the 33 there had been when the province reopened on July 1 by August 11, with 37 people in intensive care. While the second wave was the deadliest, the upcoming fourth wave put the greatest strain on Alberta's hospital system.

Kenney went on a three-week-long vacation on August 12, disappearing as ICU admissions steadily escalated, surpassing 100 for the first time since June upon his August 30 return. The premier claimed he was in contact "every single day" with staff and government officials while he was away, but a copy of his calendar obtained by *CTV News* in October suggested

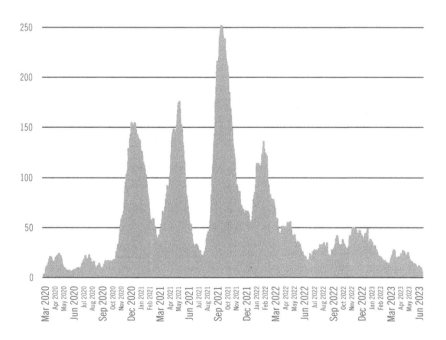

ICU admissions reached their peak in the fall of 2021 after Kenney made the catastrophic decision to lift all pandemic restrictions in time for the Calgary Stampede, causing the functional collapse of Alberta's health-care system. Source: COVID-19 Alberta Statistics/ Government of Alberta.

otherwise. He had "Weekly Covid Update" meetings written on the calendar on August 18 and 25. For the University of Calgary's Hardcastle, this disappearance was the lowest point of Kenney's pandemic response. "There were various points before then when, yes, we could criticize the balance that he arrived at between lives and livelihoods, and the fact that it tended to prioritize the latter, but at least he was there. At least he was available to answer questions.... That I think is the real failure, because he wasn't even making decisions then, he was just not there at all."

On September 2, Kenney made his first public appearance since August 9 on Facebook Live. With 119 ICU admissions and a seven-day average of 1,150 new cases, he said he was "concerned" but promised there would be no "lockdown," urging Albertans to simply get vaccinated. The problem was Albertans weren't heeding the call — the province had the lowest vaccination rate in the country, which might have had to do with the fact they were told the pandemic was over. As a result, the following day, Kenney launched a program giving $100 to vaccine-hesitant people who got vaccinated before October 14. He also cut alcohol sales off at 10:00 p.m. and reintroduced a province-wide mask mandate, except for in schools, offloading responsibility for that decision onto the school boards themselves.

ICU admissions surpassed 200 on September 13 for the first time in the pandemic — a potent symbol of Open for Summer's failure. Two days later, Kenney admitted he was wrong to say restrictions would be gone for good but not for lifting them when he did. The premier deflected a reporter's question on whether this policy reflected poorly on his leadership abilities: "I don't think this is about me, I think this is about protecting our hospitals, and we have to do what is necessary to do so." At the same press conference, he announced a convoluted quasi-vaccine passport system called the "restrictions exemption program," which allowed businesses to opt out of new restrictions by requiring proof of vaccination.

Introducing a vaccine passport, even if it wasn't called that, represented another major defeat for Kenney, who in the face of anti-vaccine protestors at a July 12 Stampede event, promised Alberta would never introduce one, reassuring them they "have nothing to be concerned about." His reversal was a clear sign of weakness, a tacit admission that personal responsibility could only go so far, as well as a realization that Kenney could no longer keep up his balancing act as cases continued to climb. By September 24, Alberta had 20,180 active cases, almost half of Canada's total. "Our health-care system has functionally collapsed," Dr. Schwartz from the University of Alberta told the *New York Times*. A day earlier, AHS CEO Dr. Verna Yiu said the only reason Alberta's ICU capacity hadn't overflowed was that people were dying. On September 28, Alberta reached its peak of ICU admissions with 257. All told, there were 933 Covid deaths from August 1 to November 30. While Covid cases and hospitalizations reached unseen heights during the Omicron wave in early-2022, it wouldn't replicate the number of deaths or ICU strain of previous waves. At this point, Kenney's political future came into sharper focus.

Knives Out

As a result of the failures laid bare in September, Kenney shuffled Tyler Shandro out of the Ministry of Health and replaced him with Labour Minister Jason Copping on September 21, the eve of a UCP caucus meeting to discuss his leadership. Leela Aheer, the former minister of culture, multiculturalism and status of women whom Kenney removed from Cabinet after she called on him to apologize for the Sky Palace incident, called the Shandro shuffle "an absolutely despicable move to try to save himself [and] shift the blame" in an interview with *Calgary Herald* columnist Don Braid. Seeing a chance for revenge, she wanted Kenney gone, and she was far from the only one. At the five-hour September 22 meeting, the caucus agreed to move up the party's annual general meeting from fall to spring, forcing Kenney to make the case for his leadership sooner rather than later.

The forces mobilized against Kenney, for the most part, weren't those who thought his Covid restrictions were too tepid. The issue was that he imposed them at all, focusing on "lives and livelihoods" rather than "livelihoods and freedom." Kenney's "more or less ad hoc" approach to pandemic management, Timothy Caulfield, the University of Alberta's Canada Research Chair in Health Law and Policy, told me, contributed to an "information chaos," empowering those who thought the pandemic wasn't as serious as it was presented to be.

The exigencies of the pandemic no doubt pushed Kenney outside his comfort zone. He adopted a confused stance, at first embracing the same harsh policies he pursued throughout his career to maintain some semblance of business as usual. But he eventually caved to public criticism, tempering his instincts to avoid what he calculated were the political costs of inaction. This was a fatal miscalculation. What he thought was politically costly was, in fact, an asset to the very forces he recruited into his authoritarian populist project to bring him into power in 2019. Kenney abandoned the base he had spent the past six years firing up, and they needed a new champion. They found this champion in someone who had spent the past several years on the political sidelines.

11

THE FALL

WHEN JASON KENNEY RETURNED TO ALBERTA in 2016 in his big blue pickup truck, travelling across the province to rile up rural Albertans against the federal government, he unleashed forces he couldn't control, who eventually turned on him when he couldn't satiate their desires. They sought to tear down the elite institutions Kenney spent his entire political career strengthening. "The spirits that I summoned, I now cannot rid myself of again," wrote Johann Wolfgang von Goethe in his poem *Der Zauberlehrling.* Brian Topp, NDP leader Rachel Notley's former chief of staff, aptly quoted this passage in a May 21, 2022, piece in *Policy* magazine celebrating Kenney's demise, in which he labelled Kenney a "sorcerer's apprentice." Just as the ethnocultural communities Kenney attracted to the federal Conservatives soured on the party when they started talking about a snitch line for "barbaric cultural practices," the Alberta sovereigntists abandoned ship when they realized they, too, were being used. As Kenney's political prospects were in freefall, two former rivals were waiting in the wings to harness the spirits he summoned.

Danielle Smith's political career was written off as dead since the floor-crossing debacle of 2014 when she squandered her status as Leader of Opposition to join the PC government she'd spent the past five years lambasting as out-of-touch elites. It was her second spectacular political flameout. Less than a year after her election to the Calgary Board of Education in October 1998, where she gained the moniker "Trashcan Dani" for allegedly rummaging through the garbage in search of insulting notes her progressive political opponents on the board passed around, the provincial government disbanded the board entirely in August 1999 due to dysfunction. By October, she was a *Calgary Herald* columnist, where she mused about the health benefits of cigarette smoking,[1] compared Indigenous treaty rights to apartheid,[2] proposed marketization as the solution to every problem, and scabbed during the newspaper's strike that began in November. After her defeat for the Highwood PC nomination in 2015, she swore off electoral politics, instructing *Global News* reporter Vassy Kapelos, who inquired about her political future, to "piss off."[3] Smith returned to her previous career at the *Herald* and hosting a talk radio show on Corus, the owner of Global. In June 2019, she became a corporate lobbyist for the Alberta Enterprise Group. And then the pandemic happened.

While Kenney was torn between using the pandemic as an opportunity to further his long-term political project, on the one hand, and taking what he thought was a pragmatic approach to maintain unity in the UCP on the other, Smith had no such inhibitions. She wholeheartedly embraced anti-restrictions and the anti-vaxx crowd, which suited her well as a consistent neoliberal ideologue. She lacked Kenney's neoconservative baggage, with its statist, moralistic inclinations toward traditionalist notions of the collective good. For Smith, it's all about freedom; there are no responsibilities, only rights.

Right off the bat, Smith endorsed quack treatments for the pandemic. She touted hydroxychloroquine as a 100 percent surefire Covid treatment and drinking tonic water as a means of developing immunity, for which Corus forced her to apologize. She quit Global in January 2021, claiming "far too many topics have become unchallengeable and the mob of political correctness thinks nothing of destroying a person's career and reputation over some perceived slight, real or imagined." Her final guest was Jason Kenney,[4] who appeared on her radio show repeatedly throughout the pandemic, a symbol of him engaging in dialogue with his most persistent critics on the right.

Unconstrained by Corus, Smith went deeper into the Covid conspiracist rabbit hole, starting an account on the private social media platform Locals and an email newsletter, where she mused about cancel culture, cryptocurrency, Alberta separatism, and Kenney's bungling of the pandemic from the perspective that he was taking a far too activist approach. In March 2021, she took to the *Calgary Herald* to compare mandatory vaccination, which at that point wasn't being explored in Alberta, to Nazi experiments on Jews during the Shoah. She hadn't yet revealed her intention to mount a political comeback; that would come soon, as Kenney's political fortunes waned.

The 2021 federal election, in which Prime Minister Justin Trudeau used Conservative leader Erin O'Toole's praise of Kenney's early pandemic response to his advantage in eastern Canada, produced a vacancy in the provincial Fort McMurray–Lac La Biche riding after UCP backbencher Laila Goodridge was elected Conservative MP for the federal Fort McMurray–Cold Lake riding. This provided an opening for Kenney's old rival, Brian Jean, to return to Alberta politics, filing his paperwork for the UCP nomination in November. He was a one-issue candidate and that was to remove Kenney from power. In pursuit of this end, he engaged in wild conspiracism, shrieking from the top of his lungs about globalists, the World Economic Forum, and the Great Reset, and later insinuated vaccines were as deadly as Covid. Jean won the nomination in December 2021 after engaging in some nasty race-baiting against Kenney's preferred candidate, Joshua Gogo. Jean referred to Gogo as a "Nigerian economist who lives in Fort McMurray,"[5] which suited his far-right conspiracist campaign messaging. Winning the by-election handily on March 15, 2022, Jean promised to take the fight to the UCP leadership review the following month in Red Deer.

The so-called Freedom Convoy, which began in Prince Rupert, British Columbia, and took over Ottawa for a month in January and February 2022, provided further ammunition for the forces aligned against Kenney, who lamented his weakness in backtracking on his Open for Summer plans as ICU admissions soared. A blockade in support of the convoy at the Coutts, Alberta, border crossing with Montana, which resulted in multiple arrests, including charges of conspiracy to murder a federal officer, posed further difficulty for Kenney's long-standing law-and-order neoconservatism.

Asked during a February 12 appearance on Global TV's *The West Block* about the full-throated support of the convoy offered by Conservative MP Pierre Poilievre, Kenney suggested Poilievre was being "held hostage by groups that are breaking the law." A week later, sensing which way the conservative winds were blowing, Kenney announced the province would launch a challenge against Prime Minister Justin Trudeau using the Emergencies Act to break up the convoy's Ottawa occupation, but after condemning the convoy's most extreme elements, this move appeared half-hearted at best.

The convoy produced two important outcomes for Kenney's fate — he lifted all remaining pandemic restrictions in Alberta, which furthered the perception among his base that he was weak and indecisive, and Erin O'Toole, whose half-hearted convoy support lit the spark on brewing caucus discontent, was turfed as federal Conservative leader. O'Toole's ouster mirrored Kenney's, with a shared top-down approach to caucus relations and inconsistent messaging on the convoy that alienated a significant portion of their bases. Both would be replaced by staunch opponents of pandemic restrictions.

While Jean's by-election campaign was underway, a shadowy organization called Take Back Alberta (TBA) formed, which described itself in explicitly populist terms as a "grassroots movement built to advance freedom and transfer power from the ruling elite to the people of our province." It proved a key player in dislodging Kenney from power, mobilizing Albertans in the same communities Kenney travelled across in 2016 to create a united right-wing coalition. The public didn't learn of TBA's existence until a March 3 *Calgary Sun* column from Rick Bell, which quoted one of its organizers, failed Calgary mayoral candidate Zane Novack, who lamented the "mental and physical health" impacts of pandemic restrictions. TBA founder David Parker later said he was originally a Kenney supporter but turned on him during the pandemic. He was an enthusiastic backer of the Coutts blockade, where he delivered a speech and was introduced by Fort Macleod town councillor and TBA associate Marco Van Huigenbos, who faces a mischief charge in relation to the blockade.

On March 24, less than a fortnight after Jean's by-election win, audio was leaked to the CBC of Kenney telling caucus staffers he had considered calling it quits. "I don't need this job. I could go to the private sector, have my evenings, weekends off," he told them. But, Kenney added, he determined this course of action would be "grossly irresponsible," citing a need to guard against the "hostile takeover of our party by fringe elements." Kenney characterized these elements as "kooky people" and "lunatics" who he said, echoing Prime Minister Justin Trudeau, hold "extreme, hateful, intolerant, bigoted, and crazy views." Kenney's goose was cooked.

A week after those remarks leaked, having seen Brian Jean's success running for the UCP as an anti-Kenney, Danielle Smith announced she would seek the UCP leadership if Kenney failed his review, criticizing his "Ottawa-style" approach to leadership and his characterization of a large fraction of the party's base as "lunatics." She told the *Calgary Sun's* Rick Bell: "They are people with legitimate grievances. They're angry and hurt and need some understanding and some respect." Smith also apologized for the 2014 floor crossing, acknowledging she should have stayed with Wildrose to hold Premier Jim Prentice accountable. "That's what people wanted me to do and I let them down."

Weeks before Kenney's scheduled leadership review, the party changed it to a mail-in ballot, which Jean, harking back to the 2017 UCP leadership race, called a "formula for fraud and cheating"[6] after membership almost doubled in the days leading up to the March 19 registration deadline. When the results came in on May 18, Kenney received 51.4 percent support — technically a victory, but not enough to justify his continued leadership. He announced his intention to stay on as leader until the results of the leadership race, which was contested by Smith and Jean, as well as by former Cabinet ministers Travis Toews, Rebecca Schulz, Leela Aheer, Rajan Sawhney, and Todd Loewen, who was booted from the UCP caucus after calling on Kenney to resign. All candidates attempted to distance themselves from Kenney's decisions, a sign that his slight majority of support in the leadership review obscured a deep unpopularity with the membership. It was likely some members, disapproving of Kenney's top-down leadership approach, voted for his leadership anyway, because they were concerned about the threat to the UCP's electoral prospects posed by figures such as Smith and Jean. These members shifted their support to Toews.

Smith, speaking at packed rural town halls across the province, promised to "never again" impose public health restrictions. She vowed to fire the entire board of Alberta Health Services and the College of Physicians and Surgeons, whom she previously accused of covering up the efficacy of horse dewormer ivermectin as a Covid treatment.[7] Smith stood alongside Theo Fleury, the former Calgary Flames star and mental health advocate turned far-right conspiracist as he likened Covid restrictions to sexual abuse.

Beyond Covid, Smith was roundly denounced by her political opponents within and without the UCP leadership race for suggesting a cancer diagnosis was "completely within your control and there's something you can do about that that is different."[8] She advocated an Uber-like app where the government would deposit $300 so Albertans could "just begin the process of ... buy[ing] the healthcare of their choice."[9] Smith's perspective on health policy is no doubt informed by her hard-core libertarianism, which rejects out of hand any collective solutions, viewing every health problem as being within an individual's purview. Kenney's neocon inclinations, by contrast, leave plenty of room for statist intervention in the name of public order. For all his faults, it's inconceivable Kenney would ever suggest cancer as a matter of personal responsibility. But he paved the way for Smith when he dragged his heels on implementing further Covid restrictions, citing the dangers of lockdowns, or when he dismissed Covid as a mere influenza, or his repeated efforts at health-care privatization.

It wasn't just on Covid-related issues that Kenney disappointed the party's grassroots, making them ripe for Smith's taking. He failed to "put Alberta first," as Smith put it, by not implementing the recommendations of his own Fair Deal Panel, which travelled the province cataloguing grievances Albertans had with Ottawa. Smith liked the panel's idea of setting up an Alberta police force to replace the RCMP, which Kenney said he'd look into, but she wanted to go further than the panel recommendations, advocating Alberta collect its own income taxes and opt out of the federal employment insurance program. With a goal of forging a "new relationship with the rest of the country,"[10] she touted the Alberta Sovereignty Act — the centrepiece of the 2021 "Free Alberta Strategy" outlined by the Calgary School's Barry Cooper, lawyer Erik From, and former Wildrose

MLA Rob Anderson — which calls for the province to dismiss any federal law the province deems as treading on its own turf. This would become her signature policy proposal, helping her stand out from the rest of the candidates.

In the runup to the October 2022 leadership vote, as Smith's momentum became increasingly evident, Kenney lashed out at the Sovereignty Act, calling it a "cockamamie" plot that would create economic uncertainty in Alberta,[11] but he set the stage for it with his raging against the purported injustices of Ottawa's treatment of Alberta. It was the logical outcome of constantly harping on the structure of Confederation and Alberta's role in it. Given Kenney's unpopularity, it was also unlikely his interventions against Smith's proposal would have their intended effect. It was, however, somewhat personal for Kenney, who as a lame-duck premier unveiled a new ad campaign to attract workers from Toronto and Vancouver fed up with high housing costs to come live in Alberta, where housing was cheaper, wages higher, and everything else more expensive. His pitch was solely economic, making the plan vulnerable to the risks posed by Smith's top policy preference. This highlights a key difference between Kenney and Smith — Kenney wanted to keep the wheels of capitalism turning through the very elite institutions he purported to oppose, whereas Smith was more than willing to burn it all down to serve the same end.

Smith won the leadership race on October 8, although it took her until the final ballot to defeat establishment favourite Travis Toews, reflecting some unease within the party about her radical agenda. She outlined her main priorities in her victory speech: "No longer will Alberta ask permission from Ottawa to be prosperous and free. We will not have our voices silenced or censored. We will not be told what we must put in our bodies in order that we may work or travel." She brought in Rob Anderson as her top adviser and passed the renamed Alberta Sovereignty within a United Canada Act in December, which in effect gives the Legislative Assembly the power to override the courts and runs roughshod over Indigenous treaty rights, which are negotiated with the Crown. All her opponents in the UCP leadership race, save for Leela Aheer, who finished last, were rewarded with Cabinet posts and reversed their opposition to the act.

Jason Kenney, pictured in May 2023, has landed several jobs after his resignation.

An hour after the act was first introduced, Kenney announced he was quitting politics, evading the consequences of his actions for one final time.

As of August 2023, Jason Kenney worked as an adviser to online event planning company Eventcombo and law firm Bennett Jones, sat on the board of the power company Atco, and was a senior fellow at the right-leaning C.D. Howe Institute think tank.

With Smith firmly in the driver's seat, TBA outlined its plan to take over the UCP board, which consists of the party leader and 18 directors, purging it of the remnants of Kenneyism. Its agenda of ruling out any future vaccine mandates or pandemic restrictions, banning electronic voting, and "restructuring" AHS dovetailed almost entirely with Smith's. At the UCP AGM shortly after Smith's victory, all nine candidates for the board endorsed by TBA won, giving TBA and Smith a majority on the party's 18-member board. They took over constituency associations in Livingstone-Macleod, Innisfail–Sylvan Lake, and Rimbey–Rocky Mountain. Most symbolically, Eric Bouchard, a candidate who shared TBA's views, became the MLA for Kenney's former Calgary-Lougheed riding in the 2023 election.

Why Did Kenney Fail?

Kenney's populist pitch was based on a tacit agreement. He would give the former Wildrose base his establishment legitimacy, and they would give him their votes. He used populist rhetoric of deferring to the party grassroots to seize power. Once in power, when the party's grassroots attempted to undermine his authority, he made it clear that he was the ultimate decision-maker. It took a crisis to bring this contrast into sharp focus. Kenney could play a populist on TV, but that isn't who he really is, because at the end of the day, he's a firm believer in institutions — at least insofar as they serve his authoritarian project. Smith, on the other hand, is a true believer in tearing it all down in the name of freedom.

Vito Marciano, Brian Jean's chief of staff, wrote in a May 2022 *National Post* op-ed that Kenney's problems with his party predated the pandemic. "Everyone knew that Kenney wasn't *really* a blue truck guy ... but no one expected Kenney to shamelessly jettison blue truck populism once elected. Yet that is exactly what he did." His first sin, according to Marciano, was recruiting advisers who hadn't lived in Alberta for years and didn't understand the province. Marciano doesn't name them, but Kenney's chief of staff Jamie Huckaby and adviser David Knight Legg certainly fitted the bill. Kenney then instituted tight control over his caucus, whose constituents' concerns were cast aside.

By sheer recklessness, Marciano writes, Kenney picked fights with teachers through a preposterous curriculum rewrite and doctors by ripping up the province's agreement with the Alberta Medical Association. "Albertans had hired Jason Kenney to fight the Liberals in Ottawa, but instead found him fighting the things that mattered to them in their own communities." Marciano's conclusion that "Covid was the least of the reasons" for Kenney's downfall is unsurprising, given his boss's views on the pandemic, but his point that Kenney's deficiencies as a leader were well known prior to the pandemic stands.

Derek Fildebrandt, who was one of Kenney's staunchest proponents on the Wildrose ledger before a series of scandals led to his abrupt political downfall, now edits the hard-right *Western Standard* online news site. He told me Kenney's conception of the conservative base is "largely frozen in time, from the mid-to-late '90s." Kenney conflated the "Alberta first" crowd constituting the Wildrose base with the social conservatives he cultivated with ease as a federal Reformer and Conservative. "Social conservatives are the most low-maintenance voter group in the democratic world," Fildebrandt said. "All you have to do is give them nice words. They don't expect you to actually take any hard actions."

Alberta firsters, by contrast, mean business. Provincial conservative politicians, unlike their federal counterparts, aren't weighed down by the need to create an electoral coalition spanning from the suburbs of Vancouver to the suburbs of Toronto. They do need to win over some swing voters in Calgary, but that can easily be done with neoliberal economic policies. When Kenney promised the Fair Deal Panel, those who sympathized with notions of Alberta separatism expected him to actually implement its recommendations, not just use them as a talking point to earn their votes in the next election. When it came to the pandemic, Kenney assumed his reluctance to impose restrictions would be enough to win over those who didn't want restrictions. It wasn't.

Marciano's and Fildebrandt's insights are valuable as members of the former Wildrose grassroots Kenney used for electoral gain and discarded as soon as he thought they stood in his way. Their critiques of Kenney from the perspective of those he dismissed as lunatics and kooks largely ring true. Kenney didn't lose his grip over the party he created because of his attacks on the province's social safety net, its public-sector workers, public education system, harm-reduction infrastructure, or public health-care system — these are all instances of "promise made, promise kept," although some may have objected to the way he pursued his agenda. It was the promises he couldn't deliver on Alberta's place in Confederation and pandemic management that did him in with his party's grassroots, the only people whose support he needed to lead the party. Had he lost the 2023 election, it would be a different story, and we could talk about the corrosive effects of his neoliberal policies as reasons for his failure, but the grassroots supported those policies. Kenney failed because he had nothing but disdain for his own supporters. It's as simple as that.

Kenney's authoritarian populism, which used populist framing in service of a fundamentally elitist project, has been a consistent throughline in his political career. It finally caught up to him in Alberta where he played with fire and got burned. He was unable to deliver what he promised to the UCP grassroots beyond defeating the NDP, because he didn't actually believe in upsetting the established order, of which he was a product. Once he came to power, Kenney aggressively pursued his neoliberal agenda, which was both something the PC and Wildrose elements of the UCP could agree on and consistent with Kenney's beliefs. When it came to the pandemic and questions of Alberta's role in Confederation, his coalition's contradictions proved insurmountable, with Kenney being pulled in multiple directions, leaving nobody satisfied. The main faction he needed to satisfy to remain in power, however, was the party's grassroots, whom he held in contempt, a sentiment they came to reciprocate. It was an ignominious end for someone who played a crucial role in taking ideas once considered far to the right of the Canadian political consensus into the mainstream.

EPILOGUE

IT'S FITTING THAT IN HIS FINAL month as premier, Jason decided to fly to the United Kingdom to stand in line for 14 hours to pay his final respects to Queen Elizabeth II, taking him back full circle to his days as a teenager in Victoria waking up in the middle of the night to get a good spot to see her outside the B.C. Legislative Assembly. Kenney, in a surreal display, did live hits via Skype from the queue. He told *Global News* on September 16 that he paid for the trip out of his own pocket and claimed to be doing conference calls from the line, but hoped to have "some quiet time for prayerful reflection" once he got closer to the queen's corpse, calling Westminster Hall, where Her Majesty was lying in state, a "sacred place."

In another interview, Kenney described the people from various walks of life in the queue to see the queen lying in state, from people wearing top hats to those sporting mohawk haircuts, in a way that reveals his ideal vision of society. Kenney likened this display to "people of all social classes, together, in common purpose" on a journey to visit the grave of Thomas à Becket in Geoffrey Chaucer's *The Canterbury Tales*. "It's about this amazing mishmash of society and the changes they have, but all of them, in the great equalizer of the humility of their pilgrimage."[1] For Kenney, people are equalized not through their socio-economic conditions but in shared devotion to an institution that upholds their inequality.

His trip to the United Kingdom to pay respects to the queen, whose loss he likened to that of a close friend or relative, was no doubt a weird way to cap off a 25-year-long political career, but it was extremely on brand. The monarchy is an important symbol for a figure like Kenney. On the one hand, the Crown represents a reflexive deference to authority and tradition that is central to neoconservative politics. On the other, these sorts of traditional institutions — the Vatican is another — provide an empty vessel for attaching deeper meaning to a political agenda that is at its core materialistic. It's easier to justify rewarding the rich and punishing the poor when it's in the name of a higher purpose. Kenney's Crown fetishism further demonstrates the hollow nature of his populist pretenses, which were always a means of tricking the masses into supporting his agenda. There are few institutions more elite than the British Crown. Venerating this archaic institution is entirely incomprehensible to an unemployed oil and gas worker who supported the creation of the UCP, wants to separate from Canada, thinks Covid is a hoax, and rejoined the UCP to vote for Danielle Smith. Kenney was so gifted a retail politician that he was able to convince these types of people for a time that he was their best shot at achieving power.

His skill for tapping into the energy of populism, purporting to represent the disenchanted masses against those in power, was always used to serve the interests of the very elites he raged against. That's a fundamental paradox of Kenneyism, which is highly emblematic of the modern political right. It's a project that seeks to offload the state's capacity to provide for citizens to the private sector. Those who depended on the state to get by are then taunted with meaningless notions of personal responsibility. Meanwhile, what remains of the state is used to uphold this hierarchy. The harshest edges of this agenda are sometimes tempered by pragmatic electoral considerations, but when you strip all the ideology away, you have one thing left — power. Not just the maintenance, but the strengthening of existing power relations, whether between citizens and the state, employees and their bosses, men and women, rich and poor, has been consistent throughout Kenney's career.

Since Kenney announced his intention to step down, there's been a concerted effort in conservative media to rewrite the history of his time in power, casting him as a tragic hero. In a cartoonishly charitable appraisal, columnist John Ivison, writing in the *National Post* on October 6, argued that Kenney's downfall was the result of a "fatal character flaw for any political figure: integrity." Paraphrasing Mark Twain, Ivison wrote of Kenney, "honesty in politics shines more there than elsewhere," as if the kamikaze scandal never occurred. *Post* comment editor Carson Jerema wrote on May 18, just after Kenney announced his impending resignation, that Kenney sowed his demise when he "emboldened" his caucus critics by allowing them to criticize him publicly without consequence, ignoring his expulsion of Drew Barnes and Todd Loewen for defying him.

Don Martin, writing in a May 19 *CTV News* column, argued Kenney, as a "mere mortal," couldn't overcome a "black-and-white polarization without any grey areas," as if Kenney existed outside the polarization he perpetuated. At the *Edmonton Sun*, Kenney loyalist Lorne Gunter wrote on November 24 that Kenney didn't show enough of his "tough-guy side" toward Ottawa, referring solely to his rhetoric, which his internal critics had no problem with — they despised his lack of action.

Through all these revisionist efforts, one mustn't lose sight of Kenney's uniquely pernicious political influence. His public life began with efforts to deny women who wanted to get abortions and LGBTQ+ people who wanted to visit their partners dying of AIDS the same rights as everyone else, which he first boasted about and then downplayed his role in. It ended with a total abdication of leadership during the worst public health crisis of our lifetimes, lying about his whereabouts as ICUs reached maximum capacity.

Kenney's major legacy was shifting the contours of political debate rightward, narrowing the horizons of political possibility. Nowhere is this more evident than in the Alberta NDP's failed 2023 election campaign. To compete with the united right Kenney built and tore apart before Danielle Smith brought it back together, the NDP attempted to win over disaffected conservative voters with a series of half measures that would maintain much of the damage Kenney wrought. Notley advocated for a return to an 11 percent corporate tax rate — one percentage point lower than it was before Kenney was elected — to ensure it would remain the lowest in Canada. She promised to freeze post-secondary tuition at 2023–24 levels, leaving it considerably higher than before Kenney lifted the previous freeze, and offered no promises to reverse his draconian cuts to this sector. The NDP vowed to balance the budget, leaving the door open to severe austerity measures once the price of oil inevitably declined. It's little wonder that the progressive alternative to the UCP was unable to win over enough voters to push it past the finish line. Margaret Thatcher, one of Kenney's political heroes, once said her greatest accomplishment was Tony Blair's New Labour, which accepted the neoliberal consensus she forged. It could similarly be said that Kenney's greatest accomplishment was turning the Alberta NDP into a conservative party.

I certainly don't want to leave readers with the impression that Kenney was responsible for all the problems that plague Alberta and Canada, but there's no doubt he played a key role in putting policies into practice that did incalculable harm. Canada in general, and Alberta in particular, are worse off due to his interventions, which despite his ultimate failure, provided a template for future leaders to pursue damaging policies with popular support from the very people they harm. The next Jason Kenney will learn from his failures and become even more effective in making the state serve the interests of those who already have power.

Progressive parties, whether it's the NDP or Liberals, don't appear to be up to the task of challenging the threat this style of politics poses to the social fabric. It's not enough to simply denounce the other side for every outrage they create. The New Right agenda that Kenney embodies seeks to uproot any sense of social solidarity that exists outside strict hierarchical confines. Progressives need a compelling vision to address the myriad problems we face collectively — the climate crisis, systemic racism, public health, and growing inequality. They need to accept the premise that there's something fundamentally rotten about the system as it is and point to a better future. Otherwise, we're in for a world of pain.

ACKNOWLEDGEMENTS

THERE WERE MANY PEOPLE WHO HELPED turn the book you've just read into a reality. I had the privilege of guidance and support from journalists and academics I respect greatly, and the wonderful team at Dundurn.

Roberta Lexier was the first person to encourage me to stop arguing with people on Twitter and focus those energies toward writing a book.

I met Dundurn president and publisher Kwame Scott Fraser through Nora Loreto at her 2022 book event in Calgary where I told him about my idea to write the first single, cohesive narrative on Jason Kenney's brief tenure as Alberta premier and his larger impact on Canadian conservative politics. Kwame took a chance on me as a first-time author; for that, I am eternally grateful.

Taylor Lambert, David Climenhaga, Scott Schmidt, Shama Rangwala, Ted McCoy, Bridget Stirling, Kim Siever, and Lisa Young provided valuable feedback on the book's earliest drafts, as did Roberta and Nora, helping to shape the book's structure and frame of analysis.

John Carlaw deserves full credit for first conceiving of Kenneyism as a distinct political ideology in his 2015 Ph.D. dissertation at York University, identifying Kenney's embrace of neoliberalism, neoconservatism, and authoritarian populism throughout his tenure at the Ministry of Citizenship, Immigration, and Multiculturalism.

Elena Radic oversaw this project for Dundurn, ensuring everything came together on time while providing crucial guidance throughout the process. Rudi Garcia assisted me with technical issues. Laura Boyle oversaw Karen Alexiou's design of the book's lovely cover, which I think nails Kenney's faux cowboy aesthetic. Editor Michael Carroll saved me from some of my worst writerly excesses and made the book much more cohesive and coherent with each passing draft.

The Marian Hebb Research grant from the Access Copyright Foundation enabled me to travel to Wilcox, Victoria, and San Francisco.

To all the people who spoke to me on background for this work — you know who you are — thank you.

My parents, Gail and Aubrie, and my brother, Josh, have always been some of the strongest supporters of my work, even if they don't necessarily agree with every word I write. And last, but certainly not least, is my partner Lauren. I wouldn't be able to have written this book without her patience with my erratic schedule, as well as her critiques and insights of its contents.

NOTES

Prologue

1   Jeff McMahon, "What Would You Do About Climate Change? Tax Carbon," *Forbes*, October 12, 2014, forbes.com/sites/jeffmcmahon/2014/10/12/what -would-milton-friedman-do-about-climate-change-tax-carbon/?sh =5263d0f06928.

Introduction: Defining Kenneyism

1   Tom Flanagan, "The Worst Choice, Except for All the Others," *Globe and Mail*, June 18, 2008, theglobeandmail.com/opinion/the-worst-choice-except -for-all-the-others/article25579890.

2   *Hub Podcasts*, "Episode #125: Dialogue with Jason Kenney," October 5, 2022, thehub.ca/2022-10-05/whats-next-for-jason-kenney-the-alberta-premier -reflects-on-his-record-and-plans-for-post-political-life.

3   "Margaret Thatcher: A Life in Quotes," *Guardian*, April 8, 2013, theguardian.com/politics/2013/apr/08/margaret-thatcher-quotes.

4   Jared Wesley, "The Dramatic Fall of Jason Kenney," *Alberta Views*, September 1, 2022, albertaviews.ca/dramatic-fall-jason-kenney.

5   Linda Diebel, "'Minister for Curry,'" *Toronto Star*, February 20, 2011, IN1.

6   Martin Lawrence, "Calgary's Youthful Reform MP Puts Youthful Passion into Politics," *Calgary Herald*, March 11, 1999, A7.

7   John Carlaw, "The Conservative Party of Canada and the Politics of Citizenship, Immigration and Multiculturalism" (Ph.D. diss., York University, Toronto, 2019), 53, yorkspace.library.yorku.ca/xmlui/bitstream/handle/10315/37387/Carlaw_John_WJ_2019_PhD.pdf?sequence=2&isAllowed=y.

8   Corey Robin, *The Reactionary Mind: Conservatism from Edmund Burke to Donald Trump* (New York: Oxford University Press, 2018), 9.

9   Steve Paikin, *The Life: The Seductive Call of Politics* (Toronto: Viking, 2001), 169.

10 Rick Pedersen, "The Persuaders," *Edmonton Journal*, April 12, 1993, A1.

1: Culture Warrior

1   Paikin, *The Life*, 140.

2   "Two Indians Seek Liberal Backing in Pearson's Old Seat," *Globe and Mail*, May 9, 1968, 4.

3   Diebel, "'Minister for Curry.'"

4   Diebel, "'Minister for Curry.'"

5   "Kenney, R. Martin," *Legacy Remembers*, April 13, 2010, legacy.com/us/obituaries/legacyremembers/martin-kenney-obituary?id=41326003.

6   Alison Armstrong, "Meet Martin Kenney, International Fraud Fighter," *Toronto Star*, May 24, 2013, thestar.com/news/world/2013/05/24/meet_martin_kenney_international_fraud_fighter.html.

7   "Kelowna Youth Treatment Centre Shut Down by Government," *CBC News*, February 13, 2014, cbc.ca/news/canada/british-columbia/kelowna-youth-treatment-centre-shut-down-by-government-1.2534979.

8   Murray Peterson, *Balmoral Hall 1901–2001: An Exceptional School Celebrates Its First Century* (Balmoral Hall, 2001), 69.

9   Paikin, *The Life*, 139.

10 Angela Hall, "Legacy of Learning Series: 100 Years 100 Towns," *Regina Leader-Post*, May 17, 2005, B2.

11 Ted Byfield, "If Father Athol Murray Were Still Around, the Alliance Wouldn't Be in This Mess," *Alberta Report*, March 18, 2002, 60.

12 Lorne Brown and Doug Taylor, "The Birth of Medicare," *Canadian Dimension*, July 3, 2012, canadiandimension.com/articles/view/the-birth-of-medicare.

13 "Medicare," *Calgary Herald*, July 10, 1962, 2.

14 Marci McDonald, "Is Jason Kenney Too Extreme for the Conservatives?" *Walrus*, May 28, 2014, thewalrus.ca/true-blue.
15 Rick Bell, "Calm Before Storm," *Calgary Sun*, May 12, 2022, A5.
16 E. Kaye Fulton, "The Tax Fighter," *Maclean's*, March 6, 1995, 52–54.
17 Diebel, "'Minister for Curry.'"
18 Paikin, *The Life*, 141.
19 Jenkins insisted this occurred the day after the Liberals lost the 1984 election, demonstrating the depth of Kenney's political commitments at the time, but this timeline doesn't add up. By September 1984, Kenney was back in Wilcox.
20 Paikin, *The Life*, 140.
21 Jason Markusoff, "Jason Kenney Has Everything to Lose," *Maclean's*, March 6, 2018, macleans.ca/politics/ottawa/jason-kenney-everything-lose.
22 Paikin, *The Life*, 166.
23 Paikin, *The Life*, 166.
24 Jason Kenney, "A View from the Outside," *San Francisco Foghorn*, September 12, 1987, 12.
25 Diebel, "'Minister for Curry.'"
26 Lynn Ritzman, "Students File Suit Against USF," *San Francisco Foghorn*, February 23, 1989, 1.
27 Markusoff, "Jason Kenney Has Everything to Lose."
28 Anne Dawson, "Gays Can Marry — but Not Each Other: Calgary MP," *Calgary Herald*, February 15, 2005, A5.
29 "Alberta Premier Apologizes for Comparing Plight of Unvaccinated to Stigma Faced by 1980s AIDS Patients," *Radio-Canada International*, February 9, 2022, ici.radio-canada.ca/rci/en/news/1861025/alberta-premier-apologizes-for-comparing-plight-of-unvaccinated-to-stigma-faced-by-1980s-aids-patients.

2: Tax Slayer

1 *Hub Podcasts*, "Episode #125."
2 Membership is a bit of a misnomer, since those who give the CTF money don't get a say in its operations, but for simplicity's sake, they'll be referred to as members.
3 Miro Cernetig, "Out of the West They Rode, the Anti-Tax Gang," *Globe and Mail*, April 17, 1993, D3.
4 Brock Ketcham, "MLAs Can Afford to Retire in Style," *Calgary Herald*, November 15, 1991, A1.

5   Richard Helm, "Getty Scolds Pension Study Authors," *Edmonton Journal*, December 13, 1991, B11.

6   Don Retson, "Anti-Tax Canvassers Keep Half the Cash," *Edmonton Journal*, July 10, 1991, A8.

7   Kenneth Whyte, "Premier Ralph Squares Off with the Taxpayer Gang," *Globe and Mail*, April 24, 1993, D2.

8   Rick Pederson, "Taxpayer Lobby Defends Work," *Edmonton Journal*, April 30, 1993, A5.

9   Sheldon Alberts, "Group to Hear Sales Tax Pitch," *Calgary Herald*, January 22, 1993, B4.

10 Joan Crockatt, "Pensions, Perks Make Klein a Target on Talk Show," *Edmonton Journal*, March 4, 1993, A6.

11 Joan Crockatt and Rick McConnell, "Retroactive Pension Cuts Shock MLAs; Some PCs Look to Quit," *Edmonton Journal*, April 29, 1993, A1.

12 Ashley Geddes, "Klein Vows to Scrap Pensions," *Calgary Herald*, May 1, 1993, A1.

13 Jim Cunningham and Sheldon Alberts, "Nothing New, Say Critics," *Calgary Herald*, May 7, 1993, A2.

14 Fulton, "The Tax Fighter."

15 Sheldon Alberts, "Unions Pitch Novel Solution to the Deficit: Spend More," *Calgary Herald*, November 20, 1994, A3.

16 J.J. Moskau, "IMF Slams Ottawa's Deficit-Cutting Target as Insufficient," *Globe and Mail*, November 29, 1994, B1.

17 Fulton, "The Tax Fighter."

18 Kevin Bell, "Tax Revolt! The Great Tax Revolution of 1995," *Victoria Times Colonist*, February 13, 1995, A1.

19 Ed Struzik, "Anti-Tax Rally Draws 1,700," *Edmonton Journal*, February 7, 1995, A1.

20 Allan Freeman, "Ottawa Aims to Shrink Deficit," *Globe and Mail*, February 28, 1995, A1.

21 Thomas Walkom, "Budget Harks Back to 19th Century Realities," *Toronto Star*, March 2, 1995, A27.

22 Peter C. Newman, "A Budget That Changed a Nation's Psychology," *Maclean's*, March 20, 1995, 41.

23 "Reform MPs Take Back Pay Cuts, Say They Need Cash," Canadian Press, July 30, 1995.

24 Peter Stockland, "Reform's Death Greatly Exaggerated," *Calgary Herald*, December 6, 1996, A22.

25 "Business Group Criticizes Reform Budget," Canadian Press, February 22, 1995.

3 : The Snack Pack

1 Sean Speer, "Canada's Embattled Conservatives Should Remember That the Winds of Change Originate in Ideas," *Hub*, June 1, 2022, thehub.ca/2022 -06-01/canadas-embattled-conservatives-should-remember-that-the-winds -of-change-originate-in-ideas.
2 Ric Dolphin, "Young Reform MPs Out to Change Party's Image," *Edmonton Journal*, August 13, 1997, B5.
3 Ron Eade, "Homesick Reformers Find Comfort at the Grill," *Calgary Herald*, June 7, 1998, D12.
4 Don Martin, "Alberta 'Snack Pack' Has Big Fish to Fry in Ottawa," *Calgary Herald*, September 26, 1997, A21.
5 Peter Stockland, "Reform Hopeful Senses Closed Door," *Calgary Herald*, December 27, 1996, A12.
6 Ezra Levant, "Equality Doesn't Mean Rigging the System for Women," *Edmonton Journal*, January 26, 1994, A13.
7 Don Martin, "Voters Lack Urgency," *Calgary Herald*, May 31, 1997, A9.
8 Chris Casteel, "McCurdy Campaign Not Laughing at Paid Inhofe Heckler," *Oklahoman*, October 28, 1994, oklahoman.com/story/news/1994/10/28 /mccurdy-camp-not-laughing-at-paid-inhofe-heckler/62410321007.
9 Lisa Dempster, "Debate Hot at Raucous Candidates' Forum," *Calgary Herald*, May 22, 1997, A8.
10 Peter Stockland, "Youthful Reformer Emerging as a New Force," *Calgary Herald*, December 21, 1996, C5.
11 Paikin, *The Life*, 167.
12 William Lysak, "Are Sheep Straying from the Liberal Fold?" *Alberta Report*, April 28, 1997, 34–35.
13 Lysak, "Are Sheep Straying from the Liberal Fold?"
14 Lysak, "Are Sheep Straying from the Liberal Fold?"
15 "Preston Manning was in Calgary Today," *CTV National News*, May 17, 1997.
16 Allan Chambers, "Plain Talk, Strong Feelings," *Edmonton Journal*, June 7, 1997, F1.
17 Kim Lunman, "Manning in Line for a Raise," *Calgary Herald*, June 5, 1997, A3.
18 Sheldon Alberts, "A Caring Preston Manning Hits Ottawa," *Calgary Herald*, September 21, 1997, A9.

19 Bruce Wallace, "Preston Power," *Maclean's*, September 22, 1997, 14.

20 Scott Feschuk, "'Snack Pack' Carries Weight in Reform," *Globe and Mail*, September 20, 1997, A10.

21 Miro Cernetig, "Reform Party: The Knives Come Out," *Globe and Mail*, May 3, 1997, D1.

22 Sheldon Alberts and Peter O'Neil, "Manning Should Resign, Says MP," *Edmonton Journal*, August 13, 1998, A1.

23 Canadian Press, "Relevant Bills Would Be Tested for Family Values," *Calgary Herald*, May 31, 1998, A3.

24 Sheldon Alberts, "Clark Spurns Conservative Alliance," *Calgary Herald*, September 22, 1998, A5.

25 Sheldon Alberts, "'We Have to Go Out and Earn Our Way Riding by Riding,'" *Calgary Herald*, September 23, 1998, A15.

26 Rod Love, "Adapt or Perish, Rod Love Advises Joe Clark," *Calgary Herald*, September 29, 1998, A19.

27 William Walker and Tim Harper, "Tory Leader Sends Letter to Reform: Join with Us," *Toronto Star*, October 1, 1999, A1.

28 Gloria Galloway, "It's No Go, Joe Clark Says," *Hamilton Spectator*, October 2, 1999, D1.

29 Joel-Denis Bellavance, "Clark Orders Recruitment Drive to Boost Falling Party Memberships," *National Post*, October 2, 1999, A7.

30 Glen McGregor, "'The Problem Is Preston,'" *Ottawa Citizen*, May 1, 1999, B2.

31 Norm Ovenden, "Alberta's Day Packs in Ontario Tory Crowd," *Edmonton Journal*, April 16, 1999, A13.

32 "Day's Defamation Suit Cost Albertans $800 Gs," *CBC News*, January 16, 2001, cbc.ca/news/canada/day-s-defamation-suit-costs-albertans-800-gs-1.282230.

33 Tim Harper, "Presto! It's Back to the Future," *Toronto Star*, October 15, 1999, A1.

34 Tim Harper, "Justice System Too Soft, Day Says," *Toronto Star*, March 29, 2000, A1.

35 Justine Hunter, "Is Loyalty Enough for Manning?" *National Post*, March 24, 2000, A7.

36 Don Martin, "Leadership Race Splits Alberta's Snack Pack," *Calgary Herald*, May 22, 2000, A3.

37 Justine Hunter, "Ultra-Conservative Group to Work on Day's Behalf," *National Post*, May 26, 2000, A7.

38 Norma Greenaway, "Playing the Moral-Issue Card," *Montreal Gazette*, June 3, 2000, B1.

39 Ron Csillag, "Will Our Faith(s) Define Us?" *Canadian Jewish News*, June 29, 2000, 39.

40 "Day Concerned About Morning-After Pill," *CBC News*, October 28, 2000, cbc.ca/news/canada/day-concerned-about-morning-after-pill-1.246021.

41 Jack Aubry and Mike Tricky, "Liberals Boost Majority," *Ottawa Citizen*, November 28, 2000, A1.

42 Norm Ovenden, "Alliance Knives Sharpening with Eastern Shutout," *Edmonton Journal*, November 28, 2000, A3.

43 Sheldon Alberts, "Harper Mounts Campaign to Lead the Right," *National Post*, June 30, 2001, A6.

44 Larry Johnsrude, "Alliance Race Is On — but Will Day Run?" *Edmonton Journal*, July 18, 2001, A1.

45 Norm Ovenden, "Harper First into Race to Lead Alliance," *Edmonton Journal*, December 4, 2001, A5.

46 Brian Laghi, "Stephen Harper Embarks on Campaign for Canadian Alliance Leadership," Canadian Press, December 4, 2001.

47 Joe Paraskevas, "Harper Faces Fight for Seat," *Calgary Herald*, March 22, 2002, A1.

48 Joe Paraskevas, "Hanger Heads Harper Campaign," *Calgary Herald*, April 5, 2002, A4.

49 Ben Li, "Calgarians Show Support for War Effort," *Gauntlet*, April 3, 2003, archive.thegauntlet.ca/2003/04/calgarians-show-support-war-effort/.

50 Robert Fife and David Heyman, "Goodale Tells West Vote Grit or Miss Out," *National Post*, May 25, 2004, A6.

51 Tom Zytaruk, "Canada Not Pulling Its Weight Says MP," *Surrey Now*, May 26, 2004, 4.

52 Jason Fekete and David Heyman, "Pupils Quiz Candidates on Terror Threat," *Calgary Herald*, June 11, 2004, A4.

53 Dawn Walton, "Western Tories Greet Grit Win with Disappointment, Disgust," *Globe and Mail*, June 29, 2004, A18.

54 Jason Van Rassel, "Tory Snack Packers Get First Taste of Power," *Calgary Herald*, January 31, 2006, A4.

4: Weaponized Immigrants

1 Alex Castonguay, "The Inside Story of Jason Kenney's Campaign to Win Over Ethnic Votes," *Maclean's*, February 2, 2013, macleans.ca/news/canada/welcome -to-my-world.

2 Jason Fekete and Allan Woods, "Calgary Stalwarts Left Out of New Harper Cabinet," *Calgary Herald*, February 7, 2006, A3.

3 Carlaw, "The Conservative Party of Canada and the Politics of Citizenship, Immigration and Multiculturalism," 57.

4 Diebel, "'Minister for Curry.'"

5 Castonguay, "The Inside Story."

6 Paul Wells, *The Longer I'm Prime Minister: Stephen Harper and Canada* (Toronto: Random House Canada, 2013), 340–41.

7 Yasha Levine, "Immigrants as a Weapon: Global Nationalism and American Power," *Yasha Levine*, September 19, 2019, yasha.substack.com/p/immigrants-as -a-weapon-global-nationalism.

8 John Carlaw, "A Party for New Canadians? The Rhetoric and Reality of Neoconservative Immigration Policy," in *The Harper Record: 2008–2015*, eds. Teresa Healy and Stuart Trew (Ottawa: Canadian Centre for Policy Alternatives, 2015), 108.

9 Susan Riley, "Opposition 'Fanning Fears' over Immigration," *Windsor Star*, April 8, 2006, A8.

10 John Carlaw, "Coalition of the Winning: Neoconservative Multiculturalism in Canada," *Ethnic Aisle*, September 25, 2015, theethnicaisle.com/new-blog /2015/9/24/moving-multiculturalism-to-the-right.

11 Prithi Yelaja, "PM Plans for Ties That Bind," *Toronto Star*, June 15, 2007, A14.

12 Andrew Mayeda, "Tory Hopes Buoyed by GTA Turnout," *National Post*, March 19, 2007, A10.

13 Althia Raj, "'Canada Isn't a Hotel,'" *Ottawa Sun*, April 4, 2009, A5.

14 "Kenney Wants Immigrants to Know English or French," Canadian Press, March 20, 2009, toronto.ctvnews.ca/kenney-wants-immigrants-to-know-english -or-french-1.381432.

15 "Rewrite of Citizenship Guide Ordered," Canadian Press, April 29, 2009, proquest.com/docview/270334191/3149C1C42589413EPQ/2 ?accountid=46585.

16 Laura Stone, "Poppies Trump Potash in New Citizens' Guide," *National Post*, November 11, 2009, A10.

17 "Government Unveils New Citizenship Guidebook," *CBC News*, November 12, 2009, cbc.ca/news/politics/government-unveils-new-citizenship-guidebook -1.784599.

18 "Kenney Nixed Gay Rights in Citizenship Guide: Documents," Canadian Press, March 2, 2010, ctvnews.ca/kenney-nixed-gay-rights-in-citizenship-guide -documents-1.488071.

19 Government of Canada, "Updated Discover Canada Citizenship Study Guide Now Available," March 14, 2011, canada.ca/en/news/archive/2011/03/updated -discover-canada-citizenship-study-guide-now-available.html.

20 Immigration, Refugees and Citizenship Canada, *Discover Canada: The Rights and Responsibilities of Citizenship*, 2021, 9, canada.ca/content/dam/ircc /migration/ircc/english/pdf/pub/discover.pdf.

21 Laura Stone, "Citizenship Guide Takes Tough Stand on 'Barbaric' Cultural Practices," *Ottawa Citizen*, November 13, 2009, A3.

22 Joanne Chianello, "Jason Kenney Fires Up the Melting Pot," *Ottawa Citizen*, April 18, 2009, B1.

23 Brooke Jeffrey, *Dismantling Canada: Stephen Harper's New Conservative Agenda* (Montreal and Kingston: McGill-Queen's University Press, 2015), 225.

24 Harsha Walia, *Border and Rule: Global Migration, Capitalism, and the Rise of Racist Nationalism* (Winnipeg: Fernwood Publishing, 2021), 5.

25 Walia, *Border and Rule*, 7.

26 Tom Godfrey, "Thais to Be Deported," *Toronto Sun*, April 14, 2009, 10.

27 "Budget Watchdog Data Shows Bureaucracy Grew Under Harper," Canadian Press, June 29, 2013, cbc.ca/news/politics/budget-watchdog-data-shows -bureaucracy-grew-under-harper-1.1319927.

28 Marta Gold, "Government 'Abandoning' Foreign Workers: Lawyer," *CanWest News*, October 11, 2009.

29 UFCW Canada, "Real Protection for Temporary Foreign Workers Requires Real Solutions, Not Unenforced Paper Protocols," October 14, 2009, ufcw.ca /index.php?option=com_content&view=article&id=667:2014-02-25-02-55 -58&catid=5&Itemid=6&lang=en.

30 Marianne White, "Far from Family," *Montreal Gazette*, January 4, 2009, A7.

31 Peter O'Neil, "Czech Refugee Claims Flood Canada," *Ottawa Citizen*, April 16, 2009, A5.

32 Joe Friesen, "Minister Scolds Judges over Delays, Inconsistency in Refugee Cases," *Globe and Mail*, February 11, 2011, theglobeandmail.com/news

/politics/ottawa-notebook/minister-scolds-judges-over-delays-inconsistency
-in-refugee-cases/article611725.

33 Daniel Leblanc, "Jason Kenney Re-Hires Aide Who Sent Tory Appeal on
Commons Letterhead," *Globe and Mail*, May 30, 2011, theglobeandmail.com
/news/politics/ottawa-notebook/jason-kenney-re-hires-aide-who-sent-tory
-appeal-on-commons-letterhead/article614743.

34 Wells, *The Longer I'm Prime Minister*, 340–41.

35 Wells, *The Longer I'm Prime Minister*, 355.

36 Megan O'Toole, "'Immigrant Voters' Help Tory Majority," *National Post*,
May 4, 2011, A12.

37 Kim Mackerel, "Citizenship to Be Revoked for Thousands in Historic
Crackdown on Immigration Fraud," *Globe and Mail*, December 9, 2011,
theglobeandmail.com/news/politics/citizenship-to-be-revoked-for-thousands
-in-historic-crackdown-on-immigration-fraud/article4247733.

38 Althia Raj, "Ottawa to Strip 1,800 of Citizenship," *National Post*, July 20,
2011, A1.

39 Stephanie Levitz, "Only 12 Citizenships Revoked So Far in 18-Month
Crackdown on Fraud," Canadian Press, February 28, 2013.

40 Jeffrey, *Dismantling Canada*, 229.

41 Nicholas Keung, "Only 'Rich' Can Afford Super Visa," *Toronto Star*,
December 31, 2011, A13.

42 Harsha Walia, "Canada's Managed Migration Program," in *The Harper
Record: 2008–15*, eds. Teresa Healy and Stuart Trew (Ottawa: Canadian
Centre for Policy Alternatives, 2016), 160.

43 Ian Robertson, "Bridal Party Over," *Toronto Sun*, October 27, 2012, 27.

44 This is not to be confused with the Canada-U.S. Safe Third Country
Agreement, which is entirely separate.

45 Steve Rennie, "Tories Say New Bill Will Make It Easier to Deal with Bogus
Refugee Claims," Canadian Press, February 16, 2012.

46 Nicholas Keung, "Roma Refugees: Canadian Billboards in Hungary Warn
of Deportation," *Toronto Star*, January 25, 2013, thestar.com/news/canada
/2013/01/25/roma_refugees_canadian_billboards_in_hungary_warn_of
_deportation.html.

47 Andy Levy-Ajzenkopf, "Kenney Lists Hungary, Slovak Republic as 'Safe,'"
Canadian Jewish News, December 20, 2012, 18.

48 "Doctors Protest 'Disastrous' Cuts to Refugee Health," Canadian Press,
June 18, 2012, cbc.ca/news/politics/doctors-protest-disastrous-cuts-to
-refugee-health-1.1136633.

49   Haroon Siddiqui, "Jason Kenney Has Become the Chief Headhunter for Business," *Toronto Star*, April 28, 2013, thestar.com/opinion/commentary/2013 /04/28/jason_kenney_has_become_the_chief_headhunter_for_business _siddiqui.html.

5: Big Blue Pickup Truck

1   *Hub Podcasts*, "Episode #125."

2   Jared Wesley, *Code Politics: Campaigns and Culture on the Canadian Prairies* (Vancouver: University of British Columbia Press, 2011), 9–10.

3   Wesley, *Code Politics*, 236.

4   Wesley, "The Dramatic Fall of Jason Kenney."

5   Clark Banack, *God's Province: Evangelical Christianity, Political Thought, and Conservatism in Alberta* (Montreal and Kingston: McGill-Queen's University Press, 2016), 6.

6   Banack, *God's Province*, 8.

7   Markusoff, "Jason Kenney Has Everything to Lose."

8   Duncan Kinney, "Jason Kenney Is Wrong: Unite Alberta Is Not a Non-Profit at All," *Progress Alberta*, August 24, 2016, web.archive.org/web/20210802214702 /progressalberta.ca/jason_kenney_is_wrong_unite_alberta_is_actually_a _for_profit_corporation.

9   Rob Drinkwater, "Alberta PC Leadership Hopeful Jason Kenney Launches 'Unite Alberta Truck Tour,'" Canadian Press, August 1, 2016.

10 Michael Hall, "Looking Under the Hood of Jason Kenney's Iconic Campaign Truck," Royal Roads University, March 1, 2022, royalroads.ca/news/looking -under-hood-jason-kenneys-iconic-campaign-truck.

11 Bill Kauffman, "Kenney Says Disillusioned NDP Supporters Will Back His Bid," *Calgary Herald*, August 16, 2016, A4.

12 Carrie Tait, "Female Candidates Quitting Alberta PC Leadership Race a 'Step Back' for Women: Notley," *Globe and Mail*, November 9, 2016, theglobeandmail.com/news/alberta/female-candidates-quitting-alberta-pc -leadership-race-a-step-back-for-women-notley/article32782999.

13 These remarks were likely overshadowed by a joke he made bemoaning how it was "against the law to beat Rachel Notley," which he promptly apologized for.

14 "Strathmore-Brooks Wildrose Association Tops Fundraising in 2016," *Bassano Times*, January 24, 2017, A17.

15 Laura Stone, "Jason Kenney Vows Repercussions Against B.C. over Trans Mountain Pipeline," *Globe and Mail*, August 4, 2017.

16 "Alberta PC Leadership Candidate Jason Kenney Hit with $5,000 Fine," Canadian Press, November 21, 2016, thestar.com/news/canada/2016/11/21 /alberta-pc-leadership-candidate-jason-kenney-hit-with-5000-fine.html.

17 "Calgary Herald Retracts Licia Corbella's Columns Promoting Jason Kenney's 2017 UCP Leadership Bid," *PressProgress*, August 12, 2019, pressprogress.ca/calgary-herald-retracts-licia-corbellas-columns-promoting -jason-kenneys-2017-ucp-leadership-bid.

18 Charles Rusnell and Jennie Russell, "Unravelling the Controversy Behind the 2017 UCP Leadership Race," *CBC News*, March 28, 2019, cbc.ca/news /canada/edmonton/kenney-galloway-kamikaze-campaign-1.5073789.

19 Drew Anderson and Carolyn Dunn et al., "'Left with Fines, Charges and Shame': Calgary Political Insider Alleges Voter Fraud in UCP Leadership Campaign," *CBC News*, March 7, 2019, cbc.ca/news/canada/calgary/alberta -election-commissioner-findings-hardyal-mann-irregular-political-contributions -voter-fraud-1.5066753.

20 Meghan Grant, "Alberta Kamikaze Candidate Suffered 'Severe Reputational Harm,' Lawyer Argues in Fine Appeal," *CBC News*, November 25, 2022, cbc.ca/news/canada/calgary/kamikaze-campaign-callaway-fine-appeal -calgary-ucp-1.6664983.

21 Erika Tucker, "Jeff Callaway Drops Out of UCP Race, Alleges Bullying from Man Falsely Characterized as Brian Jean Appointee," *Global News*, October 4, 2017, globalnews.ca/news/3785433/jeff-callaway-drops-out-of -ucp-leadership-race-endorses-jason-kenney.

22 "'I'm a Flawed Man': Embattled Alberta MLA Derek Fildebrandt Quits UCP Caucus," *CBC News*, August 15, 2017, cbc.ca/news/canada/edmonton /derek-fildebrandt-resignation-ucp-1.4249001.

23 Meghan Grant, "MLA Derek Fildebrandt Won't Be Allowed to Rejoin UCP After Pleading Guilty to Illegally Shooting Deer," *CBC News*, February 2, 2018, cbc.ca/news/canada/calgary/derek-fildebrandt-deer-kill-charges -didsbury-court-1.4516638.

24 James Wood, "UCP Leadership Candidates Vow to Push Past Voting Controversy as Race Ends," *Calgary Herald*, October 28, 2017, A4.

25 "Former UCP MLA Tells RCMP Jason Kenney's Team Cast Fake Votes Through Illegal 'Identity Fraud' Scheme," *PressProgress*, February 3, 2019, pressprogress.ca/former-ucp-mla-tells-rcmp-jason-kenneys-team-cast-fake -votes-through-illegal-identity-fraud-scheme.

26 Drew Anderson and Carolyn Dunn et al., "Fraudulent Emails Used to Cast Votes in UCP Leadership Race, CBC Finds," *CBC News*, April 10, 2019, cbc.ca /news/canada/calgary/ucp-leadership-voter-fraud-membership-lists-data-1 .5091952.

27 "Some Listed as UCP Leadership Voters Never Signed Up, Leaked Documents Show," *PressProgress*, April 16, 2019, pressprogress.ca/some-listed -as-ucp-leadership-voters-never-signed-up-leaked-documents-show.

28 Svjetlana Milnarevic, "Wildrose Leader Holds Town Hall," *Daily Herald-Tribune* (Grande Prairie), February 27, 2017.

29 Eric Bowling, "UCP Leader Makes Westlock Stop," *Westlock News*, March 27, 2018, A1.

30 Kieran Leavitt, "Equalization Payments and Why Alberta Doesn't Get Them: We're Rich, Expert Says," *Toronto Star*, December 11, 2018, thestar.com /edmonton/2018/12/11/equalization-payments-and-why-alberta-doesnt-get -them-were-rich-expert-says.html.

31 Mario Canseco, "Negligible Public Support for Separation in Alberta," *Research Co.,* December 20, 2018, researchco.ca/2018/12/20/alberta-separation.

32 Madeline Smith, "Lake of Fire 2.0? Why UCP Bozo Eruptions Show 'Alberta at a Crossroads,'" *Star Calgary*, April 3, 2019, thestar.com/calgary/2019/04/03 /lake-of-fire-20-why-ucp-bozo-eruptions-show-alberta-at-a-crossroads.html.

6: Waging War on the Public Sector

1 Rachel Maclean, "Alberta's Carbon Tax Brought in Billions: See Where It Went," *CBC News*, April 8, 2019, cbc.ca/news/canada/calgary/carbon-tax-alberta -election-climate-leadership-plan-revenue-generated-1.5050438.

2 Kim Trynacity, "Union Membership in Alberta Creeping Up," *CBC News*, June 20, 2018, cbc.ca/news/canada/edmonton/union-membership -grows-alberta-notley-barnetson-mcgowan-1.4713431.

3 Ian Hussey, "Job Creation or Job Loss? Big Companies Use Tax Cut to Automate Away Jobs in the Oil Sands," Parkland Institute, September 2022, assets.nationbuilder.com/parklandinstitute/pages/1984/attachments /original/1664129845/parkland-report-job_creation_or_job_loss.pdf?1664129845.

4 Emma Graney, "Janice MacKinnon Made 'Draconian' Cuts in Saskatchewan, but Says Alberta Is in Much Better Shape," *Edmonton Journal*, July 25, 2019, edmontonjournal.com/news/politics/janice-mackinnon-the -woman-charged-with-fixing-albertas-finances.

5   "Report and Recommendations of the Blue Ribbon Panel on Alberta's Finances," August 2019, 12, open.alberta.ca/dataset/081ba74d-95c8-43ab-9097 -cef17a9fb59c/resource/257f040a-2645-49e7-b40b-462e4b5c059c/download /blue-ribbon-panel-report.pdf.

6   "Report and Recommendations," 22.

7   Colby Cosh, "Is the MacKinnon Report a New Direction for Alberta or Are We Just Muddling Through?" *National Post*, September 4, 2019, nationalpost.com /opinion/colby-cosh-is-the-mackinnon-report-a-new-direction-for-alberta -or-are-we-just-muddling-through.

8   Scott Schmidt, "Push for Better Pay in the Private Sector," *Medicine Hat News*, October 2, 2019, medicinehatnews.com/commentary/opinions/2019/10/02 /push-for-better-pay-in-the-private-sector.

9   Graham Thomson, "Opinion: MacKinnon Report Gives Kenney Roadmap for Klein-Style Cuts," *CBC News*, September 4, 2019, cbc.ca/news/canada /edmonton/opinion-mackinnon-report-cuts-1.5269337.

10 Dean Bennett, "Unions Vow to 'Fight Back' as Alberta Lawmakers Introduce Bill That Strips Bargaining Rights," Canadian Press, June 13, 2019, thestar.com /edmonton/2019/06/13/unions-vow-to-fight-back-as-alberta-lawmakers -introduce-bill-that-strips-bargaining-rights.html.

7: Burning Down the House

1   "Tobacco Lobbying Preceded Label Retreat," *CBC News*, December 8, 2010, cbc.ca/news/canada/tobacco-lobbying-preceded-label-retreat-1.875187.

2   A note on style. You might have noticed me using *oil sands* and *tar sands* interchangeably, as they refer to the same resources in the Athabasca fields surrounding Fort McMurray in northeastern Alberta. Industry boosters prefer the sanitized *oil sands* to make the resources sound more banal. Environmentalists use *tar sands* in reference to the fact that Alberta bitumen is heavier and thus more energy-intensive than other forms of oil.

3   Ezra Levant, *Ethical Oil: The Case for Canada's Oil Sands* (Toronto: McClelland & Stewart), 2010, Loc 119 of 4242, Kindle.

4   Levant, *Ethical Oil*, Loc 3437 of 4242, Kindle.

5   Steven Chase, "Harper's Embrace of 'Ethical' Oil Sands Reignites 'Dirty' Arguments," *Globe and Mail*, January 7, 2011, theglobeandmail.com/news /politics/harpers-embrace-of-ethical-oil-sands-reignites-dirty-arguments /article563356.

6   Jane Taber, "Meet Harper's Oil Sands Muse," *Globe and Mail*, January 11, 2011, theglobeandmail.com/news/politics/ottawa-notebook/meet-harpers-oil-sands-muse/article610888.

7   "Vivian Krause," *Narwhal*, thenarwhal.ca/topics/vivian-krause.

8   "Bitumen Production," *Oil Sands Magazine*, December 12, 2022, oilsandsmagazine.com/projects/bitumen-production.

9   Fatima Syed, "Canada's Supreme Court Rules Carbon Price Constitutional. Here's What You Need to Know," *Narwhal*, March 25, 2021, thenarwhal.ca/carbon-tax-supreme-court-canada.

10 Alberta's NDP, "A New Fiscal Plan, Where Everyone Contributes Fairly," *Leadership for What Matters*, 22.

11 Claudia Cattaneo, "Oilpatch Support for Notley Climate Deal Running on Fumes as CEOs Depart," *Financial Post*, June 21, 2017, financialpost.com/commodities/energy/and-then-there-was-one-final-ceo-who-made-climate-deal-with-notley-left-to-defend-it.

12 "Premier Notley Praised by Alberta's Energy Industry for Tough Stance in Pipeline Dispute," *CBC News*, February 15, 2018, cbc.ca/news/canada/calgary/alberta-energy-panel-trans-mountain-1.4537745.

13 Krause, Vivian, "The Tar Sands Campaign Against the Overseas Export of Canadian Oil: Activism or Economic Sabotage?" *Fair Questions*, January 12, 2018, 3, fairquestions.typepad.com/files/tar-sands-campaign-vivian-krause-12jan2018-excerpts-1.pdf.

14 Krause, "The Tar Sands Campaign," 9.

15 Krause, "The Tar Sands Campaign," 13.

16 "Campaign Against Alberta Oil Sands Not Helping the Environment, Argues Researcher," *CBC News*, November 9, 2018, cbc.ca/news/canada/calgary/vivian-krause-tar-sands-campaign-canada-oil-1.4895487.

17 The notoriously litigious Krause sued Garossino and the *Observer* in 2017 over an earlier article tying her to the Mike Duffy expense scandal. "*National Observer* Defends Against Defamation Lawsuit," *Canada's National Observer*, June 27, 2017, nationalobserver.com/2017/06/27/news/national-observer-defends-against-defamation-lawsuit.

18 Sandy Garossino, "A Data-Based Dismantling of Jason Kenney's Foreign Funding Conspiracy Theory," *Canada's National Observer*, October 3, 2019, nationalobserver.com/2019/10/03/analysis/data-based-dismantling-jason-kenneys-foreign-funding-conspiracy-theory.

19 David Staples, "Alberta Needs Notley's Wisdom and Kenney's Fight to Win Oilsands Campaign," *Edmonton Journal*, April 12, 2019, edmontonjournal.com

/news/local-news/david-staples-alberta-needs-notleys-wisdom-and-kenneys
-fight-to-win-oilsands-campaign.

20 Chase, "Harper's Embrace of 'Ethical' Oil Sands."

21 "Jason Kenney: Vladimir Putin's Jailing of Dissidents Is 'Instructive' on How to
Deal with Environmentalists," *PressProgress*, September 11, 2019, pressprogress
.ca/jason-kenney-vladimir-putins-jailing-of-dissidents-is-instructive-on-how
-to-deal-with-environmentalists.

22 Kieran Leavitt, "Postmedia Wants in on United Conservative 'War Room,'
Hires Former Kenney Staffer to Lobby Government," *Star Edmonton*, May
17, 2019, thestar.com/edmonton/2019/05/17/postmedia-wants-in-on-united
-conservative-war-room-hires-former-kenney-staffer-to-lobby-government.html.

23 James Keller, "Vancouver Chef Featured in Article by Alberta 'Energy War
Room' Furious He Wasn't Told of Links to Government," *Globe and Mail*,
December 25, 2019, theglobeandmail.com/canada/alberta/article-vancouver
-chef-featured-in-article-by-alberta-energy-war-room.

24 Alex Boyd, "Alberta's War Room Accuses Netflix Cartoon *Bigfoot Family* of
'Peddling Lies' About Oil Industry," *Toronto Star*, March 12, 2021, thestar.com
/news/canada/2021/03/12/albertas-war-room-accuses-netflix-cartoon-bigfoot
-family-of-peddling-lies-about-oil-industry.html.

25 "Alberta Politicians Slam 'Vicious' Netflix Cartoon for Kids," *Al Jazeera,* March
7, 2021, aljazeera.com/news/2021/3/17/alberta-politicians-slam-vicious
-netflix-cartoon-for-kids.

26 Amy Tucker, "Battle of the War Rooms: Climate Change Activists Fundraise
for Their Own Group to Combat Jason Kenney's," *Star Calgary*, April 18, 2019,
thestar.com/calgary/2019/04/18/battle-of-the-war-rooms-climate-change
-activists-fundraise-for-their-own-group-to-combat-jason-kenneys.html.

27 Sharon J. Riley, "Inside Another Kind of 'War Room' — Meet the Alberta
Climate Activists Who Say They're Not Scared of Jason Kenney," *Narwhal*,
December 20, 2019, thenarwhal.ca/inside-another-kind-of-war-room
-meet-the-alberta-climate-activists-who-say-theyre-not-scared-of-jason
-kenney.

28 Tyler Dawson, "Alberta Announces Public Inquiry into 'Shadowy' Foreign
Funding of Environmental Groups," *National Post*, July 4, 2019, nationalpost
.com/news/politics/alberta-announces-public-inquiry-into-shadowy-foreign
-funding-of-environmental-groups.

29 Lisa Johnson, "Alberta Inquiry into Funding of Foreign Environmental Groups
Alters Course Again," *Edmonton Journal*, August 6, 2020, edmontonjournal

.com/news/politics/alberta-inquiry-into-foreign-environmental-group
-funding-changes-terms-of-reference-again.

30 Sarah Rieger, "Inquiry into Alleged Anti-Alberta Energy Campaigns
Doesn't Have Time to Fact-Check Statements: Commissioner," *CBC News*,
September 16, 2020, cbc.ca/news/canada/calgary/foreign-funded-anti-alberta
-energy-inquiry-1.5725780.

31 "4th Deadline Extension Granted to Steve Allan's Alberta Inquiry into Oil & Gas
Critics," Canadian Press, May 19, 2021, globalnews.ca/news/7877009/alberta
-inquiry-4th-deadline-extension.

32 Jeremy Appel, "Jason Kenney's Anti-environmentalist Campaign Is Winning,"
Passage, August 5, 2021, readpassage.com/jason-kenneys-anti-environmentalist
-campaign-is-winning.

33 Lisa Johnson, "Allan Inquiry's Report Triggers War of Words with
Alberta's Energy War Room," *Edmonton Journal*, October 22, 2021,
edmontonjournal.com/news/politics/allan-inquirys-report-triggers-war-of
-words-with-albertas-energy-war-room.

34 Jonathan Swift, "The Examiner," *Gulliver's Travels and Other Writings* (New
York: Bantam Books, 1962), 474.

35 "Environmental Organizations Sue Premier Kenney for Defamation,"
Environmental Defence, February 3, 2022, environmentaldefence.ca/2022/02
/03/environmental-organizations-sue-premier-kenney-for-defamation.

36 Mike De Souza and Heather Yourex-West, "Alberta Government Took Six
Months to Release Alarming Climate Report," *Global News*, February 6,
2020, globalnews.ca/news/6600989/alberta-buried-climate-report.

8: Education for the Few

1 Janet French, "Alberta Social Studies Curriculum Adviser Says Kamloops
Unmarked Burial Site No Evidence of Genocide," *CBC News*, June 17,
2021, cbc.ca/news/canada/edmonton/alberta-social-studies-curriculum
-adviser-says-kamloops-unmarked-burial-site-no-evidence-of-genocide-1
.6070407.

2 Duncan Kinney, "FOIP Shows Likely Political Interference in Curriculum
Drafting Process," *Progress Report*, August 18, 2021, theprogressreport.ca
/foip_shows_possible_political_interference_in_curriculum_drafting
_process.

3   Janet French, "Education Experts Slam Leaked Alberta Curriculum Proposals," *CBC News*, October 21, 2020, cbc.ca/news/canada/edmonton /education-experts-slam-leaked-alberta-curriculum-proposals-1.5766570.

4   Lisa Johnson, "LaGrange Defends Value of K–6 Draft Curriculum Pilot, Despite Only Two Per Cent of Alberta Students Participating," *Edmonton Journal*, November 8, 2021, edmontonjournal.com/news/politics/lagrange-defends -value-of-k-6-draft-curriculum-pilot-despite-only-two-per-cent-of-alberta -students-participating.

5   "Teachers Call for Stop to Curriculum Implementation," The Alberta Teachers' Association, April 15, 2021, legacy.teachers.ab.ca/News%20Room/NewsReleases /Pages/Teachers-Call-for-Stop-to-Curriculum-Implementation.aspx.

6   Milton Friedman, "The Role of Government in Education," in *Economics and the Public Interest*, ed. Robert A. Solo (New Brunswick, NJ: Rutgers University Press, 1955), la.utexas.edu/users/hcleaver/330T /350kPEEFriedmanRoleOfGovttable.pdf.

7   Anthony Johnson, "Klein's Cuts Shock Alberta," *Calgary Herald*, January 19, 1994, A1.

8   Diana Coulter, "Public Schools Need Competition — Dinning," *Edmonton Journal*, January 29, 1994, A5.

9   "Budget Highlights," *Calgary Herald*, February 25, 1994, A1.

10 Andy Marshall, "Limits on Charter Schools Criticized," *Calgary Herald*, November 24, 1994, B8.

11 Curtis Riep, "Privatizing Public Choice: The Past, Present, and Future of Charter Schools in Alberta," *Public School Boards Association of Alberta*, September 2020, 5, public-schools.ab.ca/wp-content/uploads/2020/12 /PrivatizingPublicChoice-ThePastPresentandFutureofCharteSchoolsin Alberta.pdf.

12 Eva Ferguson, "Choice in Education Act Raises Concerns of Eroding Public System," *Calgary Herald*, May 28, 2020, calgaryherald.com/news/choice-in -education-act-raises-concerns-of-eroding-public-system.

13 "Education Minister Orders Audit of Calgary Board of Education, Accusing It of 'Mismanagement,'" *CBC News*, November 20, 2019, cbc.ca/news/canada /calgary/lagrange-minister-education-alberta-calgary-board-education-audit -1.5366272.

14 Jonathan Teghtmeyer, "Documents Prove Education Funding Has Been Cut," *ATA News*, February 25, 2020, legacy.teachers.ab.ca/News%20Room /ata%20news/Vol54/Number-9/Pages/Documents-prove-education-funding -has-been-cut.aspx.

15 Janet French, "Cutting Through Confusion: Explaining Alberta's Changing Rules for School Board Funding," *CBC News*, August 23, 2020, cbc.ca/news /canada/edmonton/explaining-alberta-school-funding-1.5696222.

16 Lauren Boothby, "Alberta Budget 2021: Province Says It Won't 'Penalize' School Boards for Lower Enrolment, but Nearly 2,000 Jobs Lost to Pandemic Won't Return," *Edmonton Journal*, February 26, 2021, edmontonjournal.com /news/politics/alberta-budget-2021-province-will-not-penalize-school-boards -amid-covid-19-enrolment-drop.

17 "Report and Recommendations of the Blue Ribbon Panel on Alberta's Finances," August 2019, 40, open.alberta.ca/dataset/081ba74d-95c8-43ab -9097-cef17a9fb59c/resource/257f040a-2645-49e7-b40b-462e4b5c059c /download/blue-ribbon-panel-report.pdf.

18 Moira Wyton, "Alberta Budget 2019: Tuition Fee Freeze Lifted as Post-Secondary Grants Cut," *Edmonton Journal*, October 25, 2019, edmontonjournal.com /news/politics/alberta-budget-2019-tuition-fee-freeze-lifted-as-post-secondary -grants-cut.

19 Lisa Johnson, "Alberta Budget 2020: Advanced Education Funding Cut 6.3 Per Cent, Tuition to Rise," *Edmonton Journal*, February 28, 2020, edmontonjournal .com/news/politics/alberta-budget-2020-advanced-education-funding-cut -6-3-per-cent-tuition-to-rise.

20 Janet French, "Some Alberta Post-Secondary Institutions Left Relatively Unscathed While U of A Funds Slashed, New Data Shows," *CBC News*, June 28, 2021, cbc.ca/news/canada/edmonton/some-alberta-post-secondary-institutions -left-relatively-unscathed-while-u-of-a-funds-slashed-new-data-shows-1.6081029.

21 UASU Staff, "The 2022 Budget: What It Means for Us," *Flame*, February 25, 2022, theflame.su.ualberta.ca/en/blog/2022/02/25/the-2022 -provincial-budget-and-what-it-means-for-you.

9: Rejecting Harm Reduction

1 Nadine Yousif, "A Small Alberta City Is Home to the Busiest Drug Consumption Site in North America: We Spent 12 Hours Inside," *StarMetro Edmonton*, August 18, 2019, thestar.com/edmonton/2019/08/18/a-small-alberta -city-is-home-to-the-busiest-drug-consumption-site-in-north-america-we -spent-12-hours-inside.html.

2 John Ibbitson, "How Harper Created a More Conservative Canada," *Globe and Mail*, February 6, 2015, theglobeandmail.com/news/politics/globe

-politics-insider/how-harper-created-a-more-conservative-canada
/article22829480.

3 Roshini Nair and Jon Hernandez, "Liberal Government's Refusal to Repeal Bill C-2 'Disappointing,' Supervised Injection Site Advocate Says," *CBC News*, August 24, 2016, cbc.ca/news/canada/british-columbia/supervised -injection-hurdles-1.3733942.

4 Simon Little, "'I'm Not Saying I'm Opposed': Kenney Walks Back Tough Talk on Supervised Consumption Site," *Global News*, March 5, 2018, globalnews.ca/news/4064454/im-not-saying-im-opposed-kenney-walks-back -tough-talk-on-supervised-consumption-sites.

5 Kieran Leavitt, "Expert Cited by Jason Kenney in 'NDP Drug Sites' Tweet Criticizes Him for Being 'Inflammatory,'" *Toronto Star*, January 23, 2020, thestar.com/news/canada/2020/01/23/expert-cited-by-jason-kenney-in-ndp -drug-sites-tweet-criticizes-him-for-being-inflammatory.html.

6 Meghan Potkins, "Farkas Wants Mental Health Funding Diverted to Businesses, Residents in 'Drug Use Hot Spots,'" *Calgary Herald*, July 15, 2019, calgaryherald.com/news/local-news/farkas-wants-addictions-funding -diverted-to-businesses-residents-in-drug-use-hot-spots.

7 Meghan Potkins, "'We're Basically at War': Sheldon Chumir's Zone of Overdoses, Needles and Fear," *Calgary Herald*, February 14, 2019, calgaryherald .com/news/local-news/you-should-be-ashamed-concerns-around-safe-drug -site-aired-at-emotional-city-hall-meeting.

8 Potkins, "'We're Basically at War.'"

9 Madeline Smith, "Lethbridge Councillor Plans to Request City's Supervised Drug Consumption Site Be Defunded, *StarMetro Calgary*, August 9, 2019, thestar.com/calgary/2019/08/09/lethbridge-councillor-plans-to-request-citys -supervised-drug-consumption-site-be-defunded.html.

10 Danica Ferris, "Lethbridge City Council Defeats Controversial Supervised Consumption Site Motion," *Global News*, August 19, 2019, globalnews.ca /news/5786889/lethbridge-city-council-defeats-supervised-consumption -site-motion.

11 Jon Watson, "'There Are No Consequences for Them': Split Opinions over Supervised Consumption Sites," *Daily Herald Tribune* (Grande Prairie), September 18, 2019, dailyheraldtribune.com/news/local-news/there-are-no -consequences-for-them-split-opinions-over-supervised-consumption-sites.

12 "Report on Social Impacts of Injection Sites a 'Wake-Up Call': Alberta Minister," Canadian Press, March 5, 2020, globalnews.ca/news/6635968/alberta -supervised-consumption-site-review-report.

13 Jordan Omstead, "Alberta's Safe Consumption Site Review Biased and Flawed, Researcher Says," *CBC News*, January 8, 2021, cbc.ca/news/canada /edmonton/alberta-s-safe-consumption-review-biased-and-flawed-researcher -says-1.5867053.

14 James D. Livingston, "Supervised Consumption Sites and Crime: Scrutinizing the Methodological Weaknesses and Aberrant Results of a Government Report in Alberta, Canada," *Harm Reduction Journal* 18, no. 4 (January 6, 2021), harmreductionjournal.biomedcentral.com/articles/10.1186/s12954 -020-00456-2.

15 Terry Vogt and Jillian Code, "Missing ARCHES Funds Accounted For: Lethbridge Police," *CTV News*, December 22, 2020, calgary.ctvnews.ca /missing-arches-funds-accounted-for-lethbridge-police-1.5241779.

16 Emily Olsen, "Lethbridge Patrol Notes Increased Overdoses, Needle Debris Since ARCHES Closure," *Global News*, September 14, 2020, globalnews.ca /news/7334894/lethbridge-arches-closure-drug-crisis.

17 Dustin Cook and Anna Junker, "Requirement to Provide Health Number for Accessing Supervised Consumption Sites in Alberta Postponed Until New Year," *Edmonton Journal*, September 7, 2021, edmontonjournal.com/news /local-news/requirement-to-provide-health-number-for-accessing-supervised -consumption-sites-in-alberta-postponed-until-new-year.

18 Paul Willcocks, "The Recovery Success That Wasn't," *Tyee*, August 10, 2023, thetyee.ca/Opinion/2023/08/10/Marshall-Smith-Recovery-Success.

19 Jeremy Hainsworth, "Investigation: B.C.-Owned Addiction Rehab Allegedly Used for Liberal Politicking, Contract Awards," *Glacier Investigates*, April 27, 2021, vancouverisawesome.com/bc-news/investigation-bc-owned-addiction -rehab-allegedly-used-for-liberal-politicking-contract-awards-3670052.

20 Jeremy Appel, "'Just Say No to Drugs': The UCP Government's Approach to Alberta's Overdose Crisis," *Alberta Views*, June 1, 2022, albertaviews.ca/just -say-no-drugs.

21 "Recovery-Oriented Systems of Care (AB)," *Canada's Premiers*, May 19, 2021, canadaspremiers.ca/ep9-ab.

22 "Harm Reduction," Alberta Health Services, albertahealthservices.ca/info /Page15432.aspx.

23 Appel, "'Just Say No to Drugs.'"

24 Anna Junker, "Lack of Localized Data 'Leaves Communities in the Dark' in Alberta's Drug Poisoning Crisis," *Edmonton Journal*, July 18, 2022, edmontonjournal.com/news/local-news/lack-of-localized-data-leaves -communities-in-the-dark-in-albertas-drug-poisoning-crisis.

25 Paul Wells, "'Just Like They're Doing in Alberta,'" *Paul Wells*, November 17, 2022, paulwells.substack.com/p/just-like-theyre-doing-in-alberta.

10: The Plague

1   James Keller and Laura Stone, "How Prepared Are Our Hospitals for the Coronavirus Outbreak?" *Globe and Mail*, March 15, 2020, theglobeandmail.com/canada/article-how-prepared-are-our-hospitals-for-the-coronavirus-outbreak.

2   Paris Marx, "PM Trudeau, There's Nothing 'Innovative' About Privatized Health Care," *Breach*, February 1, 2023, breachmedia.ca/pm-trudeau-theres-nothing-innovative-about-privatized-health-care.

3   Lisa Young, "'With Comorbidities': The Politics of COVID-19 and the Kenney Government," in *Blue Storm: The Rise and Fall of Jason Kenney*, ed. Duane Bratt et al. (Calgary: University of Calgary Press, 2023), 435.

4   Wesley, "The Dramatic Fall of Jason Kenney."

5   "Alberta's Health Minister Holds Shares in a Private Company That Connects Customers to Things He Recently Cut," *PressProgress*, April 7, 2020, pressprogress.ca/albertas-health-minister-holds-shares-in-a-private-company-that-connects-customers-to-things-he-recently-cut.

6   *Hub Podcasts*, "Episode #125."

7   Madeline Smith, "Alberta Doctors Reach New Funding Contract with the Province," *Edmonton Journal*, September 29, 2022, edmontonjournal.com/news/local-news/alberta-health-minister-to-detail-new-deal-with-ama.

8   Bob Weber, "Limits on Gatherings Make It a 'Great Time to Be Building a Pipeline,' Says Alberta Energy Minister," Canadian Press, May 25, 2020, cbc.ca/news/canada/edmonton/pipelines-alberta-protests-physical-distancing-1.5584025.

9   Carl Meyer and Drew Anderson, "Documents Reveal How Alberta Oil and Gas Industry Used Pandemic to Push 'Wish List,'" *Narwhal*, December 19, 2022, thenarwhal.ca/capp-oil-lobbying-alberta-government.

10 Joel Dryden and Sarah Rieger, "Inside the Slaughterhouse," *CBC News*, May 6, 2020, newsinteractives.cbc.ca/longform/cargill-covid19-outbreak.

11 Jason Herring, "Immigrant Workers at Alberta Meat Plants Vulnerable to Dangerous Conditions, Research Finds," *Calgary Herald*, November 25, 2021, calgaryherald.com/news/local-news/alberta-meat-plant-workers-vulnerable-to-dangerous-conditions-new-research.

12 "Workers at Cargill's Alberta Meat Plant Were Offered Special 'Bonus' Pay for Perfect Attendance During Pandemic," *PressProgress*, May 6, 2020, pressprogress.ca/workers-at-cargills-alberta-meat-plant-were-offered-special -bonus-pay-for-perfect-attendance-during-pandemic.

13 David Climenhaga, "Alberta Safety Inspection of Cargill Slaughterhouse Done by Facetime, with No Actual Inspector on Site," *Alberta Politics*, April 22, 2020, albertapolitics.ca/2020/04/alberta-safety-inspection-of-cargill -slaughterhouse-done-by-facetime-with-no-actual-inspector-on-site.

14 Charles Rusnell and Jennie Russell, "Union Group Says Documents Show Alberta Government Prioritized Cargill Plant Operation over Worker Safety," *CBC News*, March 30, 2021, cbc.ca/news/canada/edmonton/union -group-says-documents-show-alberta-government-prioritized-cargill-plant -operation-over-worker-safety-1.5968428.

15 Kent Fletcher, "Critics Describe Premier Jason Kenney's COVID-19 Speech as 'Trumpian,'" *Global News*, May 28, 2020, globalnews.ca/news/7000260 /alberta-premier-jason-kenney-covid-19-speech-trumpian.

16 Ashley Joannou and Anna Junker, "AHS Workers' Wildcat Strike Declared Illegal by Alberta Labour Relations Board," *Edmonton Journal*, October 27, 2020, edmontonjournal.com/news/local-news/alberta-health-care-workers-walk -off-the-job-aupe.

17 Rick Bell, "No Lockdown Yet," *Calgary Sun*, October 21, 2020, A10.

18 Allison Bench, "Kenney Warns Stronger Measures Could Be in Store for Alberta as COVID-19 Cases Rise by 991 Sunday," *Global News*, November 15, 2020, globalnews.ca/news/7464288/alberta-covid-19-cases-nov-15.

19 Helen Pike, "Headhunters Promise 'Escape' from Alberta for Doctors, Health-Care Workers," *CBC News*, November 6, 2020, cbc.ca/news/canada/calgary /alberta-health-care-workers-doctors-lured-to-jobs-across-canada-1.5777334.

20 Jason Herring, "Kenney Pleads with Albertans to Follow Public Health Orders, but Won't Add Restrictions," *Calgary Herald*, April 1, 2021, calgaryherald.com/news/local-news/live-at-330-p-m-kenney-hinshaw-to -give-covid-19-update-amid-surge-in-variants.

21 Karen Bartko, "17 UCP MLAs Revolt Against Alberta Government's Renewed COVID-19 Restrictions," *Global News*, April 7, 2021, globalnews.ca /news/7744125/alberta-covid-restrictions-ucp-mlas-letter.

22 Michael Franklin, "'Slap in the Face': Kenney Posts Statement About Huge Crowds at Bowden, Alta. Rodeo," *CTV News*, May 2, 2021, calgary.ctvnews.ca /slap-in-the-face-kenney-posts-statement-about-huge-crowds-at-bowden-alta -rodeo-1.5411190.

23   Tom Yun, "'It'll Crash Tremendously,'" *CTV News*, May 3, 2021, ctvnews.ca
      /health/coronavirus/it-ll-crash-tremendously-alberta-now-leads-canada-and
      -u-s-in-per-capita-covid-19-cases-1.5412090.

24   Bartko, "17 UCP MLAs."

25   Young, "'With Comorbidities,'" 449.

26   Alex Boyd, "'Don't Live in Fear': Alberta to Drop All Major COVID
      Restrictions for Canada Day." *Toronto Star*, June 18, 2021, thestar.com/news
      /canada/2021/06/15/on-canada-day-alberta-will-become-the-first-province
      -to-drop-all-major-covid-restrictions.html.

11: The Fall

1   Stephen Magusiak, "Danielle Smith Claimed Smoking Cigarettes Had Positive
      Health Benefits," *PressProgress*, July 26, 2022, pressprogress.ca/danielle
      -smith-claimed-smoking-cigarettes-had-positive-health-benefits.

2   Jeremy Appel, "Danielle Smith's Record of Anti-Indigenous Punditry,"
      Orchard, December 21, 2022, theorchard.substack.com/p/danielle-smiths
      -record-of-anti-indigenous.

3   David Climenhaga, "Get Ready to Welcome Danielle Smith to Alberta's
      Blogging Elite!" *Alberta Politics*, March 31, 2015, albertapolitics.ca/2015/03
      /get-ready-to-welcome-danielle-smith-to-albertas-blogging-elite.

4   Jason Kenney, "Live: On the Last Danielle Smith Show," Facebook, February
      19, 2021, facebook.com/kenneyjasont/videos/187823076447841.

5   Jamie Malbeuf, "Brian Jean Apologizes for Social Media Post Highlighting
      Ethnicity of Political Opponent," *CBC News*, November 15, 2021, cbc.ca/news
      /canada/edmonton/brian-jean-mla-ucp-1.6250227.

6   Wallis Snowdon, "Alberta Premier Jason Kenney's Rival Slams Shift to Mail-
      In Ballot for Leadership Review," *CBC News*, March 23, 2022, cbc.ca/news
      /canada/edmonton/jason-kenney-leadership-vote-1.6394733.

7   "Alberta Feed Stores Inundated with Calls For Ivermectin over False Claims
      Livestock Dewormer Treats COVID," *Radio-Canada International*, August
      30, 2021, ici.radio-canada.ca/rci/en/news/1820261/alberta-feed-stores
      -inundated-with-calls-for-ivermectin-over-false-claims-livestock-dewormer
      -treats-covid.

8   Tyson Fedor, "UCP Leadership Candidate Danielle Smith Under Fire by All
      Political Stripes for Cancer Comments," *CTV News*, July 26, 2022, calgary

.ctvnews.ca/ucp-leadership-candidate-danielle-smith-under-fire-by-all-political
-stripes-for-cancer-comments.

9   Jeremy Appel, "Lunatics Take Over UCP Asylum," *Orchard*, August 26,
2022, theorchard.substack.com/p/lunatics-take-over-ucp-asylum.

10 Rick Bell, "Danielle Smith Fires Back, Insists She's No Separatist," *Calgary Sun*,
June 30, 2022, calgarysun.com/opinion/columnists/bell-danielle-smith-fires
-back-insists-shes-no-separatist.

11 Dean Bennett, "Kenney Defends Alberta Lieutenant-Governor, Attacks
'Cockamamie' Sovereignty Bill," Canadian Press, September 2, 2022.

Epilogue

1   *Hub Podcasts*, "Episode #125."

IMAGE CREDITS

INDEX

ABOUT THE AUTHOR

Jeremy Appel is an independent Edmonton-based journalist who has covered Alberta politics since he arrived in the province in 2017, when Jason Kenney was in the midst of his plan to take over the faltering PC Party and merge it with the Wildrose. First coming to prominence as a reporter and columnist for the *Medicine Hat News*, his work has appeared in mainstream and independent news outlets, including *CBC News*, the *Globe and Mail*, the *Canadian Jewish News*, *Tablet*, the *Tyee*, *Jacobin*, the *Maple*, the *Breach*, *Ricochet*, and elsewhere. Appel co-hosts the *Forgotten Corner* and *Big Shiny Takes* podcasts, and has appeared on *Canadaland*, *Alberta Advantage*, *The Big Story*, *Haus of Decline*, *The Insurgents*, *Left Reckoning*, and more. Beyond Alberta, his work focuses on Canadian politics, Indigenous issues, the climate crisis, labour relations, Canadian and U.S. foreign policy, and the intersection of media, politics, and corporate power.